Probabilistic Databases

Synthesis Lectures on Data Management

Editor
M. Tamer Özsu, *University of Waterloo*

Synthesis Lectures on Data Management is edited by Tamer Özsu of the University of Waterloo. The series will publish 50- to 125 page publications on topics pertaining to data management. The scope will largely follow the purview of premier information and computer science conferences, such as ACM SIGMOD, VLDB, ICDE, PODS, ICDT, and ACM KDD. Potential topics include, but not are limited to: query languages, database system architectures, transaction management, data warehousing, XML and databases, data stream systems, wide scale data distribution, multimedia data management, data mining, and related subjects.

Probabilistic Databases
Dan Suciu, Dan Olteanu, Christopher Ré, and Christoph Koch
2011

Peer-to-Peer Data Management
Karl Aberer
2011

Probabilistic Ranking Techniques in Relational Databases
Ihab F. Ilyas and Mohamed A. Soliman
2011

Uncertain Schema Matching
Avigdor Gal
2011

Fundamentals of Object Databases: Object-Oriented and Object-Relational Design
Suzanne W. Dietrich and Susan D. Urban
2010

Advanced Metasearch Engine Technology
Weiyi Meng and Clement T. Yu
2010

Probabilistic Databases
Dan Suciu, Dan Olteanu, Christopher Ré, and Christoph Koch

ISBN: 978-3-031-00751-4   paperback
ISBN: 978-3-031-01879-4   ebook

DOI 10.1007/978-3-031-01879-4

A Publication in the Springer series
SYNTHESIS LECTURES ON DATA MANAGEMENT

Lecture #16
Series Editor: M. Tamer Özsu, *University of Waterloo*
Series ISSN
Synthesis Lectures on Data Management
Print 2153-5418   Electronic 2153-5426

Probabilistic Databases

Dan Suciu
University of Washington

Dan Olteanu
University of Oxford

Christopher Ré
University of Wisconsin-Madison

Christoph Koch
École Polytechnique Fédérale de Lausanne

SYNTHESIS LECTURES ON DATA MANAGEMENT #16

ABSTRACT

Probabilistic databases are databases where the value of some attributes or the presence of some records are uncertain and known only with some probability. Applications in many areas such as information extraction, RFID and scientific data management, data cleaning, data integration, and financial risk assessment produce large volumes of uncertain data, which are best modeled and processed by a probabilistic database.

This book presents the state of the art in representation formalisms and query processing techniques for probabilistic data. It starts by discussing the basic principles for representing large probabilistic databases, by decomposing them into tuple-independent tables, block-independent-disjoint tables, or U-databases. Then it discusses two classes of techniques for query evaluation on probabilistic databases. In *extensional query evaluation*, the entire probabilistic inference can be pushed into the database engine and, therefore, processed as effectively as the evaluation of standard SQL queries. The relational queries that can be evaluated this way are called safe queries. In *intensional query evaluation*, the probabilistic inference is performed over a propositional formula called *lineage expression*: every relational query can be evaluated this way, but the data complexity dramatically depends on the query being evaluated, and can be #P-hard. The book also discusses some advanced topics in probabilistic data management such as top-k query processing, sequential probabilistic databases, indexing and materialized views, and Monte Carlo databases.

KEYWORDS

query language, query evaluation, query plan, data complexity, probabilistic database, polynomial time, sharp p, incomplete data, uncertain information

Contents

Preface: A Great Promise

Traditional relational databases are *deterministic*. Every record stored in the database is meant to be present with *certainty*, and every field in that record has a precise, unambiguous value. The theoretical foundations and the intellectual roots of relational databases are in First Order Logic, which is essentially the relational calculus, the foundation of query languages such as SQL. In First Order Logic, the fundamental question is whether a logical sentence is true or false. Logical formulas under first-order semantics can be used to assert that a record is, or is not, in a relation, or in a query result, but they cannot make any less precise statement. The original applications that motivated the creation of relational databases required certain query results: accounting, inventory, airline reservations, and payroll. Database systems use a variety of tools and techniques to enforce this, such as integrity constraints and transactions.

Today, however, data management needs to include new data sources, where data are uncertain, and which are difficult or impossible to model with traditional semantics or to manage with a traditional Relational Database Management System (RDBMS). For an illustration, consider *Business Intelligence* (BI), whose goal is to extract and analyze business data by mining a large collection of databases. BI systems can be made more useful by including *external data*, such as twitter feeds or blogs, or email messages in order to extract even more valuable business information. For example, by analyzing blogs or twitter feeds and merging them with offline databases of products, companies can obtain early feedback about the quality of a new product or its degree of adoption, such as for a new car model, a new electronic gadget, or a new movie; such knowledge is very valuable, both for manufacturers and for investors. However, a traditional RDBMS requires the data to be precise: for each tweet, the system needs to know precisely what product it mentions and whether the comment is favorable or unfavorable. The data must be cleaned before it can be used in a traditional RDBMS.

The goal of *Probabilistic Databases* is to extend today's database technology to handle *uncertain* data. The uncertainty is expressed in terms of probabilities: a tuple is present only with some probability, or the value of an attribute is given by a probability distribution. Probabilistic databases are expected to scale as well as traditional database systems, and they should support queries as complex as those supported by advanced query processors today; however, but they will do this while allowing the data to be uncertain, or probabilistic. Both the data and their probabilities are stored in standard relations. The semantics, however, is *probabilistic*: the exact state of the entire database is not known with precision; instead, it is given by a probability distribution. When an SQL query is executed, the system returns a set of answers and it annotates each answer with a probability, representing the degree of confidence in that output. Typically, the answers are ranked in decreasing order of their output probability, so that users can inspect the top, most credible answers first. Thus, the main use of probabilities is to record the degree of uncertainty in the data and to rank the outputs to a query; in some applications, the exact output probabilities matter less to the user than the ranking of the outputs. Probabilistic databases have a major advantage in processing uncertain data over their traditional counterparts. The data can be simply stored in the database without having to be cleaned first. Queries can be run immediately on the data. Cleaning can proceed gradually if and when more information becomes available by simply adjusting the probability value until it becomes 1.0, in which case the data becomes certain, or 0.0, in which case the data item can be removed. Even data that cannot be cleaned at all and will remain forever uncertain can still be stored and queried in a probabilistic database system.

Probabilistic databases take an evolutionary approach: the idea is to extend relational technology with a probabilistic semantics, rather than to develop a new artifact from scratch. All popular database techniques should carry over automatically to a probabilistic database: indexes, query optimization, advanced join algorithms, parallel query processing, etc. The goal is to extend the existing semantics of relational data to represent uncertainties but keep all the tools and techniques that have been proven so effective on deterministic data. As we will see in this book, this is not an easy task at all. The foundations of probabilistic databases are in First Order Logic *extended* with probabilities where the computational complexity of inference and model checking problems has only recently started to be understood.

The AI literature has studied probabilistic inference over *Graphical Models*, GM, such as Bayesian Networks and Markov Networks, which are described in several textbooks [Darwiche, 2009, Jordan, 1998, Koller and Friedman, 2009, Pearl, 1989]. There, the computational complexity is well understood: inference is exponential in the size of the network, and, to be more exact, in the *tree-width* of the network [Lauritzen and Spiegelhalter, 1990, Pearl, 1989]. Tree-width is a fundamental notion also in database theory: in particular, most interesting classes of queries require time exponential in the size of the query and, specifically, in the tree-width of its fundamental combinatorial structure, a graph [Abiteboul et al., 1995, Flum et al., 2002] or hypergraph [Chekuri and Rajaraman, 1997, Gottlob et al., 1999], formed by the relations occurring in the query as nodes and edges that represent joins. The difference here is that queries are usually small compared to the database, and query evaluation is easy under this assumption. By contrast, the network of a GM represents the data itself, and thus it can be very large.

The separation between query and data is a fundamental characteristics that distinguishes probabilistic databases from graphical models. The size of the data may be very large, but the queries are, by comparison, quite small. At a conceptual level, this distinction has been crisply articulated by Vardi [1982], who introduced the term *data complexity*. The query evaluation problem, both in traditional databases and in probabilistic databases, has two inputs: the query Q and the database instance D. In data complexity, the query Q is fixed, and the complexity is measured only as a function of the size of the database instance D. All modern query languages (SQL, XQuery) have polynomial time data complexity on deterministic databases[1], meaning that for any fixed Q, the

---

[1]The complexity of these languages becomes higher when extended with recursive functions, such as permitted in XQuery.

data complexity is in polynomial time in the size of the database. In contrast, there is no similar separation of query and data in GMs, where the entire network represents the data.

While it is possible to model a probabilistic database as a large graphical model, and reduce query evaluation to inference in GM [Sen and Deshpande, 2007], in this book we define and study probabilistic databases differently from GM. In our study, we separate the query from the data. We represent the uncertain data by a combination of classical database relations and propositional formulas, sometimes called *lineage*, which is an approach first introduced by Imieliński and Lipski [1984]. This approach leads us to probabilistic inference on propositional formulas, which, although being a special case of inference in GMs, has been investigated separately in the verification community by Bryant [1986] and in the AI literature by Darwiche [2009].

There are several reasons and advantages to this model of probabilistic databases over general GM.

First, under this model the database has a simple probabilistic model, which can scale easily. If a more complex probabilistic model is needed by the application, the correlations are expressed by the query (or view), which has a relatively small expression. This is a design principle that is well established in standard database modeling and schema normalization theory. In schema normalization, a deterministic table that has unwanted dependencies is decomposed into simpler tables that remove those dependencies and can be recovered from the decomposed tables using a view (usually a natural join). The same design principle exists in graphical models where a probability distribution on a large number of random variables is decomposed into a product of factors over smaller subsets of variables. The connection between database normalization and factor decomposition in graphical models was described by Verma and Pearl [1988]. Thus, in a probabilistic database, the base tables have a very simple probabilistic model, often consisting only of independent or disjoint tuples but can be very large, while the query may introduce complex correlations, but its expression is small. Independence properties in the data are in a strong sense certified by the representation and do not need to be discovered in the network structure of a GM by the inference algorithm. We explore representation formalisms for probabilistic databases in Chapter 2.

Second, the separation into query and data leads both to new inference techniques, specific to probabilistic databases, and to a better insight into the complexity of the probabilistic inference problem. We will describe a probabilistic inference method that is guided by the query expression and not by the database instance. In particular, one of the inference rules, the inclusion-exclusion formula or, more generally, the Möbius inversion function, has an exponential cost in the query yet a polynomial cost in the data: for that reason, inclusion-exclusion has no analog in traditional approaches for probabilistic inference on propositional formulas or in graphical models, yet, as we shall see, it proves to be very effective in probabilistic databases. The rule is possible only through the separation between the query and the data. At a theoretical level, the *data complexity* of probabilistic inference has an interesting dichotomy property: some queries Q have polynomial time data complexity, while others are provably hard for #P; every Union of Conjunctive Queries falls into one of these two categories; hence, the data complexity forms a dichotomy. This phenomenon does not have a correspondence in other probabilistic inference settings since there is no distinction between the data and the query. We describe query evaluation on probabilistic databases in Chapter 3, Chapter 4, and Chapter 5.

Third, this query-centric approach to probabilistic inference allows us to build on decades of research on database management systems by reusing and extending database technology for data representation, storage, and query processing. It is a common theme in research on probabilistic database systems to build on existing database technology. Some of these approaches are surveyed in Chapter 6. Case studies of the TRIO and MayBMS systems can be found in the book by Aggarwal [2008].

This book contains a survey of the main concepts in probabilistic databases: representation formalisms for probabilistic data, query evaluation, and some advanced topics including sequential probabilistic databases, indexes, and Monte Carlo databases. Many applications today need to query large amounts of uncertain data, yet achieving scalability remains challenging. The techniques and concepts described in this book represent the state of the art in query processing on probabilistic databases. The new approach to probabilistic inference described in this book, based on the separation of the data and the query, holds a great promise for extending traditional, scalable database processing techniques with probabilistic inference. The book is intended for researchers, either in database or probabilistic inference, or as a textbook for an advanced graduate class.

Dan Suciu, Dan Olteanu, Christopher Ré, and Christoph Koch
May 2011

Acknowledgments

The authors would like to acknowledge many collaborators and friends who, through their discussions and comments have helped shape our thinking and, thus, have directly or indirectly influenced this book: Lyublena Antova, Magdalena Balazinska, Michael Benedikt, Nilesh Dalvi, Adnan Darwiche, Amol Deshpande, Daniel Deutch, Pedro Domingos, Robert Fink, Wolfgang Gatterbauer, Johannes Gehrke, Rainer Gemulla, Lise Getoor, Vibhav Gogate, Michaela Götz, Joseph Halpern, Andrew Hogue, Jiewen Huang, Thomas Jansen, Abhay Jha, Evgeny Kharlamov, Benny Kimelfeld, Phokion Kolaitis, Gerome Miklau, Tova Milo, Alexandra Meliou, Swaroop Rath, Karl Schnaitter, Pierre Senellart, Val Tannen, and Rasmus Wissmann.

Finally, the authors would like to acknowledge their funding agencies: Dan Suciu's work is supported by NSF IIS-0911036, IIS-0915054, IIS-0713576, and IIS-0627585. Dan Olteanu's work is supported by EPSRC under grant ADEPT number EP/I000194/1, and by the Future and Emerging Technologies (FET) programme within the Seventh Framework Programme for Research of the European Commission, under the FET-Open grant agreements FOX number FP7-ICT-233599 and HiPerDNO number FP7-ICT-248135. Christopher Ré's work is supported by the Air Force Research Laboratory (AFRL) under prime contract no. FA8750-09-C-0181, the National Science Foundation under IIS-1054009, and gifts from Google, Microsoft, Physical Layer Systems, and Johnson Controls, Inc. Christoph Koch's work was supported by German Science Foundation (DFG) grant KO 3491/1-1, NSF grants IIS-0812272 and IIS-0911036, a KDD grant, a Google Research Award, and a gift from Intel. Any opinions, findings, conclusions, or recommendations expressed in this work do not necessarily reflect the views of DARPA, AFRL, or the US government.

Dan Suciu, Dan Olteanu, Christopher Ré, and Christoph Koch
May 2011

CHAPTER 1

Overview

1.1 TWO EXAMPLES

NELL[1], the Never-Ending Language Learner, is a research project from CMU that learns over time to read the Web. It has been running continuously since January 2010. It crawls hundreds of millions of Web pages and extracts facts of the form (`entity, relation, value`). Some facts are shown in Figure 1.1. For example, NELL believes that "Mozart is a person who died at the age of 35" and that "biscutate_swift is an animal".

NELL is an example of a large scale Information Extraction (IE) system. An IE system extracts *structured data*, such as triples in the case of NELL, from a collection of *unstructured data*, such as Web pages, blogs, emails, twitter feeds, etc. Data analytics tools today reach out to such external sources because it contains valuable and timely information.

The data extracted by an IE system is structured and therefore can be imported in a standard relational database system. For example, as of February 2011, NELL had extracted 537K triples of the form (`entity, relation, value`), which can be downloaded (in CSV format) and imported in, say, PostgreSQL. The relational schema for NELL can be either a single table of triples, or the data can be partitioned into distinct tables, one table for each distinct relation. For presentation purposes, we took the latter approach in Figure 1.2 and show a few tuples in two relations, `ProducesProduct` and `HeadquarteredIn`. For example, the triple (`sony, ProducesProduct, walkman`) extracted by Nell is inserted in the database table `ProducesProduct` as the tuple (`sony, walkman`). Data analytics can now be performed by merging the NELL data with other, offline database instances.

Most IE systems, including NELL, produce data that are *probabilistic*. Each fact has a probability, representing the system's confidence that the extraction is correct. While some facts have probability 1.0, most tuples have a probability that is < 1.0. In fact 87% of the 537K tuples in NELL have a probability that is less than 1.0. *Most of the data in NELL is uncertain.* Traditional data cleaning methods simply remove tuples that are uncertain and cannot be repaired; this is clearly not applicable to large scale IE systems because it would remove a lot of valuable data items. To use such data at its full potential, a database system must understand and process data with probabilistic semantics.

Consider a simple query over the NELL database: "Retrieve all products manufactured by a company headquartered in San Jose":

```
select x.Product, x.Company
```

[1]http://rtw.ml.cmu.edu/rtw/

Recently-Learned Facts twitter   (Refresh)

instance	iteration	date learned	confidence
biscutate_swift is an animal	211	18-feb-2011	100.0 👍 👎
pedigree_animals is a mammal	210	17-feb-2011	99.5 👍 👎
poppy_seed_holiday_bread is a baked_good	212	20-feb-2011	100.0 👍 👎
manuel_criado_de_val is a South_American_person	210	17-feb-2011	99.5 👍 👎
dillon_county_airport is an airport	210	17-feb-2011	93.8 👍 👎
the sports team toronto_blue_jays was the winner_of n1993_world_series	212	20-feb-2011	96.9 👍 👎
mozart is a person who died_at_the_age_of 35	210	17-feb-2011	96.9 👍 👎
peoria and arizona are proxies for eachother	210	17-feb-2011	99.9 👍 👎
wutv_tv is a TV_affiliate_of the network fox	210	17-feb-2011	96.9 👍 👎
white_stripes collaborates with jack_white	210	17-feb-2011	93.8 👍 👎

Figure 1.1: Facts extracted by NELL from the WWW. The thumbs-up and thumbs-down icons are intended to solicit users' input for cleaning the data.

```
from ProducesProduct x, HeadquarteredIn y
where x.Company=y.Company and y.City='san_jose'
```

This is a join of the two tables in Figure 1.2, and a fragment of the result is the following:

Product	Company	P
personal_computer	ibm	0.95
adobe_indesign	adobe	0.83
adobe_dreamweaver	adobe	0.80

The first answer, (personal_computer, ibm), is obtained by joining the tuples marked with X_1 and Y_1 in Figure 1.2, and its probability is the product of the two probabilities: $0.96 \cdot 0.99 \approx 0.95$. Similarly, (adobe_dreamweaver, adobe) is obtained by joining the tuples X_2, Y_2. Distinct tuples in NELL are considered independent probabilistic events; this is quite a reasonable assumption to make, for example, the tuple X_1 was extracted from a different document than Y_1, and, therefore, the two tuples can be treated as independent probabilistic events. As a consequence, the probabilities of the answers to our query are computed by multiplying the probabilities of the tuples that contributed to these answers. This computation can be expressed directly in SQL in a standard relational database:

```
select distinct x.Product, x.Company, x.P * y.P as P
from ProducesProduct x, HeadquarteredIn y
where x.Company = y.Company and y.City = 'san_jose'
order by P desc
```

ProducesProduct

Company	Product	P
sony	walkman	0.96
microsoft	mac_os_x	0.96
ibm	personal_computer	0.96
adobe	adobe_illustrator	0.96
microsoft	mac_os	0.9
adobe	adobe_indesign	0.9
adobe	adobe_dreamweaver	0.87
...	...	...

X_1 spans the first four data rows; X_2 spans the lower rows.

HeadquarteredIn

Company	City	P
microsoft	redmond	1.00
ibm	san_jose	0.99
emirates_airlines	dubai	0.93
honda	torrance	0.93
horizon	seattle	0.93
egyptair	cairo	0.93
adobe	san_jose	0.93
...	...	...

Y_1 marks the upper rows; Y_2 marks the adobe row.

Figure 1.2: NELL data stored in a relational database.

Thus, we can use an off-the-shelf relational database system to represent probabilistic data by simply adding a probability attribute, then use regular SQL to compute the output probabilities and to rank them by their output probabilities.

The goal of a probabilistic database system is to be a general platform for managing data with probabilistic semantics. Such a system needs to scale to large database instances and needs to support complex SQL queries, evaluated using probabilistic semantics. The system needs to perform probabilistic inference in order to compute query answers. The probabilistic inference component represents a major challenge. As we will see in subsequent chapters, most SQL queries require quite complex probabilistic reasoning, even if all input tuples are independent, because the SQL query itself introduces correlations between the intermediate results, and this makes probabilistic reasoning difficult.

The type of data uncertainty that we have seen in NELL is called *tuple-level uncertainty* and is defined by the fact that for each tuple the system has a degree of confidence in the correctness of that tuple. Thus, each tuple is a random variable. In other settings, one finds *attribute-level uncertainty*, where the value of an attribute is a random variable: it can have one of several choices, and each choice has an associated probability.

We illustrate attribute-level uncertainty with a second example. Google Squared[2] is an online service that presents tabular views over unstructured data that are collected and aggregated from public Web pages. It organizes the data into tables, where rows correspond to tuples and columns correspond to attributes, but each value has a number of possible choices. For example, the square in Figure 1.3 is computed by Google Squared in response to the keyword query "comedy movies". The default answer has 20 rows and 8 columns: each row represents a movie ("The Mask", "Scary Movie", "Superbad", etc.) and each column represents an attribute ("Item Name", "Language", "Director",

[2]http://www.google.com/squared

Figure 1.3: Google square *comedy movies* (left figure) as of November 2010. By clicking on the language and director fields of *The Mask*, pop-ups are shown with possible languages and directors of this movie (right figure).

"Release Date", etc.). For each attribute value, Google Squared displays only the value with the highest degree of confidence. However, if the user clicks on that value, then alternative choices are shown. For example, the most likely director of "The Mask" is Chuck Russell, but Google Squared has found other possible values ("John R. Dilworth," etc.) with lower confidence, and the user can see them by clicking on the director value (as shown in the figure). Similarly, for the language, English is the most likely, but a few other possible values exists.

In attribute-level uncertainty, the value of an attribute is a random variable that can take one of several possible outcomes. For example, the Director attribute of "The Mask" can be "Chuck Russell", "John R. Dilworth", etc. Assuming each movie has only one director, these choices are *mutually exclusive* probabilistic events. On the other hand, the choices of different attribute values are considered to be independent. For example, we assume that the Director attribute and the Language attribute are independent, and, similarly, we assume that Director attributes of different movies are also independent.

The power of external data sources such as NELL or Google Squared comes from merging them and further integrating them with other offline data sources, using relational queries. For instance, one can ask for birthplaces of directors of comedy movies with a budget of over $20M by joining the square for *comedy movies* (where we can ask for the budget) with some other external dataset like NELL (to obtain the directors' birthplaces). To do this, one needs a system that supports complex SQL queries over databases with uncertain data. Such a system is, of course, a probabilistic database system.

1.2   KEY CONCEPTS

1.2.1   PROBABILITIES AND THEIR MEANING IN DATABASES

How I stopped worrying and started to love probabilities[3].

Where do the probabilities in a probabilistic database come from? And what exactly do they mean? The answer to these questions may differ from application to application, but it is rarely satisfactory. Information extraction systems are based on probabilistic models, so the data they extract is probabilistic [Gupta and Sarawagi, 2006, Lafferty et al., 2001]; RFID readings are cleaned using particle filters that also produce probability distributions [Ré et al., 2008]; data analytics in financial prediction rely on statistical models that often generate probabilistic data [Jampani et al., 2008]. In some cases, the probability values have a precise semantics, but that semantics is often associated with the way the data is derived and not necessarily with how the data will be used. In other cases we have no probabilistic semantics at all but only a subjective confidence level that needs to be converted into a probability: for example, Google Squared does not even associate numerical scores, but defines a fixed number of confidence levels (high, low, etc.), which need to be converted into a probabilistic score in order to be merged with other data and queried. Another example is BioRank [Detwiler et al., 2009], which uses as input subjective and relative weights of evidence and converts those into probabilistic weights in order to compute relevance scores to rank most likely functions for proteins.

No matter how they were derived, we always map a confidence score to the interval [0, 1] and interpret it as a probability value. The important invariant is that a larger value always represents a higher degree of confidence, and this carries over to the query output: answers with a higher (computed) probability are more credible than answers with a lower probability. Typically, a probabilistic database ranks the answers to a query by their probabilities: the ranking is often more informative than the absolute values of their probabilities.

1.2.2   POSSIBLE WORLDS SEMANTICS

The meaning of a probabilistic database is surprisingly simple: it means that the database instance can be in one of several states, and each state has a probability. That is, we are not given a single database instance but several possible instances, and each has some probability. For example, in the case of NELL, the content of the database can be any subset of the 537K tuples. We don't know which ones are correct and which ones are wrong. Each subset of tuples is called a *possible world* and has a probability: the sum of probabilities of all possible worlds is 1.0. Similarly, for a database where the uncertainty is at the attribute level, a possible world is obtained by choosing a possible value for each uncertain attribute, in each tuple.

Thus, a probabilistic database is simply a probability distribution over a set of possible worlds. While the number of possible worlds is astronomical, e.g., 2^{537000} possible worlds for NELL, this

---

[3]One of the coauthors.

is only the semantics: in practice we use much more compact ways to represent the probabilistic database, as we discuss in Chapter 2.

1.2.3   TYPES OF UNCERTAINTY

Two types of uncertainty are used in probabilistic databases: tuple-level uncertainty and attribute-level uncertainty.

In *tuple-level uncertainty*, a tuple is a random variable; we do not know whether the tuple belongs to the database instance or not. The random variable associated to the tuple has a Boolean domain: it is *true* when the tuple is present and *false* if it is absent. Such a tuple is also called a *maybe tuple* [Widom, 2008]. In *attribute-level uncertainty*, the value of an attribute A is uncertain: for each tuple, the attribute A represents a random variable, and its domain is the set of values that the attribute may take for that tuple.

We will find it convenient to convert attribute-level uncertainty into tuple-level uncertainty and consider only tuple-level uncertainty during query processing. This translation is done as follows. For every tuple t, where the attribute A takes possible values $a_1, a_2, a_3, \ldots$, we create several clone tuples $t_1, t_2, t_3, \ldots$ that are identical to t except for the attribute A, whose values are $t_1.A = a_1$, $t_2.A = a_2$, etc. Now each tuple t_i is uncertain and described by a random variable, and the tuples $t_1, t_2, \ldots$ are mutually exclusive. A block of exclusive tuples is also called an *X-tuple* [Widom, 2008].

1.2.4   TYPES OF PROBABILISTIC DATABASES

The simplest probabilistic database is a *tuple-independent* database, where the tuples are independent probabilistic events. Another popular kind is the *block independent-disjoint* probabilistic database, or BID, where the tuples are partitioned into blocks, such that all tuples within a block are disjoint (i.e., mutually exclusive) events, and all tuples from different blocks are independent events. Attribute level uncertainty can be naturally represented as a BID table. While sometimes one needs to represent more complex correlations between the tuples in a database, this is usually achieved by decomposing the database into independent and disjoint components, in a process much like traditional database normalization. Another classification of probabilistic databases is into *discrete* and *continuous*. In the former, attributes are discrete random variables; in the latter, they are continuous random variables. In this book, we focus on discrete probabilistic databases and discuss the continuous case in a chapter on advanced techniques (Section 6.3).

1.2.5   QUERY SEMANTICS

Recall that the answer of a query Q on a *deterministic* database D is a set of tuples, denoted $Q(D)$. The semantics of the query on a *probabilistic* database is a set of pairs (t, p), where t is a possible tuple, i.e., it is in the query's answer in one of the possible worlds W, and p is the probability that t is in $Q(W)$ when W is chosen randomly from the set of possible worlds. In other words, p represents the marginal probability of the event "the query returns the answer t" over the space of possible worlds; p is sometimes called the *marginal probability* of the tuple t. In practice, Q returns an ordered set of pairs $(t_1, p_1), (t_2, p_2), \ldots$ where $t_1, t_2, \ldots$ are distinct tuples and $p_1, p_2, \ldots$ are their marginal probabilities, such that the answers are ranked by $p_1 \geq p_2 \geq \ldots$

This semantics does not report how distinct tuples are correlated. Thus, we know that t_1 is an answer with probability p_1 and that t_2 is an answer with probability p_2, but we do not know the probability that *both* t_1 and t_2 are answers. This probability can be 0 if t_1, t_2 are mutually exclusive; it can be $p_1 p_2$ if t_1 and t_2 are independent events; or it can be $\min(p_1, p_2)$ if the set of worlds where one of the tuples is an answer is contained in the set of worlds where the other tuple is an answer. The probability that both t_1, t_2 occur in the answer minus $p_1 p_2$ is called the *covariance*[4] of t_1, t_2: the tuples are independent iff the covariance is 0. Probabilistic database systems prefer to drop any correlation information from the query's output because it is difficult to represent for a large number of tuples. Users, however, can still inquire about the correlation, by asking explicitly for the probability of both t_1 and t_2. For example, consider the earlier query *Retrieve all products manufactured by a company headquartered in San Jose*, and suppose we want to know the probability that both `adobe_indesign` *and* `adobe_dreamweaver` are in the answer. We can compute that by running a second query, *Retrieve all pairs of products, each manufactured by a company headquartered in San Jose*, and looking up the probability of the pair `adobe_indesign`, `adobe_dreamweaver` in the answer. Thus, while one single query does not convey information about the correlations between the tuples in its answer, this information can always be obtained later, by asking additional, more complex queries on the probabilistic database.

1.2.6   LINEAGE

The *lineage* of a possible output tuple to a query is a propositional formula over the input tuples in the database, which says which input tuples must be present in order for the query to return that output. Consider again the query "Retrieve all products manufactured by a company headquartered in `San Jose`" on the database in Figure 1.2. The output tuple (`personal_computer`, `ibm`) has lineage expression $X_1 \wedge Y_1$, where X_1 and Y_1 represent the two input tuples shown in Figure 1.2; this is because both X_1 and Y_1 must be in the database to ensure that output. For another example, consider the query *find all cities that are headquarters of some companies*: the answer `san_jose` has lineage $Y_1 \vee Y_2$ because any of Y_1 or Y_2 are sufficient to produce the answer `san_jose`. Query evaluation on probabilistic databases essentially reduces to the problem of computing the probability of propositional formulas, representing lineage expressions. We discuss this in detail in Chapter 2.

We note that the term "lineage" is sometimes used in the literature with slightly different and not always consistent meanings. In this book, we will use the term lineage to denote a propositional formula. It corresponds to the *PosBool* provenance semiring of Green et al. [2007], which is the semiring of positive Boolean expressions, except that we also allow negation.

---

[4]The covariance of two random variables X_1, X_2 is $cov(X_1, X_2) = E[(X_1 - \mu_{X_1}) \cdot (X_2 - \mu_{X_2})]$. In our case, $X_i \in \{0, 1\}$ is the random variable representing the absence/presence of the tuple t_i, $\mu_{X_i} = E[X_i] = p_i$; hence, the covariance is $E[(X_1 - \mu_{X_1}) \cdot (X_2 - \mu_{X_2})] = E[X_1 \cdot X_2] - E[X_1] \cdot p_2 - p_1 \cdot E[X_2] + p_1 \cdot p_2 = E[X_1 \cdot X_2] - p_1 \cdot p_2 - p_1 \cdot p_2 + p_1 \cdot p_2 = E[X_1 \cdot X_2] - p_1 \cdot p_2 = P(t_1 \in Q(W) \wedge t_2 \in Q(W)) - P(t_1 \in Q(W)) \cdot P(t_2 \in Q(W))$.

	Graphical Models	**Probabilistic Databases**
Probabilistic model	Complex (correlations given by a graph)	Simple (disjoint-independent tuples)
Query	Simple (e.g., $P(X_1 X_3 \| X_2 X_5 X_7)$)	Complex (e.g., $\exists x.\exists y.\exists z.R(x, y) \wedge S(x, z)$)
Network	Static (Bayesian or Markov Network)	Dynamic (database+query)
Complexity measured in size of	Network	Database
Complexity parameter	Tree-width	Query
System	Stand-alone	Extension to Relational DBMS

Figure 1.4: Comparison between Graphical Models and Probabilistic Databases.

1.2.7   PROBABILISTIC DATABASES V.S. GRAPHICAL MODELS

A graphical model (GM) is a concise way to represent a joint probability distribution over a large set of random variables $X_1, X_2, \ldots, X_n$. The "graph" has one node for each random variable X_i and an edge (X_i, X_j) between all pairs of variables that are correlated in the probability space obtained by fixing the values of all the other variables[5]. GMs have been extensively studied in knowledge representation and machine learning since they offer concise ways to represent complex probability distributions.

Any probabilistic database is a particular type of a GM, where each random variable is associated to a tuple (or to an attribute value, depending on whether we model tuple-level or attribute-level uncertainty). Query answers can also be represented as a GM, by creating new random variables corresponding to the tuples of all intermediate results, including one variable for every answer to the query. Thus, GMs can be used both to represent probabilistic databases that have non-trivial correlations between their tuples and to compute the probabilities of all query answers. However, there are some significant distinctions between the assumptions made in GMs and in probabilistic databases, which are summarized in Figure 1.4, and are discussed next.

First, the probabilistic model in probabilistic databases is simple and usually (but not always) consists of a collection of independent, or disjoint-independent tuples; we discuss in Chapter 2 how this simple model can be used as a building block for more complex probabilistic models. In contrast, the probabilistic model in GMs is complex: they were designed explicitly to represent

---

[5]This definition is sufficient for our brief discussion but is an oversimplification; we refer the reader to a standard textbook on graphical models, e.g., [Koller and Friedman, 2009].

complex correlations between the random variables. Thus, the probabilistic model in databases is simple in the sense that there are no correlations at all, or only disjoint events.

Second, the notion of a query is quite different. In GMs, the query is simple: it asks for the probability of some output variables given some evidence; a typical query is $P(X_1 X_3 | X_2 X_5 X_7)$, which asks for the probability of (certain values of) the random variables X_1, X_3, given the evidence (values for) X_2, X_5, X_7. In probabilistic databases, the query is complex: it is an expression in the Relational Calculus, or in SQL, as we have illustrated over the NELL database.

Third, the network in GMs depends only on the data and is independent on the query, while in probabilistic databases the network depends on both the data and the query. Thus, the network in GMs is static while in probabilistic databases it is dynamic. The network in probabilistic databases is the query's lineage, obtained from both the databases instance and the query and may be both large (because the database is large) and complex (because the query is complex). The distinction between a static network in GM and a dynamic network in probabilistic databases affects dramatically our approach to probabilistic inference.

The complexity of the probabilistic inference problem is measured in terms of the size of the network (for GMs) and in the size of the database (for probabilistic databases). In this respect, the network in GMs is analogous to the database instance in databases. However, the key parameter influencing the complexity is different. In GM, the main complexity parameter is the network's treewidth; all probabilistic inference algorithms for GM run in time that is exponential in the treewidth of the network. In probabilistic databases, the main complexity parameter is the query: we fix the query, then ask for the complexity of probabilistic inference in terms of the size of the database instance. This is called *data complexity* by Vardi [1982]. We will show that, depending on the query, the data complexity can range from polynomial time to #P-hard.

Finally, probabilistic databases are an evolution of standard, relational database. In particular, they must use techniques that integrate smoothly with existing query processing techniques, such as indexes, cost-based query optimizations, the use of database statistics, and parallelization. This requires both a conceptual approach to probabilistic inference that is consistent with standard query evaluation and a significant engineering effort to integrate this probabilistic inference with a relational database system. In contrast, probabilistic inference algorithms for GM are stand-alone, and they are currently not integrated with relational query processing systems.

1.2.8 SAFE QUERIES, SAFE QUERY PLANS, AND THE DICHOTOMY

An *extensional query plan* is a query plan that manipulates probabilities explicitly and computes both the answers and probabilities. Two popular examples of extended operators in extensional query plans are the *independent join* operator, $\bowtie^i$, which multiplies the probabilities of the tuples it joins, under the assumption that they are independent, and the *independent project* operator, Π^i, which computes the probability of an output tuple t as $1 - (1 - p_1) \cdots (1 - p_n)$ where $p_1, \ldots, p_n$ are the probabilities of all tuples that project into t, again assuming that these tuples are independent. In general, an extensional plan does not compute the query probabilities correctly. If the plan does compute the output probabilities correctly for any input database, then it is called a *safe query plan*. Safe plans are easily added[6] to a relational database engine, either by small modifications of the relational operators or even without any change in the engine by simply rewriting the SQL query to manipulate the probabilities explicitly.

If a query admits a safe plan, then its data complexity is in polynomial time because any safe plan can be computed in polynomial time in the size of the input database by simply evaluating its operators bottom-up. Not all queries admit safe plans; as we will show in Chapter 3, for specific queries, we can prove that their data complexity is hard for $\#P$, and these obviously will not have a safe plan (unless $P = \#P$). If a query admits a safe query plan, then it is called a *safe query*; otherwise, it is called *unsafe*.

The notion of query safety should be thought of as a syntactic notion: we are given a set of rules for generating a safe plan for a query, and, if these rules succeed, then the query is called safe; if the rules fail, then we call the query unsafe. We describe a concrete set of such rules in Chapter 4. The question is whether these rules are complete: if the query can be computed in polynomial time by *some* algorithm, will we also find a safe plan for it? We show in Chapter 4 that the answer is yes if one restricts queries to unions of conjunctive queries and the databases to tuple-independent probabilistic databases. In this case, we have a dichotomy: for every query, either its data complexity is in polynomial time (when the query is safe) or is provably hard for $\#P$ (when it is unsafe).

The terms *safe query* and *safe query plan* were introduced in the MystiQ project by Dalvi and Suciu [2004].

1.3   APPLICATIONS OF PROBABILISTIC DATABASES

In recent years, there has been an increased interest in probabilistic databases. The main reason for this has been the realization that many diverse applications need a generic platform for managing probabilistic data; while the focus of this book is on techniques for managing probabilistic databases, we describe next some of these applications accompanied by an extensive list of references for further reading.

Information extraction (IE), already mentioned in this chapter, is a very natural application for probabilistic databases because some important IE techniques already generate probabilistic data. For example, Conditional Random Fields (CRFs) [Lafferty et al., 2001] define a probability space over the possible ways to parse a text. Typically, IE systems retain the most probable extraction, but Gupta and Sarawagi [2006] show that by storing multiple (or even all) alternative extractions of a CRF in a probabilistic database, one can increase significantly the overall recall of the system, thus justifying the need for a probabilistic database. Wang et al. [2008a], Wang et al. [2010b], and Wang et al. [2010a] describe a system, BayesStore, which stores the CRF in a relational database system and pushes the probabilistic inference inside the engine. Wick et al. [2010] describe an

---

[6]One should be warned, however, that the requirement of the plan to be safe severely restricts the options of a query optimizer, which makes the engineering aspects of integrating safe plans into a relational engine much more challenging than they seem at the conceptual level.

application of probabilistic databases to the Named Entity Recognition (NER) problem. In NER, each token in a text document must be labeled with an entity, such as PER (person entity such as Bill), ORG (organization such as IBM), LOC (location such as New York City), MISC (miscellaneous entity-none of the above), and O (not a named entity). By combining Markov Chain Monte Carlo with incremental view update techniques, they show considerable speedups on a corpus of 1788 New York Times articles from the year 2004. Fink et al. [2011a] describe a system that can answer relational queries on probabilistic tables constructed by aggregating Web data using Google Squared and on other online data that can be brought in tabular form.

A related application is *wrapper induction*. Dalvi et al. [2009] describe an approach for robust wrapper induction that uses a probabilistic change model for the data. The goal of the wrapper is to remain robust under likely changes to the data sources.

RFID data management extracts and queries complex events over streams of readings of RFID tags. Due to the noisy nature of the RFID tag readings these are usually converted into probabilistic data, using techniques such particle filters, then are stored in a probabilistic database [Diao et al., 2009, Khoussainova et al., 2008, Ré et al., 2008, Tran et al., 2009].

Probabilistic data is also used in *data cleaning*. Andritsos et al. [2006] show how to use a simple BID data model to capture key violations in databases, which occur often when integrating data from multiple sources. Antova et al. [2009] and Antova et al. [2007c] study data cleaning in a general-purpose uncertain resp. probabilistic database system, by iterative removal of possible worlds from a representation of a large set of possible worlds. Given that a limited amount of resources is available to clean the database, Cheng et al. [2008] describe a technique for choosing the set of uncertain objects to be cleaned, in order to achieve the best improvement in the quality of query answers. They develop a quality metric for a probabilistic database, and they investigate how such a metric can be used for data cleaning purposes.

In *entity resolution*, entities from two different databases need to be matched, and the challenge is that the same object may be represented differently in the two databases. In *deduplication*, we need to eliminate duplicates from a collection of objects, while facing the same challenge as before, namely that an object may occur repeatedly, using different representations. Probabilistic databases have been proposed to deal with this problem too. Hassanzadeh and Miller [2009] keep duplicates when the correct cleaning strategy is not certain and utilize an efficient probabilistic query-answering technique to return query results along with probabilities of each answer being correct. Sismanis et al. [2009] propose an approach that maintains the data in an unresolved state and dynamically deals with entity uncertainty at query time. Beskales et al. [2010] describe ProbClean, a duplicate elimination system that encodes compactly the space of possible repairs.

Arumugam et al. [2010] and Jampani et al. [2008], Xu et al. [2009] describe applications of probabilistic databases to *business intelligence* and *financial risk assessment*. Deutch et al. [2010b], Deutch and Milo [2010], and Deutch [2011] consider applications of probabilistic data to *business processes*.

Scientific data management is a major application domain for probabilistic databases. One of the early works recognizing this potential is by Nierman and Jagadish [2002]. They describe a system, ProTDB (Probabilistic Tree Data Base) based on a probabilistic XML data model and they apply it to protein chemistry data from the bioinformatics domain. Detwiler et al. [2009] describe BioRank, a mediator-based data integration systems for exploratory queries that keeps track of the uncertainties introduced by joining data elements across sources and the inherent uncertainty in scientific data. The system uses the uncertainty for ranking uncertain query results, in particular for predicting protein functions. They use the uncertainty in scientific data integration for ranking uncertain query results, and they apply this to protein function prediction. They show that the use of probabilities increases the system's ability to predict less-known or previously unknown functions but is not more effective for predicting well-known functions than deterministic methods. Potamias et al. [2010] describe an application of probabilistic databases for the study of protein-protein interaction. They consider the protein-protein interaction network (PPI) created by Krogan et al. [2006] where two proteins are linked if it is likely that they interact and model it as a probabilistic graph. Another application of probabilistic graph databases to protein prediction is described by Zou et al. [2010]. Voronoi diagrams on uncertain data are considered by Cheng et al. [2010b].

Dong et al. [2009] consider uncertainty in *data integration*; they introduce the concept of probabilistic schema mappings and analyze their formal foundations. They consider two possible semantics, by-table and by-tuple. Gal et al. [2009] study how to answer aggregate queries with COUNT, AVG, SUM, MIN, and MAX over such mappings, by considering both by-table and by-tuple semantics. Cheng et al. [2010a] study the problem of managing possible mappings between two heterogeneous XML schemas, and they propose a data structure for representing these mappings that takes advantage of their high degree of overlap. van Keulen and de Keijzer [2009] consider user feedback in probabilistic data integration. Fagin et al. [2010] consider probabilistic data exchange and establish a foundational framework for this problem.

Several researchers have recognized the need to redesign major components of data management systems in order to cope with uncertain data. Cormode et al. [2009a] and Cormode and Garofalakis [2009] redesign the histogram synopses, both for internal DBMS decisions (such as indexing and query planning) and for approximate query processing. Their histograms retain the possible-worlds semantics of probabilistic data, allowing for more accurate, yet concise, representation of the uncertainty characteristics of data and query results. Zhang et al. [2008] describe a data mining algorithm on probabilistic data. They consider a collection of X-tuples and search for approximately likely frequent items, with guaranteed high probability and accuracy. Rastogi et al. [2008] describe how to redesign access control to data when the database is probabilistic. They observe that access is often controlled by data, for example, a physician may access a patient's data only if the database has a record that the physician treats that patient; but in probabilistic databases the grant/deny decision is uncertain. The authors described a new access control method that adds a degree of noise to the data that is proportional to the degree of uncertainty of the access condition. Atallah and Qi [2009] describe how to extend skyline computation to probabilistic databases, without using "thresholding", while Zhang et al. [2009] describe continuous skyline queries over sliding windows on uncertain data elements regarding given probability thresholds. Jestes et al. [2010] extend the string similarity problem, which is used in many database queries, to probabilistic strings; they consider both the "string level model", consisting of a complete distribution on the possible strings, and the "character level model", where characters are independent events, and derive solutions for the Expected Edit Distance (EED). Xu et al. [2010] generalize the simple selection problem to probabilistic databases: the attribute in the data is uncertain and given by a probabilistic histogram, and the value being searched is also uncertain. They use the Earth Mover's Distance to define the similarity between the two uncertain values and describe techniques for computing it.

A class of applications of probabilistic databases is in *inferring missing attribute values* in a deterministic database by mining portions of the data where those values are present. The result is a probabilistic database since the missing values cannot be inferred exactly, but one can derive a probability distribution on their possible values. Wolf et al. [2009] develop methods for mining attribute correlations (in terms of Approximate Functional Dependencies), value distributions (in the form of Naïve Bayes Classifiers), and selectivity estimates for that purpose. Stoyanovich et al. [2011] use *ensembles* and develop an elegant and effective theory for inferring missing values from various subsets of the defined attributes. Dasgupta et al. [2009] describe an interesting application of probabilistic data for acquiring unbiased samples from online hidden database, which offer query interfaces that return restricted answers (e.g., only top-k of the selected tuples), accompanied by a total count of the total number of tuples.

Finally, we mention an important subarea of probabilistic databases that we do not cover in this book: ranking the query answers by using both a user defined scoring criterion *and* the tuple probability, e.g., [Cormode et al., 2009b, Ge et al., 2009, Li et al., 2009a,b, Soliman et al., 2008, 2010, Zhang and Chomicki, 2008]. It is often the case that the user can specify a particular ranking criteria, for example, rank products by prices or rank locations by some distance, which has a well defined semantics even on a deterministic database. If the database is probabilistic, then ranking becomes quite challenging because the system needs to account both for the user defined criterion and for the output probability.

1.4   BIBLIOGRAPHIC AND HISTORICAL NOTES

1.4.0.1   Early Work on Probabilistic Databases

Probabilistic databases are almost as old as traditional databases. Early work from the 80's [Cavallo and Pittarelli, 1987, Gelenbe and Hébrail, 1986, Ghosh, 1986, Lefons et al., 1983] described attributes as random variables. Attribute-level uncertainty as we understand it today, as an uncertain value of an attribute, was popularized by the work of Barbará et al. [1992] who also considered query processing and described a simple evaluation method for selection-join queries.

Motivated by the desire to merge databases with information retrieval, Fuhr [1990] and Fuhr and Rölleke [1997] defined a more elaborate probabilistic data model, which is essentially equivalent to the possible worlds semantics. A similar semantics is described by Zimányi [1997].

Around the same time, ProbView, a system by Lakshmanan et al. [1997], took a different approach by relaxing the probabilistic semantics in order to ensure efficient query evaluation; the idea of relaxing the probabilistic semantics can also be found in [Dey and Sarkar, 1996].

The possible worlds model for logics of knowledge and belief was originally proposed by Hintikka [1962], and it is now most commonly formulated in a normal modal logic using the techniques developed by Kripke [1963]. It is used extensively in logics of knowledge [Fagin et al., 1995].

1.4.0.2 Incomplete Databases

Much more work has been done on databases that have a notion of uncertainty but not probability. Uncertainty in the form of NULL values is part of the SQL standard and supported by most database management systems. In an even stronger form of *labeled nulls* that represent uncertain values that have identity and can be joined on, they were already part of Codd's original definition of the relational model. The seminal research work on databases with uncertainty is by Imieliński and Lipski [1984] who introduced the notion of conditional tables and strong representation systems, which will both be discussed in more detail in this book. The expressiveness of various uncertainty models and the complexity of query evaluation has been studied in a sequence of works, e.g., [Abiteboul et al., 1991, Grahne, 1984, 1991, Libkin and Wong, 1996, Olteanu et al., 2008]. A recent paper [Koch, 2008b] shows that a natural query algebra for uncertain databases, whose probabilistic extension can also be observed as the core of the query languages of the Trio and MayBMS systems, has exactly the expressive power of second-order logic. This is a somewhat reassuring fact, because second-order logic extends first-order-logic, the foundation of relational database languages, by precisely the power to "guess relations" and thus reason about possible worlds and what-if scenarios, which is the essence of uncertain database queries.

1.4.0.3 Probabilistic Graphical Models

As explained earlier, this book is not about probabilistic graphical models but instead focuses on the *database approach* to managing probabilistic databases, yet GMs do inform the research in probabilistic databases significantly. There is a vast amount of research on inference in graphical models by a variety of communities, including researchers in Artificial Intelligence, (bio)statistics, information theory, and others [Aji and McEliece, 2000]; in fact, the volume of work on graphical models significantly exceeds that of research on probabilistic databases. We refer the reader to several books by Pearl [1989], Gilks et al. [1995], Jordan [1998], Darwiche [2009], and Koller and Friedman [2009]. The connection between probabilistic databases and graphical models was first described and studied by Sen and Deshpande [2007]. The concurrent work by Antova et al. [2007c] uses a model of probabilistic databases that can be at once seen as flat Bayesian Networks and as a product decomposition of a universal relation representation [Ullman, 1990] of the set of possible worlds representing the probability space.

1.4.0.4 Renewed Research in Probabilistic Databases

In recent years, there has been a flurry of research activity surrounding probabilistic databases, starting with the Trio project [Widom, 2005, 2008] at Stanford and the MystiQ project [Dalvi and Suciu, 2004] at the University of Washington around 2004. Further well-known probabilistic database systems development efforts include MayBMS [Antova et al., 2007c, Huang et al., 2009], PrDB [Sen et al., 2009], ORION [Cheng et al., 2003, Singh et al., 2008], MCDB [Arumugam et al., 2010, Jampani et al., 2008], and SPROUT [Fink et al., 2011a, Olteanu et al., 2009].

CHAPTER 2

Data and Query Model

Traditionally, database management systems are designed to deal with information that is completely known. In reality, however, information is often incomplete or uncertain. An *incomplete database* is a database that allows its instance to be in one of multiple states (worlds); a *probabilistic database* is an incomplete database that, furthermore, assigns a probability distribution to the possible worlds. This chapter introduces incomplete and probabilistic databases, and discusses some popular representation methods. We start with a brief review of the relational data model and queries.

2.1 BACKGROUND OF THE RELATIONAL DATA MODEL

In this book, we consider only relational data. A *relational schema* $\bar{R} = \langle R_1, \ldots, R_k \rangle$ consists of k relation names, and each relation R_j has an associated arity $r_j \geq 0$.

A *relational database instance*, also called *world W*, consists of k relations $W = \langle R_1^W, \ldots, R_k^W \rangle$, where R_j^W is a finite relation of arity r_j over some fixed, infinite universe U, $R_j^W \subseteq U^{r_j}$. We often blur the distinction between the *relation name R_j* and the *relation instance R_j^W*, and write R_j for both. When given n possible worlds $W_1, \ldots, W_n$, we abbreviate R_j^i for $R_j^{W_i}$. We write interchangeably either W or D for a database instance; in the latter case, the relation instances are denoted by $R_1^D, \ldots, R_k^D$.

The queries that we will study are expressed in the *Relational Calculus*, or RC. Equivalently, these are First Order Logic expressions over the vocabulary $\bar{R}$. A query has the form $\{\bar{x} \mid Q\}$, also written as $Q(\bar{x})$, where $\bar{x}$ are the free variables, also called *head variables*, in the relational formula Q. The formula Q is given by the following grammar:

$$Q \quad ::= \quad u = v \mid R(\bar{x}) \mid \exists x.Q_1 \mid Q_1 \wedge Q_2 \mid Q_1 \vee Q_2 \mid \neg Q \tag{2.1}$$

Here $u = v$ is an equality predicate (where u, v are variables or constants), $R(\bar{x})$ is a relational atom with variables and/or constants, whose relation symbol R is from the vocabulary $\bar{R}$. The connectives $\wedge, \vee, \neg$ and the existential quantifier $\exists$ have standard interpretation. We will often blur the distinction between the formula Q and the query $\{\bar{x} \mid Q\}$, and write simply $Q(\bar{x})$ for the query.

A query Q without free variables is called a *Boolean query*. Given a database instance D, we write $D \models Q$ whenever Q is true in D; we omit the standard definition of $D \models Q$, which can be found in any textbook on logic, model theory, or database theory, e.g., [Abiteboul et al., 1995]. If a query Q has head variables $\bar{x}$, then it defines a function from database instances to relations of arity $|\bar{x}|$: $Q(D) = \{\bar{a} \mid D \models Q[\bar{a}/\bar{x}]\}$. Here $Q[\bar{a}/\bar{z}]$ means the query expression Q where all variables $\bar{z}$ are substituted with the constants $\bar{a}$.

For a simple illustration, consider the query $Q(x, z) = \exists y.R(x, y) \wedge S(y, z)$. Given an input instance $D = \langle R^D, S^D \rangle$, the query Q returns the set of pairs (a, c) for which there exists b s.t. $(a, b) \in R^D$ and $(b, c) \in S^D$. This set is denoted by $Q(D)$. To make it concrete, if $R^D = \{(a_1, b_1), (a_2, b_2), (a_2, b_3)\}$, $S^D = \{(b_2, c_1), (b_2, c_2), (b_2, c_3), (b_3, c_3)\}$, then $Q(D) = \{(a_2, c_1), (a_2, c_2), (a_2, c_3)\}$.

By convention, we restrict queries to be domain independent [Abiteboul et al., 1995]. In that case, the semantics of a query coincides with the following *active domain semantics*. Let *ADom* be the set of all constants occurring in all relation instances of the database D; we call it the *active domain* of the database D. Under the active domain semantics, every quantifier $\exists x$ in the query Q is interpreted as ranging over the active domain $ADom(D)$, and the set of answers $\bar{a}$ is also restricted to the active domain.

A *Conjunctive Query*, or CQ, is a query constructed only using the first four production rules of the grammar given by Eq. (2.1). A *Union of Conjunctive Queries*, UCQ, is a query constructed only using the first five grammar production rules. It is well known that every UCQ query can be written equivalently as $Q_1 \vee Q_2 \vee \ldots$ where each Q_i is a conjunctive query, which justifies the name *union of conjunctive queries*. Note that UCQ does not include queries with the predicate $u \neq v$: this can be expressed as $\neg(u = v)$, but in UCQ, we do not have negation. Also, we do not consider interpreted predicates, like $u < v$, as part of the query language: both $u \neq v$ and $u < v$ can be treated as an uninterpreted relational predicate $R(u, v)$, in effect, forgetting any special properties that the interpreted predicate has, but some of the necessary-and-sufficient results in Chapter 4 no longer hold in the presence of interpreted predicates.

An alternative syntax for RC is given by a *non-recursive datalog with negation*. In this language, a query is defined by a sequence of *datalog rules*, each having the form:

$$S(\bar{x}): -L_1, L_2, \ldots, L_k$$

where the atom $S(\bar{x})$ is called the *head*, $\bar{x}$ are called the *head variables*, the expression $L_1, L_2, \ldots, L_k$ is called the *body*, and each atom L_i is either a positive relational atom $R(\bar{x}_i)$ or the negation of a relational atom $\neg R(\bar{x}_i)$. Each rule must be *domain independent*, meaning that every variable must occur in at least one non-negated atom. The program is non-recursive if the rules can be ordered such that each head symbol S does not occur in the body of the current rule or the bodies of the previous rules.

We will freely switch back and forth between the two notations. For example, the query $Q(x, z)$ above is written as follows in non-recursive datalog:

$$Q(x, z): -R(x, y), S(y, z)$$

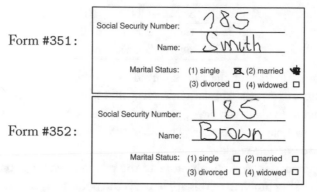

Figure 2.1: Two completed survey forms.

For another example, consider the following datalog program, which computes all paths of lengths 2 or 3 in a graph given by the binary relation $R(x, y)$:

$$S(x, y): -R(x, z), R(z, y)$$
$$Q(x, y): -S(x, y)$$
$$Q(x, y): -R(x, z), S(z, y)$$

Written as a relational formula it becomes:

$$Q = \{(x, y) \mid \exists z.(R(x, z) \wedge R(z, y)) \vee \exists z_1.\exists z_2.(R(x, z_1) \wedge R(z_1, z_2) \wedge R(z_2, y))\}$$

or, still equivalently, as:

$$Q = \{(x, y) \mid R(x, z), R(z, y) \vee R(x, z_1), R(z_1, z_2), R(z_2, y)\}$$

2.2 THE PROBABILISTIC DATA MODEL

Consider a census scenario in which a large number of individuals manually fill in forms. The data in these forms subsequently has to be put into a database, but no matter whether this is done automatically using OCR or by hand, some uncertainty may remain about the correct values for some of the answers. Figure 2.1 shows two simple filled-in forms. Each one contains the social security number, name, and marital status of one person.

The first person, Smith, seems to have checked marital status "single" after first mistakenly checking "married", but it could also be the opposite. The second person, Brown, did not answer the marital status question. The social security numbers also have several possible readings. Smith's could be 185 or 785 (depending on whether Smith originally is from the US or from Europe), and Brown's may either be 185 or 186. In total, we have $2 \cdot 2 \cdot 2 \cdot 4 = 32$ possible readings of the two census forms, which can be obtained by choosing one possible reading for each of the fields.

In an SQL database, uncertainty can be managed using null values. Our census data could be represented as in the following table.

R	FID	SSN	N	M
	351	null	Smith	null
	352	null	Brown	null

Using nulls, information about the values considered possible for the various fields is lost. Moreover, it is not possible to express correlations such as that while social security numbers may be uncertain, no two distinct individuals can have the same. In this example, we want to exclude the case that both Smith and Brown have social security number 185. Finally, we cannot store probabilities for the various alternative possible worlds.

An alternative approach is to explicitly store all the possible readings, one relation instance per reading. The most striking problem of this approach is the potentially large number of readings. If we conduct a survey of 50 questions on a population of 200 million and we assume that one in 10^4 answers can be read in just two different ways, we get 2^{10^6} possible readings. We cannot store all these readings explicitly; instead, we need to search for a more compact representation.

Example 2.1   Similar to the Google Squared representation in Chapter 1, we can represent the available information by inlining within each field all of its possibilities (here, without probabilities).

R	FID	SSN	N	M
	351	$\{185, 785\}$	Smith	$\{1, 2\}$
	352	$\{185, 186\}$	Brown	$\{1, 2, 3, 4\}$

This representation is more compact, yet it cannot account for correlations across possible readings of different fields, such as when we know that no two persons can have the same social security number.

In this chapter, we introduce formalisms that are able to compactly represent uncertain data, and start by defining the semantics of a probabilistic database. Throughout our discussion, we will consider *incomplete databases*, which allow for multiple different states of the database, and *probabilistic databases*, which specify in addition a probability distribution on those states.

Informally, our model is the following: fix a relational database schema. An *incomplete* database is a finite set of database instances of that schema (called possible worlds). A *probabilistic database* is also a finite set of possible worlds, where each world has a weight (called probability) between 0 and 1 and the weights of all worlds sum up to 1. In a subjectivist Bayesian interpretation, one of the possible worlds is "true", but we do not know which one, and the probabilities represent degrees of belief in the various possible worlds. In our census scenario, the probabilistic database consists of one world for each possible reading, which is weighted according to its likelihood.

Definition 2.2   Fix a relational schema with k relation names, $R_1, \ldots, R_k$. An *incomplete database* is a finite set of structures $\mathbf{W} = \{W^1, W^2, \ldots, W^n\}$, where each W^i is a database instance, $W^i = \langle R_1^i, \ldots, R_k^i \rangle$, called a *possible world*.

A *probabilistic database* is a probability space $\mathbf{D} = (\mathbf{W}, P)$ over an incomplete database $\mathbf{W}$, in other words $P : \mathbf{W} \to (0, 1]$ is a function such that $\sum_{W \in \mathbf{W}} P(W) = 1$.

In this book, we will restrict probabilistic databases to have a finite set of possible worlds, unless otherwise stated; we will use the finiteness assumption all through this chapter and the next, but we will briefly look beyond it in Section 6.3 when we discuss Monte-Carlo databases.

Intuitively, in an incomplete database the exact database instance is not known: it can be in one of n several states, called worlds. In a probabilistic database, we furthermore consider a probability distribution over the set of worlds. The number of worlds, n, is very large, and we shall describe shortly some practical ways to represent incomplete and probabilistic databases.

If all instantiations of some relation R_j are the same in all possible worlds of $\mathbf{W}$, i.e., if $R_j^1 = \cdots = R_j^n$, then we say that R_j is *complete* or *certain* or *deterministic*.

The *marginal probability* of a tuple t, or the tuple *confidence*, refers to the probability of the event $t \in R_j$, where R_j is one of the relation names of the schema, with

$$P(t \in R_j) = \sum_{1 \leq i \leq n: \, t \in R_j^i} P(W^i)$$

2.3   QUERY SEMANTICS

Since a probabilistic database can be in one of many possible states, what does it mean to evaluate a query Q on such a database? In this section, we define the semantics of a query Q on a probabilistic database $\mathbf{D}$; as an intermediate step, we also define the semantics of the query on an incomplete database $\mathbf{W}$. In each case, we need to consider two possible semantics. In the first, the query is applied to every possible world, and the result consists of all possible answers (each answer is a set of tuples); this is called the *possible answer sets* semantics. This semantics is compositional (we can apply another query on the result) but is difficult or impossible to present to the user. In the second, the query is also applied to all possible worlds, but the set of answers are combined, and a single set of tuples is returned to the user; this is called *possible answers* semantics. This result can be easily presented to the user, as a list of tuples, but it is no longer compositional since we lose track of how tuples are grouped into worlds.

We allow the query to be any function from an input database instance to an output relation: in other words, for the definitions in this section, we do not need to restrict the query to the relational calculus.

Throughout this book, we will assume that the query is defined over a deterministic database. That is, the user assumes the database is deterministic and formulates the query accordingly, but the system needs to evaluate it over an incomplete or probabilistic database and therefore returns all possible sets of answers, or all possible answers. There is no way for the user to inquire about the probabilities or the different possible worlds of the database; also, the query never introduces uncertainty, all uncertainty is what existed in the input data. This is a limitation, which is sufficient for our book; more expressive query languages have been considered in the literature, and we will give some bibliographic references in Section 2.8.

2.3.1   VIEWS: POSSIBLE ANSWER SETS SEMANTICS

The possible answer sets semantics returns all possible sets of answers to a query. This semantics is compositional, and especially useful for defining views over incomplete or probabilistic databases: thus, here we will denote a query by V, and call it a *view* instead of a query, emphasizing that we consider it as a transformation mapping a world W to another world $V(W)$.

Definition 2.3   Let V be a view and $\mathbf{W} = \{W^1, \ldots, W^n\}$ be an incomplete database. The *possible answer set* is the incomplete database $V(\mathbf{W}) = \{V(W) \mid W \in \mathbf{W}\}$.

Let V be a view and $\mathbf{D} = (\mathbf{W}, P)$ be a probabilistic database. The *possible answer set* is the probability space $(\mathbf{W}', P')$, where $\mathbf{W}' = V(\mathbf{W})$, and P' is defined by $P'(W') = \sum_{W \in \mathbf{W}: V(W)=W'} P(W)$, for all $W' \in \mathbf{W}'$.

We denote by $V(\mathbf{W})$ (or $V(\mathbf{D})$) the possible answer sets of V on the incomplete database $\mathbf{W}$ (or on the probabilistic database $\mathbf{D}$).

This semantics is, conceptually, very simple. For an incomplete database, we simply apply V to every possible state of the database, then eliminate duplicates from the answers. It is important to note that if the input $\mathbf{W}$ has n possible worlds, then the output has $m = |V(\mathbf{W})| \le n$ possible worlds. Thus, the number of possible worlds can only decrease, never increase. For a probabilistic database, the probability of an answer W' is the sum of all probabilities of those inputs W that are mapped into W'.

The possible answer sets semantics is *compositional*: once we computed $\mathbf{D}' = V(\mathbf{D})$, we can apply a new view V', and obtain $V'(\mathbf{D}') = V'(V(\mathbf{D})) = (V' \circ V)(\mathbf{D})$.

2.3.2   QUERIES: POSSIBLE ANSWERS SEMANTICS

For a query, it is impractical to represent all possible answer sets to a query. Instead, it is more convenient to consider one answer at a time, which we call the *possible answers* semantics, or, also, the *possible tuples* semantics.

Definition 2.4   Let Q be a query and $\mathbf{W}$ be an incomplete database. A tuple t is called a *possible answer* to Q if there exists a world $W \in \mathbf{W}$ such that $t \in Q(W)$. The *possible answers semantics* of the query is $Q_{poss}(\mathbf{W}) = \{t_1, t_2, \ldots\}$, where $t_1, t_2, \ldots$ are all possible answers.

A tuple is called a *certain answer* if for every world $W \in \mathbf{W}$, $t \in Q(W)$. The *certain answers semantics* of the query is $Q_{cert}(\mathbf{W}) = \{t_1, t_2, \ldots\}$, where $t_1, t_2, \ldots$ are all certain answers.

Definition 2.5   Let Q be a query and $\mathbf{D} = (\mathbf{W}, P)$ be a probabilistic database. The *marginal probability* or *output probability* of a tuple t is $P(t \in Q) = \sum_{W \in \mathbf{W}: t \in Q(W)} P(W)$. The *possible answers* *semantics* of the query is $Q(\mathbf{D}) = \{(t_1, p_1), (t_2, p_2), \ldots\}$, where $t_1, t_2, \ldots$ are all possible answers and $p_1, p_2, \ldots$ are their marginal probabilities.

This is the semantics that will be our main focus in the next chapter. The intuition behind it is very simple. On a deterministic database, the query Q returns a set of tuples $\{t_1, t_2, \ldots\}$, while on a probabilistic database, it returns a set of tuple-probability pairs $\{(t_1, p_1), (t_2, p_2), \ldots\}$. These answers can be returned to the user in decreasing order of their probabilities, such that $p_1 \geq p_2 \geq \ldots$

Notice that while in incomplete databases, we have two variants of the tuple answer semantics, Q_{poss} and Q_{cert}; in probabilistic databases, we only have one. The connection between them is given by the following, where $\mathbf{D} = (\mathbf{W}, P)$:

$$Q_{poss}(\mathbf{W}) = \{t \mid (t, p) \in Q(\mathbf{D}), p > 0\}$$
$$Q_{cert}(\mathbf{W}) = \{t \mid (t, p) \in Q(\mathbf{D}), p = 1\}$$

The possible tuples semantics is *not* compositional. Once we compute the result of a query $Q(\mathbf{D})$, we can no longer apply a new query Q' because $Q(\mathbf{D})$ is not a probabilistic database: it is only a collection of tuples and probabilities. However, the possible tuple semantics does compose with the possible answer sets semantics for views: if $V(\mathbf{D})$ is a view computed using the possible answer sets semantics, then we can apply a query Q, under the possible tuples semantics, $Q(V(\mathbf{D}))$; this is equivalent to computing the query $Q \circ V$ on $\mathbf{D}$ under the possible tuples semantics.

2.4   C-TABLES AND PC-TABLES

Definition 2.2 does not suggest a practical representation of incomplete or probabilistic data. Indeed, the explicit enumeration of all the possible worlds is not feasible when the number of worlds is very large. To overcome this problem, several representation systems have been proposed, which are concise ways to describe an incomplete or a probabilistic database. In this section, we define the most general representation systems: *conditional tables* or c-tables, for incomplete databases and *probabilistic conditional tables* or pc-tables for probabilistic databases.

A c-table is a relation where each tuple is annotated with a propositional formula, called condition, over random variables. A pc-table further defines a probability space over the assignments of the random variables. To define them formally, we first need a brief review of discrete variables and propositional formulas.

Denote by Dom_X the finite domain of a discrete variable X. The event that X takes a value $a \in Dom_X$ is denoted by $X = a$ and is called an *atomic event*, or an *atomic formula*. If $Dom_X = \{true, false\}$, then we say that X is a Boolean variable and write X and $\neg X$ as shortcuts for the atomic events $X = true$ and $X = false$, respectively. Denote by $\mathbf{X}$ a finite set of variables $X_1, X_2, \ldots, X_n$. A *valuation*, or *assignment*, is a function θ that maps each random variable $X \in \mathbf{X}$ to a value $\theta(X) \in$

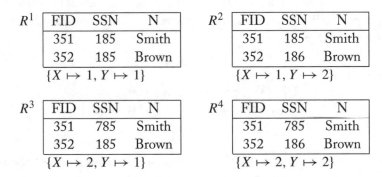

R	FID	SSN	N	
	351	185	Smith	$X = 1$
	351	785	Smith	$X \neq 1$
	352	185	Brown	$Y = 1$
	352	186	Brown	$Y \neq 1$

Figure 2.2: A Simple C-table.

R^1	FID	SSN	N
	351	185	Smith
	352	185	Brown
	$\{X \mapsto 1, Y \mapsto 1\}$		

R^2	FID	SSN	N
	351	185	Smith
	352	186	Brown
	$\{X \mapsto 1, Y \mapsto 2\}$		

R^3	FID	SSN	N
	351	785	Smith
	352	185	Brown
	$\{X \mapsto 2, Y \mapsto 1\}$		

R^4	FID	SSN	N
	351	785	Smith
	352	186	Brown
	$\{X \mapsto 2, Y \mapsto 2\}$		

Figure 2.3: The four possible worlds for C-table in Figure 2.2.

Dom_X in its domain. When $\theta(X) = a$, then we write $X \mapsto a$, or, with some abuse, $X = a$. The set of all possible valuations is denoted by $\Theta = Dom_{X_1} \times \cdots \times Dom_{X_n}$.

A *propositional formula* Φ is constructed from atomic events and the Boolean constants *true* and *false*, using the binary operations $\vee$ (logical "or") and $\wedge$ (logical "and"), and the unary operation $\neg$ (logical "not"). A formula $X \neq a$ means $\neg(X = a)$, or, equivalently, $X = a_1 \vee \ldots \vee X = a_m$ if $Dom_X - \{a\} = \{a_1, \ldots, a_m\}$. We also call Φ a *complex event*, or simply an *event*, and denote the set of satisfying assignments of Φ by

$$\omega(\Phi) = \{\theta \mid \theta \text{ is a valuation of variables in } \Phi, \Phi[\theta] = true\}$$

Consider again our census scenario. Figure 2.2 shows a c-table representing data about *name* and *social security numbers* only (we drop *marital-status* but will re-introduce it in Subsection 2.7.3). The variables X, Y are discrete, and their domains are $Dom_X = Dom_Y = \{1, 2\}$. The conditions under the columns Φ encode symbolically the assignments in which their corresponding tuples exist. For instance, the first tuple occurs in all possible worlds where $X \mapsto 1$ and does not occur in worlds where $X \mapsto 2$. Every assignment gives rise to a possible world, consisting of those tuples whose formula Φ is true. The c-table in Figure 2.2 has four distinct worlds, corresponding to possible assignments of variables X and Y. These four worlds are shown in Figure 2.3.

Now assume that we would like to enforce the integrity constraint that no two persons can have the same social security number (SSN). That is, the world R^1 in Figure 2.3 is considered wrong

R'

FID	SSN	N	
351	185	Smith	$X = 1 \wedge Z = 1$
351	785	Smith	$X \neq 1$
352	185	Brown	$Y = 1 \wedge Z \neq 1$
352	186	Brown	$Y \neq 1$

R''

FID	SSN	N	
351	185	Smith	$X = 1$
351	785	Smith	$X \neq 1$
352	185	Brown	$Y = 1 \wedge X \neq 1$
352	186	Brown	$Y \neq 1 \vee X = 1$

(a)   (b)

Figure 2.4: Two ways to enforce unique SSN in Figure 2.2.

R^2

FID	SSN	N
351	185	Smith
352	186	Brown

$\{X \mapsto 1, Y \mapsto 1\}$
$\{X \mapsto 1, Y \mapsto 2\}$

R^3

FID	SSN	N
351	785	Smith
352	185	Brown

$\{X \mapsto 2, Y \mapsto 1\}$

R^4

FID	SSN	N
351	785	Smith
352	186	Brown

$\{X \mapsto 2, Y \mapsto 2\}$

Figure 2.5: The three possible worlds for C-table in Figure 2.4 (b).

because both Smith and Brown have the same SSN. There are two options: we could repair R^1, by removing one of the two tuples, or we could remove the world R^1 altogether.

The first option is given by the c-table R' shown in Figure 2.4 (a). Here a new variable Z ensures that the first and third tuple cannot occur in the same world, by making their conditions mutually exclusive. This c-table has five possible worlds, which are derived from those in Figure 2.3 as follows: R^1 is replaced with two worlds, $\{(351, 185, \text{Smith})\}, \{(352, 185, \text{Brown})\}$, while R^2, R^3, R^4 remain unchanged. Thus, in this c-table, we enforced the constraint by repairing world R^1, and this can be done in two possible ways, by removing one of its tuples.

The second option is given by the c-table R'' in Figure 2.4 (b). In this c-table, the world R^1 does not exists at all; instead, both assignments $X \mapsto 1, Y \mapsto 1$ and $X \mapsto 1, Y \mapsto 2$ result in the same possible world R^2. This c-table has only three possible worlds, namely R^2, R^3, R^4, which are shown again in Figure 2.5, together with the assignment that generated them.

With this example in mind, we give now the definition of c-tables and pc-tables.

Definition 2.6   A *conditional database*, or *c-table* for short, is a tuple $CD = \langle R_1, \ldots, R_k, \Phi \rangle$, where $\langle R_1, \ldots, R_k \rangle$ is a relational database instance, and Φ assigns a propositional formula Φ_t to each tuple t in each relation $R_1, \ldots, R_k$.

Given a valuation θ of the variables in Φ, the *world associated with θ* is $W^\theta = \langle R_1^\theta, \ldots, R_k^\theta \rangle$ where $R_i^\theta = \{t \mid t \in R_i, \Phi_t[\theta] = true\}$ for each $i = 1, k$.

The semantics of the c-table CD, called *representation*, is the incomplete database $\mathbf{W} = \{W^\theta \mid \theta \in \Theta\}$. Recall that $\Theta = Dom_{X_1} \times \cdots \times Dom_{X_n}$ is the set of all possible valuations of the variables $X_1, \ldots, X_n$.

All three c-tables, in Figure 2.2, Figure 2.4 (a) and (b), are illustrations of this definition. In each case, the table consists of a set of tuples, and each tuple is annotated with a propositional formula. Notice that we use the term c-table somewhat abusively to denote a "c-database", consisting of several tables; we will also refer to a c-database as a "collection of c-tables".

C-tables can be represented by augmenting a standard table with a column Φ that stores the condition associated with each tuple. While in our definition, each tuple must occur at most once, in practice we sometimes find it convenient to allow a tuple t to occur multiple times and be annotated with different formulas, $\Phi_1, \Phi_2, \ldots, \Phi_m$: multiple occurrences of t are equivalent to a single occurrence of t annotated with the disjunction $\Phi_1 \vee \ldots \vee \Phi_m$.

We now move to probabilistic databases. A pc-table consists of a c-table plus a probability distribution P over the set Θ of assignments of the discrete variables $X_1, \ldots, X_n$, such that all variables are independent. Thus, P is completely specified by the numbers $P(X = a) \in [0, 1]$ that assign a probability to each atomic event $X = a$ such that, for each random variable X:

$$\sum_{a \in Dom_X} P(X = a) = 1.$$

The probability of an assignment $\theta \in \Theta$ is given by the following expression, where $\theta(X_i) = a_i$, for $i = 1, n$:

$$P(\theta) = P(X_1 = a_1) \cdot P(X_2 = a_2) \cdots P(X_n = a_n) \tag{2.2}$$

The probability of a propositional formula Φ is:

$$P(\Phi) = \sum_{\theta \in \omega(\Phi)} P(\theta) \tag{2.3}$$

where $\omega(\Phi)$ the set of satisfying assignments for Φ.

Definition 2.7   A *probabilistic conditional database*, or *pc-table* for short, is a pair $PCD = (CD, P)$ where CD is a c-table, and P is a probability space over the set of assignments.

The semantics of a pc-table is as follows. Its set of possible worlds is the set of possible worlds of the incomplete database $\mathbf{W}$ represented by CD and the probability of each possible world $W \in \mathbf{W}$ is defined as $P(W) = \sum_{\theta \in \Theta: W^\theta = W} P(\theta)$.

In practice, both the c-table CD and the probability space P are stored in standard relations. CD is stored by augmenting each tuple with a propositional formula Φ; P is stored in a separate table $W(V, D, P)$ where each row (X, a, p) represents the probability of one atomic event, $P(X = a) = p$. An example of a table W is given below:

W	V	D	P
	X	1	0.2
	X	2	0.8
	Y	1	0.3
	Y	2	0.7

The probabilities of the four possible worlds in Figure 2.3 are the following:

$$P(R^1) = 0.2 \cdot 0.3 \qquad P(R^2) = 0.2 \cdot 0.7 \qquad P(R^3) = 0.8 \cdot 0.3 \qquad P(R^4) = 0.8 \cdot 0.7$$

These four probabilities are 0.06, 0.14, 0.24, 0.56, and obviously they add up to 1.

On the other hand, the probabilities of the three possible worlds in Figure 2.5 are:

$$P(R^2) = 0.2 \cdot 0.3 + 0.2 \cdot 0.7 = 0.2 \quad P(R^3) = 0.8 \cdot 0.3 = 0.24 \quad P(R^4) = 0.8 \cdot 0.7 = 0.56.$$

In summary, pc-tables extend traditional relations in two ways: each tuple is annotated with a propositional formula, and we are given a separate table representing the probability space. This is a very general and very powerful representation mechanism: we will consider several restrictions later in this chapter.

2.5 LINEAGE

Consider a c-database $\mathbf{D}$ and a query Q in the Relational Calculus. The *lineage* of a possible answer t to Q on $\mathbf{D}$ is a propositional formula representing the event $t \in Q(W)$, over the possible worlds W of $\mathbf{D}$; we define the lineage formally in this section.

With some abuse, we will extend the definition of lineage to the case when $\mathbf{D}$ is a standard relational database (not a c-database). In that case, we introduce a new, distinct Boolean variable X_t for each tuple t in the database, and define the tuple condition to be $\Phi_t = X_t$, thus, transforming the database into a c-database. Therefore, we will freely refer to the lineage of a query on either a c-database or on a regular database.

Definition 2.8 Let $\mathbf{D}$ be a database (either a standard database, or c-database), and let Q be a Boolean query in the Relational Calculus. The *lineage* of Q on $\mathbf{D}$ is the propositional formula $\Phi_Q^{\mathbf{D}}$, or simply Φ_Q if $\mathbf{D}$ is understood from the context, defined inductively as follows. If Q is a ground tuple t, then Φ_t is the propositional formula associated with t. Otherwise, Φ_Q is defined by the following six cases:

$$\begin{aligned}
\Phi_{a=a} &= \textit{true} & \Phi_{a=b} &= \textit{false} \\
\Phi_{Q_1 \wedge Q_2} &= \Phi_{Q_1} \wedge \Phi_{Q_2} & \Phi_{Q_1 \vee Q_2} &= \Phi_{Q_1} \vee \Phi_{Q_2} \\
\Phi_{\exists x.Q} &= \bigvee_{a \in ADom(\mathbf{D})} \Phi_{Q[a/x]} & \Phi_{\neg Q} &= \neg(\Phi_Q)
\end{aligned} \qquad (2.4)$$

We denote by $ADom(\mathbf{D})$ the active domain of the database instance, i.e., the set of all constants occurring in $\mathbf{D}$.

Let Q be a (non-Boolean) query in the Relational Calculus, with head variables $\bar{x}$. For each possible answer $\bar{a}$, its lineage is defined as the lineage of the Boolean query $Q[\bar{a}/\bar{x}]$.

The lineage Φ_Q is defined by induction on the query expression Q given by Eq. (2.1). Notice that Q is always a Boolean query Q. Thus, if the query is an equality predicate $u = v$, then u and v must be two constants: if they are the same constant, then query is $a = a$, and the lineage is defined as *true*; if they are different constants, then the query is $a = b$ and then the lineage is defined as *false*. If the query is $R(\bar{x})$, then all terms in $\bar{x}$ are constants; hence, the query is a ground tuple t: the lineage is defined as Φ_t. Finally, if the query is one of the other expressions in Eq. (2.1), then the lineage is defined accordingly; this should be clear from Eq. (2.4).

Example 2.9   For a simple illustration of the lineage expression, consider the Boolean query $Q = \exists x.\exists y.R(x) \wedge S(x, y)$, and consider the following database instance with relations R and S:

R	A	
	a_1	X_1
	a_2	X_2

S	A	B	
	a_1	b_1	Y_1
	a_1	b_2	Y_2
	a_2	b_1	Y_3

We have associated a distinct Boolean variable with each tuple, in effect transforming standard relations R and S into two c-tables. Then the lineage of Q is $\Phi_Q = X_1 Y_1 \vee X_1 Y_2 \vee X_2 Y_3$. Intuitively, the lineage says when Q is true on a subset of the database: namely, Q is true if either both tuples X_1 and Y_1 are present, when both tuples X_1 and Y_2 are present, or when both tuples X_2 and Y_3 are present.

The lineage allows us to reduce the query evaluation problem to the problem of evaluating the probability of a propositional formula. More precisely:

Proposition 2.10   *Let $Q(\bar{x})$ be a query with head variables $\bar{x}$, and let $\mathbf{D}$ be a pc-database. Then the probability of a possible answer $\bar{a}$ to Q is equal to the probability of the lineage formula:*

$$P(\bar{a} \in Q) = P(\Phi_{Q[\bar{a}/\bar{x}]})$$

2.6   PROPERTIES OF A REPRESENTATION SYSTEM

We expect two useful properties from a good representation system for incomplete or for probabilistic databases. First, it should be able to represent any incomplete or probabilistic database. Second, it should be able to represent the answer to any query, under the possible answer sets semantics. The first property, called *completeness*, implies the second property, which is called *closure under a query language*.

Definition 2.11   A representation system for probabilistic databases is called *complete* if it can represent any[1] probabilistic database $\mathbf{D} = (\mathbf{W}, P)$.

Theorem 2.12   PC-tables are a complete representation system.

Proof. The proof is fairly simple. Given a finite set of possible worlds $\{\langle R_1^1, \ldots, R_k^1 \rangle, \ldots, \langle R_1^n, \ldots, R_k^n \rangle\}$, with probabilities $p_1, \ldots, p_n$, we create a pc-table $PCD = (CD, P)$ as follows. Let X be a random variable whose domain is $\{1, \ldots, n\}$ and let $P(X = i) = p_i$, for all $1 \leq i \leq n$. Intuitively, there is exactly one assignment $X = i$, corresponding to the ith possible world.

For all $1 \leq j \leq k$, the table R_j in CD is the union of all instances $R_j^1, \ldots, R_j^n$. For each tuple $t \in R_j$, the condition Φ_t is the disjunction of all conditions $X = i$, for all i s.t. $t \in R_j^i$: formally, $\Phi_t = \bigvee_{i:t \in R_j^i} (X = i)$. It is easy to verify that the constructed pc-table represents exactly the input probabilistic database. $\square$

Consider a representation formalism, like pc-tables, or one of the weaker formalisms considered in the next section. Let $\mathbf{D}$ be a probabilistic database represented in this formalism. Given a query Q, can we represent $\mathbf{V} = Q(\mathbf{D})$ in the same formalism? Here $\mathbf{V}$ is another probabilistic database, defined by the possible answer sets semantics (Subsection 2.3.1), and the question is whether it can be represented in the same representation formalism. If the answer is "yes", then we say that the representation formalism is *closed* under that particular query language.

Obviously, any complete representation system is also closed; therefore, Theorem 2.12 has the following Corollary:

Corollary 2.13   *PC-tables are closed under the Relational Calculus.*

However, using Theorem 2.12 to prove the Corollary is rather unsatisfactory because it is non-constructive. A constructive proof of Corollary 2.13 uses lineage. More precisely, let $\mathbf{D} = (CD, P)$ be a pc-database, and let $Q(\bar{x})$ be a query with k head variables. Let $A = ADom(CD)$ be the active domain of CD. Then $\mathbf{V} = Q(\mathbf{D})$ is the following pc-table. It consists of all tuples $\bar{a} \in A^k$, and each tuple $\bar{a}$ is annotated with the propositional formula $\Phi_{Q[\bar{a}/\bar{x}]}$. This defines the c-table part of $\mathbf{V}$. For

---

[1]Recall that we restrict our discussion to *finite* probabilistic databases.

the probability distribution of the Boolean variables, we simply keep the same distribution P as for **D**.

Example 2.14   Consider the following pc-database **D**. Start from the c-tables R, S defined in Example 2.9, and let P be the probability given by

$$P(X_1) = P(X_2) = P(Y_1) = P(Y_2) = P(Y_3) = 0.5 \tag{2.5}$$

Define **D** $= (\langle R, S \rangle, P)$ to be the pc-database consisting of relations R and S, and the probability distribution P.

Consider the query $Q(x, x') = R(x), S(x, y), S(x', y), R(x')$. Then, we can represent the view **V** $= Q(\mathbf{D})$ by the the following pc-table:

Q	x	x'	
	a_1	a_1	$\Phi_{Q(a_1, a_1)} = X_1 Y_1 \vee X_1 Y_2$
	a_1	a_2	$\Phi_{Q(a_1, a_2)} = X_1 X_2 Y_1 Y_3$
	a_2	a_1	$\Phi_{Q(a_2, a_1)} = X_1 X_2 Y_1 Y_3$
	a_2	a_2	$\Phi_{Q(a_2, a_2)} = X_2 Y_3$

with the same probability distribution of the propositional Boolean variables, given by Eq. (2.5).

2.7   SIMPLE PROBABILISTIC DATABASE DESIGN

A basic principle in database design theory is that a table with some undesired functional dependencies should be *normalized*, i.e., decomposed into smaller tables, where only key constraints hold. The original table can be recovered as a view from the normalized tables. The traditional motivation for database normalization is to eliminate update anomalies, but decomposition into simple components is a basic, fundamental design principle, which one should follow even when updated anomalies are not a top concern. For a simple example of database normalization, consider a schema Document(did, version, title, file): if the functional dependencies did $\rightarrow$ title and did, version $\rightarrow$ file hold, then the table should be normalized into DocumentTitle(did, title) and DocumentFile(did, version, file). The original table can be recovered as:

Document(d, v, t, f) :- DocumentTitle(d, t), DocumentFile(d, v, f)   (2.6)

By decomposing the Document table into the simpler tables DocumentTitle and DocumentFile, we have removed an undesired constraint, namely the non-key dependency did $\rightarrow$ title.

A basic principle in graphical models is that a probability distribution on a large set of random variables should be decomposed into factors of simpler probability functions, over small sets of these variables. These factors can be identified, for example, by using a set of axioms for reasoning about probabilistic independence of variables, called *graphoids* [Verma and Pearl, 1988]. For a simple illustration, consider an example [Darwiche, 2009], consisting of a probability distribution on four Boolean variables: *Burglary, Alarm, Earthquake, and Radio*. Here *Burglary* is true if there was burglary at ones' house and, similarly, for *Alarm* and *Earthquake*; the variable *Radio* is true if an earthquake is announced on the radio. The probability distribution has 16 entries, $P(B, A, E, R)$, recording the probability of each combination of states of the four variables. However, because of causal relationships known to exists between these variables, A depends only on B and E, while R depends only on E. Therefore, the probability distribution can be decomposed into a product of three functions:

$$P(B, A, E, R) = P(A|B, E) \cdot P(R|E) \cdot P(B) \cdot P(E) \qquad (2.7)$$

Thus, we have expressed the more complex probability distribution in terms of four simpler distributions.

The analogy between Eq. (2.6) and Eq. (2.7) is striking, and not accidental at all. Both databases and graphical models follow the same design principle, decomposing into the simplest components. The connection between the two decompositions was observed and studied by Verma and Pearl [1988].

The same design principle applies to probabilistic databases: the data should be decomposed into its simplest components. If there are correlations between the tuples in a table, the table should be decomposed into simpler tables; the original table can be recovered as a view from the decomposed tables. Thus, the base tables have a very simple probabilistic model, consisting of independent or disjoint tuples, but these tables can be very large. On the other hand, the view reconstructing the original table may introduce quite complex dependencies between tuples that may not even have a simple description as a graphical model, but the view expression is very small.

In this section, we discuss tuple independent and independent-disjoint tables, which are the building blocks for more complex probabilistic databases. Any probabilistic database can be derived from tuple-independent or independent-disjoint tables using a view. A *view* is simply a query, or a set of queries, over a probabilistic database **D**. We denote the view by V, and we always interpret it under the possible answer sets semantics. That is, $\mathbf{D}' = V(\mathbf{D})$ is another probabilistic database, which we call the *image*, or the *output* of V. In general, the view V consists of several queries, one for each table in the output, but to simplify our presentation, we will assume that $\mathbf{D}'$ has a single table, and thus V is a single query; the general case is a straightforward generalization. At the end of the section, we discuss U-tables, which can express efficiently the results of unions of conjunctive queries.

2.7.1   TUPLE-INDEPENDENT DATABASES

A *tuple-independent probabilistic database* is a probabilistic database where all tuples are independent probabilistic events. If the database consists of a single table, then we refer to it as a tuple-independent

ProducesProduct	Company	Product	P
	sony	walkman	0.96
	ibm	personal_computer	0.96
	adobe	adobe_dreamweaver	0.87

Figure 2.6: A tuple-independent table, which is a fragment of ProducesProduct in Figure 1.2. In a tuple-independent table, we only need to indicate the marginal tuple probabilities.

table. For a simple example, any deterministic table is a tuple-independent table. A tuple-independent table can always be represented by a pc-table whose tuples $t_1, t_2, t_3, \ldots$ are annotated with distinct Boolean variables $X_1, X_2, X_3, \ldots$. Since each variable X_i occurs only once, we don't need to store it at all; instead, in a tuple-independent table, we store the probability $p_i = P(X_i)$ next to each tuple t_i. Thus, the schema of a tuple independent table is $R(A_1, A_2, \ldots, A_m, P)$, where $A_1, A_2, \ldots, A_m$ are the regular attributes, and P is the tuple probability. Of course, a query cannot access P directly, so in a query, the relation R will appear with the schema $R(A_1, \ldots, A_m)$. Alternatively, we view a tuple-independent table as a relation $R(A_1, \ldots, A_m)$ and a probability function P mapping tuples $t \in R$ to probabilities $P(t)$. With this convention, we denote a tuple-independent probabilistic database as $\mathbf{D} = (\langle R_1, \ldots, R_k \rangle, P)$.

Figure 2.6 shows a tuple-independent table called ProducesProduct. The marginal tuple probabilities are in the right column; this is the same convention we used in Figure 1.2. In this simple example, there are 8 possible worlds, corresponding to the subsets of the table. The probability of the world consisting of the first and the third tuple is $0.96 \cdot 0.04 \cdot 0.87$.

Tuple-independent tables are good building blocks since there are no correlations and no constraints between the tuples. However, they are obviously not complete since they can only represent probabilistic databases where all tuples are independent events: for a simple counterexample, Figure 2.2 is not tuple-independent. However, more complex probabilistic databases can sometimes be decomposed into tuple independent tables, and thus "normalized"; we illustrate with an example.

Example 2.15 Consider again the NELL database. Each fact is extracted from a Webpage, called *source*. Some sources are more reliable and contain accurate facts, while other sources are less reliable and contain often incorrect facts. We want to express the fact that tuples in the probabilistic database are correlated with their source. This introduces additional correlations. For example, suppose two tuples *ProducesProduct*(a, b) and *ProducesProduct*(c, d) are extracted from the same source. If the first tuple is wrong, then it is wrong either because the source is wrong or because the extraction was wrong: in the first case, the second tuple is likely to be wrong, too. Thus, if one tuple is wrong, the probability that the other tuple is also wrong increases. For the same reason, there are now correlations between tuples in different tables, if they come from the same source. While it is possible to represent this with pc-tables, since pc-tables are a complete representation system, a better approach is to decompose the data into two tuple-independent tables with the following schemas:

```
nellSource(source, P)
nellExtraction(entity, relation, value, source, P)
```

The first table stores all the sources and their reliabilities. Source reliability is independent across sources, so the tuples in *nellSource* are independent. The second table stores the extractions, *conditioned* on the source being reliable: under this condition all extractions are independent. Thus, we have represented the entire database using two large tuple-independent tables. Our initial probabilistic database shown in Figure 1.2 can be derived from the base tables using the following views[2]:

$$ProducesProduct(x, y) \ \texttt{:-} \ \texttt{nellExtraction}(x, \text{'ProducesProduct'}, y, s), \texttt{nellSource}(s)$$
$$HeadquarteredIn(x, y) \ \texttt{:-} \ \texttt{nellExtraction}(x, \text{'HeadquarteredIn'}, y, s), \texttt{nellSource}(s)$$
...

Thus, all views are expressed over two tuple-independent tables, but they contain tuples that are correlated in complex ways.

Does this example generalize? Can we express *any* probabilistic database as a view over tuple-independent tables? The answer is "yes", but the tuple-independent tables may be very large, and even the view definition may be large too:

Proposition 2.16   *Tuple-independent tables extended with RC views are a complete representation system.*

Proof. Let $\mathbf{D} = (\mathbf{W}, P)$ be a probabilistic database with $n = |\mathbf{W}|$ possible worlds. To simplify the notations, assume that the database schema has a single relation name $R(\bar{A})$; hence, the n possible worlds in $\mathbf{D}$ are n relations, $R^1, \dots, R^n$; the general case follows immediately and is omitted. We prove the following statement by induction on n: if $\mathbf{D}$ has n possible worlds, then there exists a probabilistic database $\mathbf{ID}_n = (\langle S_n, W_n \rangle, P_n)$, over a schema $\langle S(K, \bar{A}), W(K) \rangle$, such that (a) the relation W_n is a tuple-independent probabilistic relation, with $n - 1$ independent tuples $k_1, \dots, k_{n-1}$, with probabilities $P_n(k_1), \dots, P_n(k_{n-1})$, (b) the relation S_n is a deterministic relation, and (c) there exists a query, Q_n (which depends on n), in the Relational Calculus, s.t. $\mathbf{D} = Q_n(\mathbf{ID}_n)$. Note that $\mathbf{ID}_n$ has 2^{n-1} possible worlds: the query Q_n maps them to only n possible outputs, returning exactly $\mathbf{D}$.

If $n = 1$, then $\mathbf{D}$ has a single world R^1. Choose any constant k_1 and define: $S_1 = \{k_1\} \times R^1$, $W_1 = \emptyset$, and:

$$Q_1 = \Pi_{\bar{A}}(S)$$

In other words, S_1 is exactly R^1 (plus one extra attribute), and the query Q_1 projects out that extra attribute.

---

[2]Note that the view definition does not mention the attribute P. This is standard in probabilistic databases: the query is written over the possible world, not over the representation.

Assuming the statement is true for n, we will prove it for $n + 1$. Let $\mathbf{D}'$ be a probabilistic database with $n + 1$ possible worlds, $R^1, \ldots, R^n, R^{n+1}$, and denote by $p_1, \ldots, p_n, p_{n+1}$ their probabilities. For $i = 1, \ldots, n$, let[3] $q_i = p_i / (1 - p_{n+1})$. Since $\sum_{i=1,n+1} p_i = 1$, it follows that $\sum_{i=1,n} q_i = 1$. Consider the probabilistic database $\mathbf{D}$ consisting of the first n worlds $R^1, \ldots, R^n$, with probabilities $q_1, \ldots, q_n$. By induction hypothesis, there exists a tuple-independent database $\mathbf{ID}_n = (\langle S_n, W_n \rangle, P_n)$, s.t. $W_n = \{k_1, \ldots, k_n\}$, and there exists a query Q_n s.t. $\mathbf{D} = Q_n(\mathbf{ID}_n)$. Let k_{n+1} be a new constant (not occurring in W_n): define $S_{n+1} = S_n \cup \{k_{n+1}\} \times R^{n+1}$ and $W_{n+1} = W_n \cup \{k_{n+1}\}$. Define the probabilities of its tuples as $P_{n+1}(k_i) = P_n(k_i)$ for $i \leq n$ and $P_{n+1}(k_{n+1}) = p_{n+1}$. Define Q_{n+1} to be the following[4]:

$$Q_{n+1} = \begin{cases} \Pi_{\bar{A}}(\sigma_{K=k_{n+1}}(S)) & \text{if } k_{n+1} \in W \\ Q_n(S, W) & \text{if } k_{n+1} \notin W \end{cases}$$

In other words, Q_{n+1} takes as input a possible world $\langle S, W \rangle$, where $S = S_{n+1}$ and $W \subseteq W_{n+1}$, and does the following: if $k_{n+1} \in W$ then it returns R^{n+1} (this is the first case), and if $k_{n+1} \notin W$ then it computes the query Q_n. To see why this is correct, notice that R^{n+1} is returned with probability p_{n+1}. The second case holds with probability $1 - p_{n+1}$: by induction hypothesis, Q_n returns each R^i with probability q_i, and therefore Q_{n+1} returns R^i with probability $q_i(1 - p_{n+1}) = p_i$. $\qquad\square$

Thus, tuple-independent tables, coupled with views, form a complete representation system. However, the construction in the proof is impractical, for two reasons. First, we used in the decomposition a different tuple for each possible world in $\mathbf{D}$; in general, $\mathbf{D}$ has a huge number of tuples, and for that reason, the construction in the proof is impractical. Second, the query itself (Q_n) depends on the number of worlds in $\mathbf{D}$. Proposition 2.16 is of theoretical interest only: we know that it *is* possible to decompose *any* probabilistic database into components that are tuple-independent, but it is unclear if we always want to do so. Sometimes, it is more natural to decompose the database into BID components, which we discuss next.

We end our discussion of tuple-independent probabilistic tables by showing that one needs the full power of Relational Calculus (RC) in Proposition 2.16.

Proposition 2.17 *Tuple-independent tables extended with UCQ views are not a complete representation system.*

Proof. We need a definition. We say that an incomplete database $\mathbf{W}$ has a *maximal element* if there exists a world $W \in \mathbf{W}$ that contains all other worlds: $\forall W' \in \mathbf{W}, W' \subseteq W$. It is easy to see that, for any tuple-independent probabilistic database, its incomplete database (obtained by discarding the probabilities) has a maximal element. Indeed, since all tuples are independent, we can simply include all of them and create a maximal world. Recall that every query Q in UCQ is *monotone*, meaning that, for any two database instances $W_1 \subseteq W_2$, we have $Q(W_1) \subseteq Q(W_2)$: this holds because UCQ does

---

[3]These values can be interpreted as conditional probabilities, $q_i = P(R^i | \neg R^{n+1})$.
[4]The formal expression for Q_{n+1} is $\Pi_{\emptyset}(\sigma_{K=k_{n+1}}(W)) \times \Pi_{\bar{A}}(\sigma_{K=k_{n+1}}(S)) \cup Q_n$.

R	FID	SSN	N	P
	351	185	Smith	0.2
	351	785	Smith	0.8
	352	185	Brown	0.3
	352	186	Brown	0.7

Figure 2.7: A BID table. There are two blocks (defined by the FID attribute): tuples in each block are disjoint, while tuples across blocks are independent. Note that in every possible world the attribute FID is a key (see Figure 2.3); this justifies underlining it.

not have negation. Next, one can check that, for any monotone query Q, if **W** is an incomplete database with a maximal element, then $Q(\mathbf{W})$ is also an incomplete database with a maximal element. Indeed, apply Q to the maximal world in **W**: the result is a maximal world in $Q(\mathbf{W})$, by the monotonicity of Q. Therefore, tuple-independent tables extended with UCQ views can only represent probabilistic databases that have a maximal possible world. Since there exists probabilistic databases without a maximal element (for example, consider the c-table in Figure 2.4 (b) and extend it with an arbitrary probability distribution on the assignments of X, Y), the claim of the proposition follows.   □

2.7.2 BID DATABASES

A *block-independent-disjoint database*, or BID database, is a probabilistic database where the set of possible tuples can be partitioned into blocks, such every block is included in a single relation[5], and the following property holds: all tuples in a block are *disjoint* probabilistic events, and all tuples from different blocks are *independent* probabilistic events. If the database consists of a single table, then we call it a BID-table. For a simple example, every tuple-independent table is, in particular, a BID table where each tuple is a block by itself.

Every BID table can be represented by a simple pc-table where all possible tuples in the same block, $t_1, t_2, \ldots$ are annotated with atomic events $X = 1, X = 2, \ldots$, where X is a unique variable used only for that block; this is shown, for example, in Figure 2.2. Furthermore, set the probabilities as $p_i = P(X = i) = P(t_i \in W)$.

In practice, we use a simpler representation of a BID table R, as follows. We choose a set of attributes $A_1, A_2, \ldots$ of R that uniquely identify the block to which the tuple belongs: these will be called *key attributes* because they form, indeed, a key in every possible world. Then, we add a probability attribute P. Thus, the schema of a BID table is $R(\underline{A_1, \ldots, A_k}, B_1, \ldots, B_m, P)$. For an illustration, consider representing the BID table for Figure 2.2: this is shown in Figure 2.7. The attribute FID uniquely identifies a block (this is why it is underlined); tuples within a block are disjoint, and their probabilities add up to 1.0, while tuples across blocks are independent. To help visualize the blocks, we separate them by horizontal lines.

[5]That is, a block cannot contain two tuples from two distinct relations R and S.

S	SSN	FID	P
	185	351	0.5
	185	352	0.5
	785	351	1
	186	352	1

T	FID	SSN	N	P
	351	185	Smith	0.2
	351	785	Smith	0.8
	352	185	Brown	0.3
	352	186	Brown	0.7

Figure 2.8: Normalized BID representation of the table R' in Figure 2.4 (a). The representation consists of two BID tables and a view definition, reconstructing R' from the two BID tables. The table R' is recovered by natural join, $R' = S \bowtie T$.

Of course, not every probabilistic table is a BID table; for example, none of the pc-tables in Figure 2.4 (extended with non-trivial probabilities) is a BID table. However, BID tables are complete when coupled with views expressed as conjunctive queries.

Proposition 2.18   *BID tables extended with CQ views are a complete representation system.*

Notice that we only need a view given by a conjunctive query in order to reconstruct the probabilistic relation from its decomposition into BID tables. In fact, as we show in the proof, this query is very simple, it just joins two tables. This is close in spirit to traditional schema normalization, where every table is recovered from its decomposed tables using a natural join. By contrast, in Proposition 2.16, we needed a query whose size depends on the number of possible worlds.

Proof. Let $\mathbf{D} = (\mathbf{W}, P)$ be a probabilistic database with n possible worlds $\mathbf{W} = \{W^1, \ldots, W^n\}$. Let $p_1, \ldots, p_n$ be their probabilities; thus, $p_1 + \ldots + p_n = 1$. Recall that we have assumed that the schema consists of a single relation name, $R(\bar{A})$; the proof extends straightforwardly to multiple relations. Define the following BID database $\mathbf{D}' = (\langle S, W \rangle, P)$. The first relation is deterministic, and has schema $S(K, \bar{A})$; the second relation is a BID table and has schema $W(K)$: note that the key consists of the empty set of attributes, meaning that all tuples in W are disjoint, i.e., a possible world for W contains at most one tuple. Let $k_1, \ldots, k_n$ be n distinct constants. Define the content of W as $W = \{k_1, \ldots, k_n\}$, and set the probabilities to $P(k_i) = p_i$, for $i = 1, n$ (since these tuples are disjoint, we must ensure that $\sum_i P(k_i) = 1$; indeed, this follows from $\sum_i p_i = 1$). Define the content of S as $S = \{k_1\} \times R^1 \cup \ldots \cup \{k_n\} \times R^n$. (Recall that R^i is the relation R in world W^i.) It is easy to check that the conjunctive-query view

$$R(x_1, \ldots, x_m) \;:\!-\; S(k, x_1, \ldots, x_m), W(k)$$

defined on database $\mathbf{D}'$ is precisely $\mathbf{D}$.   □

While the construction in the proof remains impractical, in general, because it needs a BID table as large as the number of possible worlds, in many concrete applications, we can find quite natural and efficient representations of the probabilistic database as views over a BID tables. We illustrate one such example, by showing how to decompose the c-table in Figure 2.4 (a) into BID tables.

Example 2.19   Extend the c-table R' in Figure 2.4 (a), to a pc-table by defining the following probabilities:

$$P(X = 1) = 0.2 \qquad P(X = 2) = 0.8$$
$$P(Y = 1) = 0.3 \qquad P(X = 2) = 0.7$$
$$P(Z = 1) = 0.5 \qquad P(Z = 2) = 0.5$$

With some abuse of notation, we also call the pc-table R'. This table has undesired constraints between tuples because two tuples are disjoint, if they have either the same *FID* or the same *SSN*. Here is a better design: decompose this table into two BID tables, *T(FID, SSN, N, P)* and *S(SSN, FID, P)*. Here, T represents the independent choices for interpreting the hand-written census forms in Figure 2.1: this is a BID table. S represents the independent choices of assigning each SSN uniquely to one person (or, more concretely, to one census form): this is also a BID table. Both BID tables S and T are shown in Figure 2.8. The original table R' can be reconstructed as:

$$R'(fid, ssn, n) :\text{-} S(\underline{ssn}, fid), T(\underline{fid}, ssn, n).$$

Thus, in this new representation, there are no more hidden constraints in S and T since these are BID tables. However, R' is not a BID table at all! Tuples with the same FID are disjoint, and so are tuples with the same SSN, but the tuples can no longer be partitioned into independent blocks of disjoint tuples; in fact, any two of the four possible tuples in Figure 2.4 (a) are correlated.

At the risk of reiterating the obvious, we note that the instances for T and S can become very large, yet their probabilistic model is very simple (BID); on the other hand, the instance R' has a complicated probabilistic model, but it is derived from the simple tables T and S by using the simple query above.

The example suggests that in many applications, the probabilistic database, even if it has a complex probability space, can be decomposed naturally into BID tables. But some probabilistic databases do not seem to have a natural decomposition. Consider, for example, the c-table in Figure 2.4 (b) (extended with some arbitrary probability distribution for the discrete variables X and Y). It seems difficult to find a natural decomposition of R'' into BID tables. Of course, we can apply the proof of Proposition 2.18, but this requires us to define a BID table that has one tuple for every possible world, which is not practical. Better designs are still possible, but it is unclear how practical they are for this particular example.

2.7.3   U-DATABASES

Neither tuple-independent nor BID databases are closed under queries in the Relational Calculus. U-relations are a convenient representation formalism, which allows us to express naturally the result of a UCQ query on a tuple-independent or BID database. U-relations are c-tables with several restrictions that ensure that they can be naturally represented in a standard relational database. First, for each tuple t in a U-relation, its annotation Φ_t must be a conjunction of k atomic events of the form $X = d$, where k is fixed by the schema. Second, unlike c-tables, in a U-relation, a tuple t may occur multiple times: if these occurrences are annotated with $\Phi_t, \Phi_t', \ldots$, then the annotation of t is taken as $\Phi_t \vee \Phi_t' \vee \cdots$ Finally, U-relations allow a table to be partitioned vertically, thus allowing independent attributes to be described separately. A U-database is a collection of U-relations. As with any pc-database, the probabilities of all atomic events $X = d$ are stored separately, in a table $W(V, D, P)$ called the *world table*; since this is similar to pc-tables, we will not discuss the world table here.

Definition 2.20   A *U-relation schema* is a relational schema $T(V_1, D_1, \ldots, V_k, D_k, A_1, \ldots, A_m)$, together with k pairs of distinguished attributes, $V_i, D_i, i = 1, k$. A *U-database schema* consists of a set of U-relation schemas.

An instance **D** of the U-relation schema T represents the following c-table, denoted by $c - \mathbf{D}$. Its schema, $c(T)$, is obtained by removing all pairs of distinguished attributes, $c(T) = R(A_1, \ldots, A_m)$, and its instance contains all tuples $t \in \Pi_{A_1, \ldots, A_m}(T)$, and each tuple $t = (a_1, \ldots, a_m)$ is annotated with the formula Φ_t:

$$\Phi_t = \bigvee_{(X_1, d_1, \ldots, X_k, d_k, a_1, \ldots, a_m) \in T} (X_1 = d_1) \wedge \cdots \wedge (X_k = d_k)$$

Similarly, an instance **D** of a U-database schema represents a conditional database $\mathbf{D}_c$ consisting of all c-tables associated with the U-relations in **D**.

In other words, a row $(X_1, d_1, X_2, d_2, \cdots, a_1, a_2, \cdots)$ in a U-relation represents (a) the tuple $(a_1, a_2, \cdots)$ and (b) the propositional formula $(X_1 = d_1) \wedge (X_2 = d_2) \wedge \cdots$. We make two simplifications to U-relations. First, if the discrete variables to be stored in a column V_i are Boolean variables and they occur only positively, then we will drop the corresponding domain attribute D_i. That is, a table $T(V_1, D_1, V_2, D_2, A)$ becomes $T(V_1, V_2, A)$: a tuple (X, Y, a) in T represents a, annotated with the formula $\Phi_a = XY$. Second, if there are fewer than k conjuncts in $\bigwedge_i (X_i = d_i)$, then we can either repeat one of them, or we can fill the extra attributes with NULLs. Continuing the example above, either tuple (Z, Z, b) or $(Z, null, b)$ represents b, annotated with $\Phi_b = Z$. In other words, a NULL value represents *true*.

Example 2.21   For a simple illustration of a U-relation, consider the pc-table in Example 2.14. This can be represented by the following U-relation:

$T(FID, M)$

V	D	FID	M
V	1	351	1
V	2	351	2
W	1	352	1
W	2	352	2
W	3	352	3
W	4	352	4

$S(FID, SSN, N)$

V	D	FID	SSN	N
X	1	351	185	Smith
X	2	351	785	Smith
Y	1	352	185	Brown
Y	2	352	186	Brown

Figure 2.9: A U-database representing the census data in Figure 2.1. It consists of two vertical partitions: the census relation is recovered by a natural join, $R(FID, SSN, N, M) = S(FID, SSN, N) \bowtie T(FID, M)$. The probability distribution function for all atomic events is stored in a separate table $W(V, D, P)$ (not shown).

Q

V_1	V_2	V_3	V_4	x	x'
X_1	Y_1	-	-	a_1	a_1
X_1	Y_2	-	-	a_1	a_1
X_1	Y_1	X_2	Y_3	a_1	a_2
X_2	Y_3	X_1	Y_1	a_2	a_1
X_2	Y_3	-	-	a_2	a_2

Each "−" means NULL. For example, the first tuple (a_1, a_1) is annotated with $X_1 Y_1$; the second tuple is also (a_1, a_1) and is annotated with $X_1 Y_2$, which means that the lineage of (a_1, a_1) is $X_1 Y_1 \vee X_1 Y_2$, the same as in Example 2.14. The third tuple is (a_1, a_2) and is annotated with $X_1 Y_1 X_2 Y_3$, etc.

Example 2.22   Consider our original census table, in Example 2.1, $R(FID, SSN, N, M)$, which has two uncertain attributes: SSN and M (marital status). Since these two attributes are independent, a U-database representation of R can consist of the two vertical partitions S and T shown in Figure 2.9. The original table R is recovered as a natural join (on attribute FID) of the two partitions: $R = S \bowtie T$.

U-databases have two important properties, which make them an attractive representation formalism. The first is that they form a complete representation system:

Proposition 2.23   *U-databases are a complete representation system.*

Proof. Recall that in the proof of Theorem 2.12, where we showed that pc-tables form a complete representation system, where a possible tuple t is annotated with $\Phi_t = \bigvee_{i:t \in R_j^i}(X = i)$. Such a pc-table can be converted into a U-database by making several copies of the tuple t, each annotated with an atomic formula $X = i$. Thus, the U-database needs a single pair (V, D) of distinguished attributes.   □

The second property is that U-databases are closed under Unions of Conjunctive Queries in a very strong sense.

Proposition 2.24   *Let* **D** *be any U-database and* $\{D^1, \ldots, D^n\}$ *be the worlds represented by* **D**. *Then, for any UCQ query* Q, *we can compute a UCQ query* Q' *in time polynomial in the size of* Q *such that the U-relation* $Q'(\mathbf{D})$ *represents* $\{Q(D^1), \ldots, Q(D^n)\}$.

In other words, we can push the computation of the representation of the answers to Q inside the database engine: all we need to do is to evaluate a standard UCQ query Q', using standard SQL semantics, on the database **D**, then interpret the answer $Q'(\mathbf{D})$ as a U-relation. Instead of a formal proof, we illustrate the proposition with an example: the proof follows by a straightforward generalization.

Example 2.25   (Continuing Example 2.14) Recall that in this example, we have two tuple-independent tables, $R(A) and S(A, B)$, and we compute the query:

$$Q(x, x') :\!- R(x), S(x, y), S(x', y), R(x')$$

Since the tables are tuple-independent, we can represent them using the following two U-relations: $T_R(V, A)$ and $T_S(V, A, B)$: for example, if $R = \{a_1, a_2\}$, then $T_R = \{(X_1, a_1), (X_2, a_2)\}$, where X_1, X_2 are two arbitrary but distinct identifiers for the two tuples. Our goal is to compute a U-relation representation of the output to the query $Q(x, x')$. As we saw, its lineage consists of conjuncts with up to four atomic predicates, and therefore we represent its output as $T_Q(V_1, V_2, V_3, V_4, A, A')$. The query that computes this representation is:

$$Q'(v_1, v_2, v_3, v_4, x, x') :\!- T_R(v_1, x), T_S(v_2, x, y), T_S(v_3, x', y), T_R(v_4, x')$$

For example, if we execute this query on the instance given in Example 2.9, then we obtain the same result as in Example 2.21, except that the NULL entries for V_3, V_4 are replaced with the values of V_1, V_2: for example, the first row $(X_1, Y_1, -, -, a_1, a_1)$ becomes now $(X_1, Y_1, X_1, Y_1, a_1, a_1)$. Clearly, this has the same meaning when interpreted as a propositional formula because by the idempotence law we have $X_1 Y_1 = X_1 Y_1 X_1 Y_1$.

This example can be generalized to a complete proof for Proposition 2.24. It also illustrates the appeal of U-databases: they can conveniently represent query answers if the query is restricted to UCQ. Note that if we allow negations in the query, then Proposition 2.24 no longer holds in this strong form. While we can always compute a U-relation that represents $Q(\mathbf{D})$, its schema may depend on the database **D**, and its instance may be exponentially larger than the input **D** and, therefore, not a natural representation of the result. The reason is because U-relations are designed to represent k-DNF formulas, for some fixed k: the negation of such a formula is no longer a k-DNF and turning it into DNF can require an exponential blowup.

2.8   BIBLIOGRAPHIC AND HISTORICAL NOTES

The seminal work on incomplete information by Imieliński and Lipski [1984] introduced three kinds of representation systems. Codd-tables are tables with nulls; v-tables are tables that may contain variables, also called *marked nulls*[6], in addition to constants; c-tables are v-tables where each tuple is annotated with a propositional formula. In addition, a c-table may specify a global condition that restricts the set of possible worlds to those defined by total valuations that satisfy this global condition. The c-tables in this book are restricted to contain only constants (no variables), and we also dropped the global condition.

The early probabilistic data model introduced by [Barbará et al., 1992] is essentially a BID data model. While the authors had been inspired by earlier work on incomplete information and c-tables, a formal connection was not established until very recently. Green and Tannen [2006] provide a rigorous discussion of the relationships between incomplete databases and probabilistic databases, and they introduced the term *pc-table*, which we also used in this book. Several researchers have proposed representation systems for probabilistic databases. The Trio system, discussed by Benjelloun et al. [2006a,b], Sarma et al. [2006, 2009b], Widom [2005], designs a model for incomplete and probabilistic databases based on maybe-tuples, X-tuples, and lineage expressions, searching for the right balance of expressiveness and simplicity. Tuple-independent probabilistic databases are discussed by Dalvi and Suciu [2004], motivated by queries with approximate predicates, which introduce an independent event for every potential match. Disjoint-independent probabilistic databases are discussed by Andritsos et al. [2006], Dalvi and Suciu [2007c]. Poole [1993] states that an arbitrary probability space can be represented by composing primitive independent-disjoint events, which captures the essence of Proposition 2.18; the proposition in the form presented here is mentioned in Dalvi and Suciu [2007c]. Proposition 2.16 and Proposition 2.17 seem folklore, but we were not able to trace them to any specific reference. U-relations have been originally introduced in the context of the MayBMS project by Antova et al. [2008].

Several other representation formalisms for probabilistic databases are discussed in the literature. *World-set decompositions* are a complete representation formalism for uncertain and probabilistic data [Antova et al., 2007c, 2009, Olteanu et al., 2008]. The decomposition used by this formalism is a prime factorization of a universal relation representation [Ullman, 1990] of the set of possible worlds representing the probability space. In their probabilistic form, such decompositions can be thought of as shallow Bayesian Networks. Li and Deshpande [2009] define the *And/Xor Tree Model*, which generalizes BID tables by allowing arbitrary interleaving of *and* (independence) and *xor* (disjointness) relationships between the tuples. The And/Xor Tree model is a special case of *WS-trees* introduced by Koch and Olteanu [2008] and, subsequently, generalized by *decomposition trees* [Olteanu et al., 2010]. Several of the data models for probabilistic databases are surveyed in the first edited collection of articles on the topic [Aggarwal, 2008]. More recent work considered extensions of c-tables with continuous probability distributions [Kennedy and Koch, 2010].

---

[6]In a Codd-table, all nulls are distinct variables; in other words, a Codd-table cannot assert that two values are equal.

Graphical model are extensively discussed in the influential book by Pearl [1989] and in recent books by Koller and Friedman [2009] and Darwiche [2009]. Sen et al. [2009] investigate the use of graphical models in probabilistic databases. The *Probabilistic Relational Model* (PRM) introduced by Koller [1999] and Friedman et al. [1999] is, in essence, a large Bayesian Network represented as a database where the probabilistic structure is captured at the schema level. For example, the Bayesian network may define a probability distribution for the Disease attribute, conditioned on other attributes such as Age, Symptoms, and Ethnicity; then, the PRM replicates this Bayesian network once for very Patient record in a database of patients. An important contribution of PRMs is that they allow the Bayesian Network to refer to keys and foreign keys; for example, the probability distribution on Diseases may also depend on the diseases of a patient's friends, which are obtained by following foreign keys. Bayesian networks were applied to optimize the representation of multidimensional histograms by Getoor et al. [2001]. In similar spirit, Deshpande et al. [2001] describe how Markov Networks can be used to optimize multidimensional histograms.

The fundamental connection between normalization theory and factor decomposition in graphical models has been discussed by Verma and Pearl [1988] but, apparently, has not been explored since then. To date, there is no formal design theory for probabilistic databases; a step towards this direction is taken by Sarma et al. [2009a], who discuss functional dependencies for uncertain databases.

The query semantics based on possible worlds that we introduced in Section 2.3 is similar to *intensional semantics* discussed by Fuhr and Rölleke [1997]. While some early work on probabilistic databases by Lakshmanan et al. [1997] and Dey and Sarkar [1996], use a simpler, less precise semantics, all recent work on probabilistic databases follows the possible world semantics for query evaluation, with the exception of the work by Li and Deshpande [2009], who propose an alternative query semantics based on the notion of a consensus answer; this is a deterministic answer world that minimizes the expected distance to the possible worlds (answers), and the work by Gatterbauer et al. [2010] who propose a semantics called *propagation* that can always be evaluated efficiently.

Throughout this book, we consider only queries that are written against a deterministic database. That is, the user writes the query with a deterministic database in mind, then the query is evaluated against a probabilistic database, by evaluating it on every possible world, as we discussed in Section 2.3. This is a restriction; in practice, one would like to have a query language that allows the user to query the probability distribution itself or to generate new uncertainty from a certain value. Several languages have been studied that go beyond these restrictions and add considerable expressive power. For example, computing conditional probabilities, maximum likelihoods, or maximum-a-posteriori (MAP) values on a probabilistic database can be supported by query languages that support probabilistic subqueries and aggregates [Koch, 2008c, Koch and Olteanu, 2008]. This additional power does not necessarily come at high cost. For example, conditional probabilities are simply ratios of probabilities computable using the techniques studied in the next section. Compositional languages for probabilistic databases are supported by both the Trio system [Widom, 2008] and the MayBMS system [Antova et al., 2007a,b, Koch, 2008c]. In both cases, probabilistic queries, closed by the *tuple confidence* (= tuple probability) operator, are supported as subqueries. Moreover, the languages of both systems support the construction of probabilistic databases from deterministic relational databases using a suitable uncertainty-introduction operator. This operator is both useful for hypothetical ("what-if") queries on deterministic databases and as a foundation for a SQL-like update language for building probabilistic databases from scratch. Koch [2008c] and Koch [2008a] discuss design principles of compositional query languages for probabilistic databases. The theoretical foundations of efficiently evaluating compositional queries are discussed by Koch [2008b] and Götz and Koch [2009].

CHAPTER 3

The Query Evaluation Problem

We now turn to the central problem in probabilistic databases: query evaluation. Given a query Q and a probabilistic database $\mathbf{D}$, evaluate Q on $\mathbf{D}$. We consider the *possible answers semantics*, Definition 2.5, under which the answer to a query Q is an ordered set of answer-probability pairs, $\{(t_1, p_1), (t_2, p_2), \ldots\}$, such that $p_1 \geq p_2 \geq \ldots$

Query evaluation is a major challenge for two reasons. On one hand, the problem is provably hard: computing the output probabilities is hard for #P (a complexity class that we review in this chapter). On the other hand, database systems are expected to scale, and we cannot restrict their functionality based on tractability considerations. Users' experience with common databases is that all queries scale to large data sets, or parallelize to large number of processors, and the same behavior is expected from probabilistic databases. We discuss in this book a number of recent advances to query evaluation on probabilistic databases that brings us closer towards that goal.

The query evaluation problem is formally defined as follows:

Query Evaluation Problem For a fixed query Q: given a probabilistic database $\mathbf{D}$ and possible answer tuple t, compute its marginal probability $P(t \in Q)$.

In this chapter we show that the query evaluation problem is #P-hard, even if the input database is a tuple-independent database. The restriction on the input is without loss of generality: query evaluation remains hard on more general inputs, as long as they allow tuple-independent databases as a special case. This applies to BID databases, U-databases, and ultimately to pc-tables. This hardness result sets the bar for probabilistic databases quite high. In the following two chapters we will describe two approaches to query evaluation, extensional evaluation, and intensional evaluation, which, together, form a powerful set of techniques for coping with the query evaluation challenge.

3.1 THE COMPLEXITY OF $P(\Phi)$

Recall from Section 2.5, that the query evaluation problem on pc-tables can be reduced to the problem of computing the probability of a lineage expression: $P(\bar{a} \in Q) = P(\Phi_{Q[\bar{a}/\bar{x}]})$. Thus, the first step towards understanding the complexity of the query evaluation problem is to understand the complexity of computing $P(\Phi)$, for a propositional formula Φ.

We assume in this section that all discrete variables are Boolean variables, and prove that computing $P(\Phi)$ is hard.

To compute $P(\Phi)$, one could apply directly its definition, Eq. (2.3), which defines $P(\Phi) = \sum_{\theta \in \omega(\Phi)} P(\theta)$, where $\omega(\Phi)$ is the set of satisfying assignments for Φ. But this leads to an algorithm whose running time is exponential in the number of Boolean variables, because one would have to iterate over all 2^n assignments θ, check if they satisfy Φ, then add the probabilities of those that do. Typically, n is the number of records in the database, hence this approach is prohibitive. It turns out that there is, essentially, no better way of computing $P(\Phi)$ in general: this problem is provably hard. In order to state this formally, we introduce two problems.

Model Counting Problem Given a propositional formula Φ, count the number of satisfying assignments $\#\Phi$, i.e., compute $\#\Phi = |\omega(\Phi)|$.

Probability Computation Problem Given a propositional formula Φ and a probability $P(X) \in [0, 1]$ for each Boolean variable X, compute the probability $P(\Phi) = \sum_{\theta \in \omega(\Phi)} P(\theta)$.

Model counting is a special case of probability computation, because any algorithm for computing $P(\Phi)$ can be used to compute $\#\Phi$. Define $P(X) = 1/2$ for every variable X: then $P(\theta) = 1/2^n$ for every assignment θ, where n is the number of variables, and therefore $\#\Phi = P(\Phi) \cdot 2^n$. A classical result, which we review here, is that the model counting problem is hard, even if Φ is restricted to a simple class of propositional formulas, as discussed next: this implies immediately that the probability computation problem is also hard.

Recall that SAT is NP-complete, where SAT is the satisfiability problem: "given Φ, check if Φ is satisfiable". The decision problem 3SAT, where Φ is restricted to a 3CNF formula, is also NP-complete, but the problem 2SAT is in polynomial time.

The complexity class #P was introduced by Valiant [1979] and consists of all function problems of the following type: given a polynomial-time, non-deterministic Turing machine, compute the number of accepting computations. The model counting problem, "given Φ, compute $\#\Phi$", is also denoted #SAT, and is obviously in #P. Note that any algorithm solving #SAT can be used to solve SAT, by simply using the former to obtain $\#\Phi$ and then testing whether $\#\Phi > 0$.

Valiant proved that #SAT is hard for #P. He also showed that computing $\#\Phi$ remains hard for #P even if Φ is restricted to be in P2CNF, the class of positive 2CNF formulas, i.e., formulas where each clause consists of two positive literals, $X_i \vee X_j$. It follows immediately that #SAT remains hard for #P even for P2DNF formulas, i.e., formulas that are disjunctions of conjuncts of the form $X_i X_j$. This has been further strengthened by Provan and Ball [1983]; they proved the following result, which is the most important hardness result used in probabilistic databases:

Theorem 3.1 Let $X_1, X_2, \ldots$ and $Y_1, Y_2, \ldots$ be two disjoint sets of Boolean variables.

- A *Positive, Partitioned 2-DNF* propositional formula is a DNF formula of the form:

$$\Phi = \bigvee_{(i,j) \in E} X_i Y_j$$

The #PP2DNF problem is "given a PP2DNF formula Φ, compute $\#\Phi$".

- A *Positive, Partitioned 2-CNF* propositional formula is a DNF formula of the form:

$$\Psi = \bigwedge_{(i,j) \in E} (X_i \vee Y_j)$$

The #PP2CNF problem is "given a PP2CNF formula Ψ, compute #Ψ".

Then, both #PP2DNF and #PP2CNF are hard for #P.

Provan and Ball [1983] proved hardness for #PP2CNF; the result for #PP2DNF follows immediately, because, if Φ and Ψ are defined by the same set E, then #$\Phi = 2^n - $#$\Psi$, where n is the total number of variables (both X_i and Y_j).

Returning to the probability computation problem, it is clear that this problem is hard for #P, but it is technically not in #P, because it is not a counting problem. To explain its relationship with #P, we start by assuming that the probability of every Boolean variable X_i is a rational number, $P(X_i) = m_i / n_i$. If $N = \prod_i n_i$ the product of all denominators, then $N \cdot P(\Phi)$ is an integer number. Then, one can check that the problem "given inputs Φ and $P(X_i) = m_i / n_i$ for $i = 1, 2, \ldots$, compute $N \cdot P(\Phi)$" is in #P (details are given by Dalvi and Suciu [2007c]). Thus, while computing $P(\Phi)$ is not in #P, computing $N \cdot P(\Phi)$ is in #P.

Finally, we note that the probability computation problem can be strictly harder than the model counting problem: more precisely, there exists families of propositional formulas Φ for which the model counting problem is easy, yet the probability computation problem is hard. Indeed, consider the following family of formulas:

$$\Psi_n = \bigvee_{i,j=1,n} X_i Z_{ij} Y_j$$

The probability computation problem is hard, by a reduction from the PP2DNF problem: given a PP2DNF formula Φ, define $P(Z_{ij}) = 1$ if the minterm $X_i Y_j$ occurs in Φ, otherwise define $P(Z_{ij}) = 0$. Then $P(\Phi) = P(\Psi_n)$. On the other hand, the reader can check, using standard combinatorics arguments[1], that the number of models of Ψ_n is given by:

$$\#\Psi_n = \sum_{k=0,n} \sum_{l=0,n} \binom{n}{k} \binom{n}{l} (2^{n^2} - 2^{n^2 - kl})$$

This is clearly computable in polynomial time.

---

[1] Fix an assignment θ of the variables $X_1, \ldots, X_n$ and $Y_1, \ldots, Y_n$. Suppose k of the X_i's are 1, and l of the Y_j's are 1. There are 2^{n^2} possible assignments to the remaining variables Z_{ij}. An assignment that does *not* make Ψ_n true is one that sets $Z_{ij} = 0$ for each i, j such that $X_i = 1$ and $Y_j = 1$: there are $2^{n^2 - kl}$ such assignments. Their difference $2^{n^2} - 2^{n^2 - kl}$ is the number of assignments to the Z-variables that make the formula true.

3.2   THE COMPLEXITY OF $P(Q)$

We now turn to the complexity of the query evaluation problem. Throughout this section we assume that the query Q is a Boolean query, thus the goal is to compute $P(Q)$. This is without loss of generality, since the probability of any possible answer $\bar{a}$ to a non-Boolean query $Q(\bar{x})$ reduces to the probability of the Boolean query $Q[\bar{a}/\bar{x}]$, more precisely, $P(\bar{a} \in Q) = P(Q[\bar{a}/\bar{x}])$. We also restrict the input probabilistic database to a tuple-independent database: if a query Q is hard on tuple-independent databases, then it remains hard over more expressive probabilistic databases, as long as these allow tuple-independent databases as a special case.

We are interested in the *data complexity* of the query evaluation problem: for a fixed query Q, what is the complexity as a function of the database D? The answer will depend on the query: for some queries, the complexity is in polynomial time, for other queries it is not. A query Q is called *tractable* if its data complexity is in polynomial time; otherwise, the query Q is called *intractable*. Recall that, over deterministic databases, for every query in the relational calculus the data complexity is in polynomial time [Vardi, 1982], hence it is tractable according to our terminology.

In this section we prove that, for each of the queries below, the evaluation problem is hard for #P:

$$H_0 = R(x), S(x, y), T(y)$$
$$H_1 = R(x_0), S(x_0, y_0) \vee S(x_1, y_1), T(y_1)$$
$$H_2 = R(x_0), S_1(x_0, y_0) \vee S_1(x_1, y_1), S_2(x_1, y_1) \vee S_2(x_2, y_2), T(y_2)$$
$$H_3 = R(x_0), S_1(x_0, y_0) \vee S_1(x_1, y_1), S_2(x_1, y_1) \vee S_2(x_2, y_2), S_3(x_2, y_2) \vee S_3(x_3, y_3), T(y_3)$$
$$\ldots$$

Each query is a Boolean query, but we have dropped the quantifiers for conciseness; that is, $H_0 = \exists x. \exists y. R(x), S(x, y), T(y)$, etc. For each query H_k, we are interested in evaluating $P(H_k)$ on a tuple-independent probabilistic database $\mathbf{D} = (\langle R, S_1, \ldots, S_k, T \rangle, P)$, and measure the complexity as a function of the size of $\mathbf{D}$ (that is, the query is fixed).

Theorem 3.2   For every $k \geq 0$, the data complexity of the query H_k is hard for #P.

Proof. We give two separate proofs, one for H_0 and one for H_1; the proof for H_k, for $k \geq 2$ is a non-trivial extension of that for H_1 and is omitted; it can be found in [Dalvi and Suciu, 2010].

The proof for H_0 is by reduction from #PP2DNF (Theorem 3.1). Consider any formula

$$\Phi = \bigvee_{(i,j) \in E} X_i Y_j \tag{3.1}$$

and construct the following probabilistic database instance $\mathbf{D} = (\langle R, S, T \rangle, P)$, where: $R = \{X_1, X_2, \ldots\}$, $T = \{Y_1, Y_2, \ldots\}$, $S = \{(X_i, Y_j) \mid (i, j) \in E\}$, and the probability function is defined as follows: $P(R(X_i)) = P(T(Y_j)) = 1/2$, $P(S(X_i, Y_j)) = 1$. Every possible world is of the form $W = \langle R^W, S, T^W \rangle$, where $R^W \subseteq R$ and $T^W \subseteq T$ (because S is deterministic). We associate the assignment θ with the possible world W such that $\theta(X_i) = true$ iff $X_i \in R^W$ and $\theta(Y_j) = true$ iff $Y_j \in T^W$. This establishes a 1-1 correspondence between possible worlds W and assignments θ. Now we note that $W \models H_0$ iff $\Phi[\theta] = true$: indeed, $W \models H_0$ iff there exists X_i, Y_j such that $R^W(X_i)$, $S(X_i, Y_j)$, $T^W(Y_j)$ is true, and this happens iff $\theta(X_i) = \theta(Y_j) = true$ and $X_i Y_j$ is a conjunct in Φ (Eq. (3.1)). Therefore, $\#\Phi = 2^n P(H_0)$, where n is the total number of Boolean variables. Thus, an oracle for computing $P(H_0)$ can be used to compute $\#\Phi$, proving that $P(H_0)$ is hard for $\#P$.

The proof for H_1 is by reduction from #PP2CNF (Theorem 3.1). Consider any formula

$$\Psi = \bigwedge_{(i,j)\in E} (X_i \vee Y_j)$$

We show how to use an Oracle for $P(H_1)$ to compute $\#\Psi$, which proves hardness for H_1. Let n be the total number of variables (both X_i and Y_j) and $m = |E|$. Given Ψ, we construct the same probabilistic database instance as before: $R = \{X_1, X_2, \ldots\}$, $T = \{Y_1, Y_2, \ldots\}$, $S = \{(X_i, Y_j) \mid (i, j) \in E\}$. We still set $P(R(X_i)) = P(T(Y_j)) = 1/2$, but now we set $P(S(X_i, Y_j)) = 1 - z$ for some $z \in (0, 1)$ to be specified below. We will compute $P(\neg H_1)$. Denote $W = \langle R^W, S^W, T^W \rangle$ a possible world, i.e., $R^W \subseteq R$, $S^W \subseteq S$, $T^W \subseteq T$. The probability of each world W depends only on S^W (if $|S^W| = c$ then $P(W) = \frac{1}{2^n}(1-z)^c z^{m-c}$). By definition, $P(\neg H_1)$ is:

$$P(\neg H_1) = \sum_{W : \neg(W \models H_1)} P(W) \tag{3.2}$$

Now consider a valuation θ for Ψ. Define E_θ the following predicate on a world $W = \langle R^W, S^W, T^W \rangle$:

$$E_\theta \equiv (X_i \in R^W \text{ iff } \theta(X_i) = true) \ \wedge \ (Y_j \in T^W \text{ iff } \theta(Y_j) = true)$$

In other words, the event E_θ fixes the relations R^W and T^W according to θ, and leaves S^W totally unspecified. Therefore its probability is:

$$P(E_\theta) = P(\theta) = \frac{1}{2^n}$$

Since the events E_θ are disjoint, we can expand Eq. (3.2) to:

$$P(\neg H_1) = \sum_\theta P(\neg H_1 | E_\theta) \cdot P(E_\theta) = \frac{1}{2^n} \sum_\theta P(\neg H_1 | E_\theta) \tag{3.3}$$

Next, we compute $P(\neg H_1 | E_\theta)$. Define:

$$C(\theta) = \{(i, j) \in E \mid \theta(X_i \vee Y_j) = true\}$$

Note that $|C(\theta)|$ is a number between 0 and m. Then, we claim that:

$$P(\neg H_1 | E_\theta) = z^{|C(\theta)|} \tag{3.4}$$

Indeed, consider a world W that satisfies E_θ. Since $H_1 = R(x_0), S(x_0, y_0) \vee S(x_1, y_1), T(y_1)$, we have $\neg(W \models H_1)$ iff both queries $R(x), S(x, y)$ and $S(x, y), T(y)$ are false on W. Consider a tuple $(X_i, Y_j) \in S$. If θ satisfies the clause $X_i \vee Y_j$, then either $R^W(X_i)$ is true, or $T^W(Y_j)$ is true (because $W \models E_\theta$), and therefore we must have $\neg S^W(X_i, Y_j)$ to ensure that both $R^W(X_i), S^W(X_i, Y_j)$ and $S^W(X_i, Y_j), T^W(Y_j)$ are false; the probability of the event $\neg S^W(X_i, Y_j)$ is z. If θ does not satisfy the clause $X_i \vee Y_j$, then both queries $R(X_i), S(X_i, Y_j)$ and $S(X_i, Y_j), T(Y_j)$ are false regardless of whether S^W contains the tuple (X_i, Y_j) or not. In other words, $\neg(W \models H_1)$ iff S^W does not contain any tuple (X_i, Y_j) for which $(i, j) \in C(\theta)$; this proves Eq. (3.4).

Finally, we compute $P(\neg H_1)$. For any number $c, 0 \leq c \leq m$, let $\#c =$ the number of valuations θ that satisfy exactly c clauses, i.e., $\#c = |\{\theta \mid c = |C(\theta)|\}|$. Then, Eq. (3.3) and Eq. (3.4) become:

$$P(\neg H_1) = \frac{1}{2^n} \sum_{c=0,m} \#c \cdot z^c$$

This is a polynomial in z of degree m, with coefficients $\#0, \#1, \ldots, \#m$. In other words, and oracle for $P(\neg H_1)$ computes the polynomial above. Note that $\#\Psi = \#m$, because in $\#\Psi$ represents the number of valuations that satisfy all m clauses. Therefore, we can compute $\#\Psi$ using an oracle for $P(\neg H_1)$ as follows. Choose any $m + 1$ distinct values for $z \in (0, 1)$, and construct $m + 1$ different database instances R, S, T (they are isomorphic, and differ only in the probabilities in S, which are set to $1 - z$). Then we call the oracle, and obtain the value of the polynomial at that point z. From these $m + 1$ values we will derive all the coefficients, e.g., by using Lagrange's polynomial interpolation formula. The leading coefficient, $\#m$, is precisely $\#\Psi$. □

As we will show in Chapter 4, not all queries are hard; in fact, many queries can be evaluated quite efficiently on tuple-independent, or on BID databases. Moreover, the list of queries H_k, $k = 0, 1, \ldots$ is not even complete: there are many other queries that are also hard. For Unions of Conjunctive Queries (UCQ), we know exactly which queries are hard, and this class includes all the queries H_k and others too; we will discuss this in Chapter 4. For the full Relational Calculus (RC), the class of hard queries is not known exactly (of course, it includes all UCQ queries that are hard).

By using the queries H_k as primitives, it is quite easy to prove that some other queries are hard. We illustrate this on the example below which is both interesting in its own right, and also illustrates one key proof technique used in the general hardness proof [Dalvi and Suciu, 2010].

Example 3.3 Consider the Boolean query

$$Q = \exists x. \exists y. \exists z. U(x, y), U(y, z)$$

We prove that it is hard for $\#P$. The query checks for the presence of a path of length 2 in the graph defined by the binary edge relation U. We will prove that it is hard even if we restrict the graph to a

k-partitioned graph, i.e., a graph where the vertices are partitioned into k disjoint sets, and every edge goes from some node in partition i to some node in partition $i + 1$, for some $i = 1, k - 1$. The question is, how large should we choose k. Clearly, if we choose $k = 2$, i.e., we consider bipartite graphs, then Q is always false, hence it is easy to compute $P(Q)$ (it is 0). If we consider 3-partite graphs, then there are two kinds of edges: from partition 1 to 2, denoted $U^1(x, y)$ and from partition 2 to 3, denoted $U^2(x, y)$. These two sets are disjoint, hence Q is equivalent to $\exists x. \exists y. \exists z. U^1(x, y), U^2(y, z)$, and this query has polynomial time data complexity (it can be computed using the rules described in the next chapter, as $P(Q) = 1 - \prod_a (1 - P(\exists x. U^1(x, a)) \cdot P(\exists z. U^2(a, z)))$, and $P(\exists x. U^1(x, a)) = 1 - (1 - \prod_b (1 - P(U^1(b, a))))$, and similarly for $P(\exists z. U^2(a, z))$.). So Q is also easy on 3-partite graphs.

Consider therefore 4-partite graphs. Now, there are three kinds of edges, denoted U^1, U^2, U^3, and the query is equivalent to the following (we omit existential quantifiers):

$$Q = U^1(x, y), U^2(y, z) \vee U^2(y, z), U^3(z, v)$$

In other words, a path of length 2 can either consist of two edges in U^1 and U^2, or of two edges in U^2 and U^3. Next, we make a further restriction on the 4-partite graph: we restrict the first partition to have a single node s (call it "source node"), and the fourth partition to have a single node t (call it "target node"). We prove that Q is hard even if the input is restricted to 4-partite graphs of this kind. Indeed, then Q becomes:

$$Q = U^1(s, y), U^2(y, z) \vee U^2(y, z), U^3(z, t)$$

This is precisely $H_1 = R(y), S(y, z) \vee S(y, z), T(z)$, up to the renaming of relations: $R(y) \equiv U^1(s, y); S(y, z) \equiv U^2(y, z)$; and $T(z) \equiv U^3(z, t)$.

3.3   BIBLIOGRAPHIC AND HISTORICAL NOTES

Valiant [1979] introduced the complexity class #P and showed, among other things, that model counting for propositional formulas is hard for #P, even when restricted to positive 2CNF (P2CNF). Provan and Ball [1983] showed that model counting for Partitioned Positive 2CNF (PP2CNF) is also hard for #P.

There exists different kinds of reductions for proving #P-hardness, which result in slightly different types of #P-hardness results: our proof of Theorem 3.2 uses a 1-Turing reduction for the hardness proof of H_0 and a Turing reduction for the hardness proof of H_1. Durand et al. [2005] discusses various notions of reductions.

The data complexity of queries on probabilistic databases was first considered by Grädel et al. [1998], which showed, in essence, that the Boolean query $R(x), S(x, y), R(y)$ is hard for #P, by reduction from P2DNF. Dalvi and Suciu [2004] consider conjunctive queries without self-joins, and prove a dichotomy into polynomial-time and #P-hard queries. In particular, they prove that $H_0 = R(x), S(x, y), T(y)$ is #P-hard by reduction from PP2DNF (same proof as in this chapter).

More, they prove that a conjunctive query without self-joins is hard iff it is *non-hierarchical* (a concept we define in the next chapter), and this happens iff the query contains three atoms of the form $R(\ldots, x, \ldots)$, $S(\ldots, x, \ldots, y, \ldots)$, $T(\ldots, y, \ldots)$. In other words, we can say, with some abuse, that the query H_0 is the *only* conjunctive query without self-joins that is hard. Note that the query $R(x), S(x, y), R(y)$ considered earlier by Grädel et al. [1998] is a conjunctive query *with* self-join, hence it does not fall under the class discussed by Dalvi and Suciu [2004].

Dalvi and Suciu [2007a] study the complexity of the evaluation problem for conjunctive queries (with or without self-joins). They establish the hardness for some queries that are related to the queries H_k. Note that H_k is not a conjunctive query, since it uses $\vee$: the queries defined by Dalvi and Suciu [2007a] are obtained from H_k by replacing the $\vee$'s with $\wedge$'s. For example, instead of H_1, they consider $H_1' = R(x_0), S(x_0, y_0), S(x_1, y_1), T(y_1)$, which is a conjunctive query with a self-join. For every k, hardness of H_k implies hardness of H_k', and vice versa, because the inclusion-exclusion formula reduces the evaluation problem for H_k to that for H_k' and several tractable queries. The details of the hardness proofs of H_k can be found in [Dalvi and Suciu, 2010], which prove the hardness result of *forbidden* queries: these include all queries H_k, but also many other queries, like $R(x, y_1), S_1(x, y_1), R(x, y_2), S_2(x, y_2) \vee S_1(x', y'), S_2(x', y'), S_3(x', y') \vee S_3(x'', y''), T(y'')$, whose hardness needs to be proven directly (it does not seem to follow from the hardness of the queries H_k).

Dalvi and Suciu [2007a] also describe an algorithm for evaluating conjunctive queries with self-joins over tuple-independent databases, but the algorithm is very complex, and is totally superseded by a new approach of Dalvi et al. [2010], which we describe in the next chapter.

Dalvi and Suciu [2007c] discuss the complexity of conjunctive queries without self-joins over BID tables, and prove a dichotomy into polynomial time and #P-hard. They show that, if one allows BID tables in the queries in addition to tuple-independent tables, then the class of hard queries is strictly larger: it includes H_0, since every tuple-independent database is, in particular, a BID database, but also includes two more patterns, which we review briefly in Subsection 4.3.1.

The complexity of several other query languages has been considered in the literature: queries with disequality joins ($\neq$) by Olteanu and Huang [2008], with inequality joins ($<$) by Olteanu and Huang [2009], with NOT EXISTS predicates by Wang et al. [2008b], with a HAVING clause by Ré and Suciu [2009], and unrestricted relational algebra queries, and in particular "quantified queries" such as relational division, by Fink et al. [2011b].

CHAPTER 4

Extensional Query Evaluation

There are two approaches to query evaluation. In *extensional query evaluation*, the evaluation process is guided entirely by the query expression Q. We discuss extensional query evaluation in this chapter. When extensional evaluation is possible, then the data complexity of Q is in polynomial time, but we have seen that some queries are provably hard, and therefore not all queries can be evaluated using the extensional approach. *Intensional query evaluation* first computes the query's lineage, then computes the probability of the lineage expression; we discuss it in the next chapter. The intensional approach reduces query evaluation to the problem of computing the probability of a propositional formula. Intensional evaluation works for every query, but by losing the information on the query expression Q, it can perform much worse than extensional query evaluation.

The queries we consider are in the Relational Calculus (RC), or one of its fragments, Unions of Conjunctive Queries (UCQ) or Conjunctive Queries (CQ), see Section 2.1. Thus, queries are built from atomic predicates using the connectives $\wedge, \vee, \exists, \neg$.

Throughout this chapter, we restrict the input database to be a tuple-independent or BID database. This will be sufficient for most practical purposes because as we argued in Section 2.7, a probabilistic database should be decomposed into a tuple-independent or BID database. In other words, if $\mathbf{D}$ is an arbitrary probabilistic database, then it should be written as $\mathbf{D} = V(\mathbf{D}_0)$, where $\mathbf{D}_0$ is tuple-independent or BID, and V is a set of relational queries (views). Then, evaluating a query Q on $\mathbf{D}$ reduces to evaluating the composed query $Q \circ V$ on $\mathbf{D}_0$. Since relational queries are closed under query composition, it means that, for all practical purposes, it suffices to study query evaluation on tuple-independent or BID tables.

We start our discussion of extensional query evaluation in Section 4.1, by describing six simple query evaluation rules. Each rule reduces the problem of evaluating Q, to the problem of evaluating some simpler queries, $Q_1, \ldots, Q_n$. Thus, each application of a rule simplifies the query, until it becomes a ground tuple; in that case, we simply look up its probability in the input database. This rule-based approach is an example of *extensional query evaluation* since it computes the query probability by examining only the query expression, without expanding its lineage.

When the rules succeed in computing the query, we say that the query is *safe*; in that case, the data complexity is in polynomial time. When the rules fail to evaluate the query, then we call the query *unsafe*; as we have seen in Chapter 3, some queries are provably hard, and these (unsurprisingly) also turn out to be unsafe. We prove that, for Unions of Conjunctive Queries, the rules are complete, in the following sense. For any unsafe query, its data complexity is provably hard for #P. This property is called a *dichotomy theorem* since every query is either in polynomial time (when the query is safe) or provably hard for #P (when the query is unsafe). Such a dichotomy is not to be expected from a theoretical point of view – for example, it is known that unless $P = NP$, there are problems strictly harder than P and not NP-hard (and thus not #P-hard). The dichotomy theorem shows that none of these intermediate problems are UCQ query evaluation problems on tuple-independent probabilistic databases. An important aspect of the dichotomy theorem is that the distinction between polynomial-time and #P-hard queries is done solely on the query expression, i.e., it is a property that can be decided based on the syntax. Thus, in the case of UCQ, the partition into polynomial time and #P-hard is done solely based on the syntax. For the full Relational Calculus, it is not known whether a similar dichotomy holds. Even checking if a query is safe is now undecidable because for the Relational Calculus checking satisfiability is undecidable [Libkin, 2004].

In some sense, extensional query evaluation is strictly more powerful than intensional evaluation, due to a new and powerful rule for evaluation, *inclusion-exclusion*. This rule is very effective when applied to a query expression, but it is not practical at all on propositional formulas because it has exponential complexity. When applied to a query, the exponential complexity is restricted to the query expression only, and the complexity remains polynomial time in the size of the data. But when applied to a propositional formula, the inclusion-exclusion rule is exponential in the size of the formula, which, in turn, depends on the size of the database. In fact, as we will see in the next chapter, inclusion-exclusion is not part of the standard set of techniques developed by the verification or AI communities for computing the probability of a propositional formula.

Next, we turn in Section 4.2 to a practical problem: how to evaluate queries by reusing standard relational techniques, query operators and query plans. An *extensional operator* is a standard relational operator (e.g., join, projection, union, selection, difference), extended to manipulate tuple probabilities explicitly. For example, a join will multiply the probabilities, etc.; typically, each extensional operator makes some assumptions on the input tuples, e.g., that they are independent, or that they are disjoint. An *extensional plan* is a query plan where each operator is an extensional operator. A *safe query plan* is an extensional plan that, furthermore, is guaranteed to compute all output probabilities correctly. The rules discussed in the previous section can be adapted to compute safe plans, and, in particular, a query is safe iff it admits a safe plan. Thus, if a query is safe, not only can we evaluate it efficiently "in theory", but we can actually push down the entire query evaluation in a relational database engine, and achieve real scalability, or (if needed) parallelize its execution. On the other hand, unsafe queries do not have any safe plans. However, in practice, we can always use an extensional plan to compute any unsafe query and obtain some approximate probabilities. We show that, under some restrictions, the probabilities returned by any extensional plan are guaranteed upper bounds of the correct probabilities.

Finally, in Section 4.3, we consider several extensions to the query evaluation problem: to BID tables, to databases where some tables are known to be deterministic, and to representations with key constraints.

4.1   QUERY EVALUATION USING RULES

Throughout this section, we assume that the input database D is tuple-independent. Therefore, each tuple t is associated with a Boolean variable X_t, and we know the probability of this Boolean variable, which we often denote $P(t) = P(X_t)$. The problem addressed in this section is the following: given a Boolean query Q, compute $P(Q)$ on some tuple-independent probabilistic database D. Recall that Φ_Q^D, or, briefly, Φ_Q, represents the lineage of Q on D, and that $P(Q) = P(\Phi_Q)$.

4.1.1   QUERY INDEPENDENCE

Consider two Boolean queries Q_1, Q_2. For a fixed probabilistic database D, they define two probabilistic events. When are these two events independent? This question is of importance because if Q_1, Q_2 are independent, then we can compute easily $P(Q_1 \wedge Q_2)$ as $P(Q_1) \cdot P(Q_2)$. In this section, we give a simple syntactic condition on Q_1, Q_2 that is sufficient for independence.

For a propositional formula Φ, let $Var(\Phi)$ denote the set of Boolean variables X that Φ depends on. A formal definition of $Var(\Phi)$ will be given in Chapter 5; for now, it suffices to assume that Φ is given as an expression, and $Var(\Phi)$ represents all Boolean variables in that expression. Clearly, if $Var(\Phi_{Q_1}) \cap Var(\Phi_{Q_2}) \neq \emptyset$, then Q_1 and Q_2 are independent.

Consider a relational atom L occurring in a RC query as defined by Eq. (2.1). The atom is of the form $L = R(v_1, \ldots, v_k)$ where R is a relational symbol, and $v_1, \ldots, v_k$ are variables and/or constants. Denote $\bar{x}$ the set of variables that occur in this atom. An *image* of the atom L is a ground tuple of the form $L[\bar{a}/\bar{x}]$ obtained by substituting all variables $\bar{x}$ in the atom with some constants $\bar{a}$. Any Boolean variable $X_t \in Var(\Phi_Q)$ corresponds to a tuple t that is the image of some atom in Q.

Definition 4.1   Two relational atoms L_1 and L_2 are said *to be unifiable*, or *to unify*, if they have a common image. In other words, there exist substitutions under which the two atoms become the same tuple: $L_1[\bar{a}_1/\bar{x}_1] = L_2[\bar{a}_2/\bar{x}_2]$, where $\bar{x}_1$ are the variables in L_1 and $\bar{x}_2$ are the variables in L_2.

Two queries Q_1, Q_2 are called *syntactically independent* if no two atoms from Q_1 and Q_2 unify.

If two atoms unify, then they must use the same relation symbol R. For example, the two R-atoms in the queries $R(x, a), S(x, b)$ and $R(b, y), S(c, y)$ unify because both have $R(b, a)$ as image, but the atom $R(x, a)$ does not unify with $S(c, y)$ because they have different relational symbols. On the other hand, the two R-atoms of $R(x, a), S(x, b)$ and $R(x, b), S(x, d)$ do not unify because they do not have a common image (assume a and b are two distinct constants).

If two queries Q_1, Q_2 are syntactically independent, then they are independent probabilistic events because, in that case, $Var(\Phi_{Q_1}) \cap Var(\Phi_{Q_2}) = \emptyset$. For example, if $Q_1 = \exists x.\exists y.R(x), S(x, y)$ and $Q_2 = \exists z.T(z)$, then these two queries are independent probabilistic events, and therefore the probability of the query $Q = R(x), S(x, y), T(z) = (\exists x.\exists y.R(x), S(x, y)) \wedge (\exists z.T(z))$ is $P(Q) = P(Q_1) \cdot P(Q_2)$. Another example is given by $Q_1 = \exists x.R(x, a, b, x)$ and $Q_2 = \exists y.\exists z.R(y, y, z, z)$.

These too are independent because the two atoms $R(x, a, b, x)$ and $R(y, y, z, z,)$ do not unify. More generally, pairwise syntactic independence implies independence as probabilistic events:

Proposition 4.2   Let $Q_1, Q_2, \ldots, Q_k$ be queries that are pairwise syntactically independent. Then $Q_1, \ldots, Q_k$ are independent probabilistic events.

The converse does not hold in general: two queries may be independent probabilistic events, yet two of their atoms unify; this is because of the absorption law. An example is given by $Q_1 = \exists x.\exists y.\exists z.\exists u.R(x, y, z, z, u) \wedge R(x, x, x, y, y)$ and $Q_2 = R(a, a, b, b, c)$. If the lineage of Q_1 contains the Boolean variable $X_{R(a,a,b,b,c)}$, then the lineage must contain the conjunct $X_{R(a,a,b,b,c)} \wedge X_{R(a,a,a,a,a)}$. This means that the database contains the tuple $R(a, a, a, a, a)$, which implies that the lineage also contains the conjunct $X_{R(a,a,a,a,a)} \wedge X_{R(a,a,a,a,a)} = X_{R(a,a,a,a,a)}$. By the absorption law $X_{R(a,a,b,b,c)} \wedge X_{R(a,a,a,a,a)} \vee X_{R(a,a,a,a,a)} = X_{R(a,a,a,a,a)}$, which means that $X_{R(a,a,b,b,c)} \notin Var(\Phi_{Q_1})$; therefore, Q_1 and Q_2 are independent, although two of their atoms unify.

It is possible to decide whether two queries Q_1 and Q_2 are independent probabilistic events (and this problem is Π_2^P-complete in the size of the queries [Miklau and Suciu, 2004]). However, we will not need that test in order to compute query probability, but we will rely only on the syntactic independence: checking if Q_1 and Q_2 are syntactically independent can be done in polynomial time in the size of the queries.

4.1.2   SIX SIMPLE RULES FOR $P(Q)$

We now describe an approach for computing $P(Q)$ on a tuple-independent probabilistic database D, by applying six simple computation rules. We will illustrate several examples in Subsection 4.1.4.

4.1.2.1   Rule 1: Independent Join

Suppose a relational query can be written as $Q_1 \wedge Q_2$ where Q_1, Q_2 are two syntactically independent queries. Then:

$$\text{Independent-join} \qquad\qquad P(Q_1 \wedge Q_2) = P(Q_1) \cdot P(Q_1) \qquad\qquad (4.1)$$

4.1.2.2   Rule 2: Independent Project

Consider an atom L in the query Q, and let x be a variable. Denote $Pos(L, x) \subseteq [arity(L)]$ the set of positions where x occurs in L; this set may be empty.

Definition 4.3   Let Q be a relational query of the form $Q = \exists x.Q'$.

- The variable x is called a *root variable* if every atom L in Q' contains the variable x; in other words, $Pos(L, x) \neq \emptyset$.

- The variable x is called a *separator variable* if for any two atoms L_1, L_2 in Q that unify, x occurs in both atoms on a common position; in other words, $Pos(L_1, x) \cap Pos(L_2, x) \neq \emptyset$.

Lemma 4.4   *Let x be a separator variable in $Q = \exists x.Q'$. Then for any two distinct constants $a \neq b$, the queries $Q'[a/x]$ and $Q'[b/x]$ are syntactically independent.*

Proof. Suppose the contrary, and let L_1', L_2' be two atoms in $Q'[a/x]$ and $Q'[b/x]$, respectively, such that L_1', L_2' unify. Let L_1, L_2 be the atoms in Q' from which L_1', L_2' are derived, i.e., $L_1' = L_1[a/x]$ and $L_2' = L_2[b/x]$. Then, obviously, L_1, L_2 unify; hence, since x is a separator variable, we must have $Pos(L_1, x) \cap Pos(L_2, x) \neq \emptyset$. But, in that case, L_1' has a on a position where L_2' has b, contradicting the fact that they unify.   □

The independent project rule is the following. Suppose a relational query can be written as $\exists x.Q$ where x is a separator variable. Then:

$$\textbf{Independent-project} \qquad P(\exists x.Q) \;=\; 1 - \prod_{a \in ADom} (1 - P(Q[a/x])) \qquad (4.2)$$

ADom is the active domain of the database D. For a simple example, consider the query $Q = \exists x.\exists y.(R(x), S(x, y))$. Here x is both root variable and a separator variable; therefore, if the active domain is $ADom = \{a_1, \ldots, a_n\}$, then the queries $Q_i = R(a_i) \wedge \exists y.S(a_i, y)$, $1 \leq i \leq n$ are independent events. Denote $p_i = P(R(a_i) \wedge \exists y.S(a_i, y))$; then, by the independent-project rule, the probability of Q is $P(Q) = 1 - \prod_i (1 - p_i)$.

While every separator variable is also a root variable, the converse is not true in general; in $\exists x.\exists y.\exists z.U(y, x), U(x, z)$, the variable x is a root variable, but not a separator variable. It is easy to see that we cannot apply the independent project rule on the variable x because the two queries $\exists y.\exists z.U(y, a), U(a, z)$ and $\exists y.\exists z.U(y, b), U(b, z)$ are dependent events; they both depend on the tuple $U(a, b)$ (and also on $U(b, a)$). We have seen in Example 3.3 that this query is hard.

To obtain separator variables, we often apply the following logical equivalence:

$$\exists x_1.Q_1 \vee \exists x_2.Q_2 = \exists x.(Q_1[x/x_1] \vee Q_2[x/x_2]) \qquad (4.3)$$

For example, consider the query:

$$Q_U = \exists x_1.\exists y_1.R(x_1), S(x_1, y_1) \vee \exists x_2.\exists y_2.T(x_2), S(x_2, y_2) \qquad (4.4)$$

The query can be written as $\exists x.(\exists y_1.R(x), S(x, y_1) \vee \exists y_2.T(x), S(x, y_2))$, and now x is a separator variable.

4.1.2.3   Rule 3: Independent Union

Suppose a relational query can be written as $Q_1 \vee Q_2$ where Q_1 and Q_2 are two syntactically independent queries. Then:

$$\textbf{Independent-union} \qquad P(Q_1 \vee Q_2) = 1 - (1 - P(Q_1)) \cdot (1 - P(Q_2)) \qquad (4.5)$$

4.1.2.4 Rule 4: Negation

If the query is $\neg Q$ then:

Negation $$P(\neg Q) = 1 - P(Q) \tag{4.6}$$

4.1.2.5 Rule 5: Inclusion-Exclusion Formula

Suppose a query can be written as $Q_1 \wedge Q_2 \wedge \ldots \wedge Q_k$. Then its probability is:

inclusion-exclusion $$P(Q_1 \wedge Q_2 \wedge \ldots \wedge Q_k) = -\sum_{s \subseteq [k], s \neq \emptyset} (-1)^{|s|} P(\bigvee_{i \in [s]} Q_i) \tag{4.7}$$

This is the dual of the popular inclusion-exclusion formula since it expresses the probability of an intersection of events in terms of the probability of unions of events. For example, when $k = 3$, then the two inclusion-exclusion formulas are:

$$
\begin{aligned}
P(Q_1 \wedge Q_2 \wedge Q_3) =& P(Q_1) + P(Q_2) + P(Q_3) \\
& - P(Q_1 \vee Q_2) - P(Q_1 \vee Q_3) - P(Q_2 \vee Q_3) \\
& + P(Q_1 \vee Q_2 \vee Q_3) \\
P(Q_1 \vee Q_2 \vee Q_3) =& P(Q_1) + P(Q_2) + P(Q_3) \\
& - P(Q_1 \wedge Q_2) - P(Q_1 \wedge Q_3) - P(Q_2 \wedge Q_3) \\
& + P(Q_1 \wedge Q_2 \wedge Q_3)
\end{aligned}
$$

We use only the former because it brings the query expression in a form in which we can apply Eq. (4.3), then find a separator variable.

4.1.2.6 Rule 6: Attribute Ranking

This rule allows us to partition the tuples of a relation instance R, according to a simple predicate. We consider two such predicates, leading to two flavors of the attribute ranking rule, which we call *Attribute-Constant Ranking* and *Attribute-Attribute Ranking*. The term "ranking" refers to the fact that we impose a partial order on the attributes; it should not be confused with tuple-ranking discussed in Section 6.1.

Attribute-attribute ranking is the following. Let A, B be two attributes of R. Partition R into three relations, $R_1 = \sigma_{A<B}(R)$, $R_2 = \sigma_{A=B}(R)$, $R_3 = \sigma_{A>B}(R)$, and substitute in the query Q all atoms referring to R with $R_1 \vee R_2 \vee R_3$. We denote Q^r the resulting query and say that Q^r is obtained from Q by "ranking" R on the attributes A, B.

Attribute-constant ranking is the following. Let A be an attribute of R and a be a constant[1] such that there exists two unifiable atoms using the relation symbol R, such that the first has the constant a in position A and the other has a variable in position A. Then we partition R into two

---

[1] If Q is a non-Boolean query, then we also do ranking w.r.t. to head variables a. In other words, for the purpose of ranking, head variables are treated as constants.

relations, $R_1 = \sigma_{A \neq a}(R)$ and $R_2 = \sigma_{A=a}(R)$, and substitute in the query Q all atoms referring to R with $R_1 \vee R_2$. We denote Q^r the resulting query and say that Q^r is obtained from Q by "ranking" R on the attribute A and the constant a.

Thus, the attribute ranking rule is:

$$\textbf{Attribute ranking} \qquad\qquad P(Q) = P(Q^r) \qquad\qquad (4.8)$$

where Q^r is obtained by ranking as explained above.

Ranking does not affect the lineage at all; it simply partitions the input tuples, but the set of tuples remains the same, and the lineage formula is also unchanged. This proves the correctness of the ranking rule:

Lemma 4.5 *If Q^r is a ranking of Q, then on any probabilistic database D, $\Phi_Q = \Phi_{Q^r}$. It follows that $P(Q^r) = P(Q)$.*

Note that Q^r is over a different vocabulary than Q. We further make the following syntactic simplifications in Q^r. In attribute-attribute ranking, the tuples in R_2 have $A = B$, so we drop the attribute B and decrease the arity of R_2 by 1; also, in R_3, where $A > B$, we switch the order of the attributes A and B. In attribute-constant ranking, the tuples in R_2 have $A = a$, so we drop the attribute A and decrease its arity by 1.

We must simplify Q^r, to remove subexpressions that become identically *false* or *true*. For example, consider the query $Q = \exists x.\exists y.R(x, y), R(y, x)$. Ranking by the two attributes of R means that we partition R into three relations, $R = R_1 \cup R_2 \cup R_3$, and obtain nine combinations, $Q = \bigvee_{i,j} R_i(x, y), R_j(y, x)$. However, only three combinations are non-empty: for example $R_1(x, y), R_1(y, x) \equiv false$, because we cannot have both $x < y$ and $y < x$. It follows that $Q = R_1(x, y), R_3(x, y) \vee R_2(x), R_2(x) \vee R_3(y, x), R_1(y, x)$, which reduces to $R_1(x, y), R_3(x, y) \vee R_2(x)$; as explained, we write $R_2(x)$ instead of $R_2(x, x)$, and define $R_3 = \Pi_{yx}\sigma_{x>y}(R(x, y))$ instead of $\sigma_{x>y}(R(x, y))$.

The number of possible ranking steps depends only on the query, not on the database instance. This is because we can rank a pair of attributes only once; once we ranked R on A, B to obtain R_1, R_2, R_3, it makes no more sense to rank R_1 again on A, B, because $\sigma_{A<B}(R_1) = R_1$ and $\sigma_{A=B}(R_1) = \sigma_{A>B}(R_1) = \emptyset$. And, similarly, we can rank an attribute with a constant at most once. If the query Q has c constants, and the maximum arity of any relational symbol is k, then any query Q' generated by the rules will have at most $c + k$ distinct constants, which places an upper bound on the number of possible attribute-constant rankings. However, we can completely avoid ranking w.r.t. to the new constants introduced by the independent-project rule as follows. Consider a query $\exists x.Q$ where x is a separator variable. Before applying the independent-project rule, we check if there exists an atom $R(\dots, x, \dots, x, \dots)$ where x occurs in two distinct positions; in that case, we perform an attribute-attribute ranking w.r.t. to these two attributes (x continues to be a separator variable in the ranked query $\exists x.Q^r$). Repeating this process, we can ensure that x occurs only once in each atom. In any of the new queries $Q^r[a/x]$ created by the independent-project rule, the constant a is not eligible for ranking because if it occurs on some position in one atom $R(\ldots, a, \ldots)$, then every R-atom has a on that position.

4.1.2.7 General Remarks About the Rules

Every rule starts from a query Q and expresses $P(Q)$ in terms of simpler queries $P(Q_1), P(Q_2), \ldots$ For each of the queries Q_i, we apply another rule, and again, until we reach ground tuples, at which point, we simply look up their probability in the database. This process succeeds only if *all* branches of the rewriting end in ground tuples. If the rules succeed in computing the query, then we call it a *safe query*; otherwise, we call it an *unsafe query*. The rules are non-deterministic: for example, whenever we can apply an independent join, we can also apply inclusion-exclusion. No matter in what order we apply the rules; if they terminate, then the result $P(Q)$ is guaranteed to be correct. We will illustrate several examples of unsafe queries (Subsection 4.1.3) and safe queries (Subsection 4.1.4).

What is the data complexity of computing $P(Q)$ using the rules? Five of the rewrite rules do not mention the database at all: the *independent-project* rule is the only rule that depends on the active domain of the database, and it increases by a factor of $n = |ADom|$ the number of queries that need to be evaluated, while reducing by 1 the arity of all relational symbols; therefore, if the maximum arity of any relational symbol in Q is k, then the data complexity of computing $P(Q)$ is $O(n^k)$. Thus, if we can evaluate $P(Q)$ using these rules, then it has polynomial time data complexity.

For queries in the Relational Calculus (RC), safety is not a decidable property. This follows from Trakthenbrot's theorem, which states that it is undecidable to check whether a Boolean RC expression is satisfiable over finite models Libkin [2004]. For example, consider $H_0 = R(x), S(x, y), T(y)$, the query defined in Section 3.2. Clearly, H_0 is unsafe (we will examine it closer in the next section). Let Q be an arbitrary query in RC, which does not use the relational symbols R, S, T; note that Q may use negation. Then the query $H_0 \wedge Q$ is safe iff Q is not satisfiable: hence, safety is undecidable.

For UCQ queries, safety is decidable because the rules can be applied in a systematic way, as follows. First, rank all attribute-constant pairs, then repeat the following sequence of steps. (1) Convert Q from a DNF expression $Q'_1 \vee Q'_2 \vee \ldots$ to a CNF expression $Q = Q_1 \wedge Q_2 \wedge \ldots$ by applying the distributivity law. Each query Q_i is called a *disjunctive query* (it is a disjunction of connected conjunctive queries, see Figure 4.2). Apply the independent-join rule (Eq. (4.1)), $P(Q) = P(Q_{i_{11}} \wedge Q_{i_{12}} \ldots) \cdot P(Q_{i_{21}} \wedge Q_{i_{22}} \ldots) \cdots$, if possible. (2) Apply the inclusion-exclusion formula, Eq. (4.7), to the remaining conjunctions. This results in several disjunctive queries $Q_{j_1} \vee Q_{j_2} \vee \ldots$: the number of such disjunctive queries is exponential in the size of the query (of course, it is independent on the size of the database). (3) Apply independent union Eq. (4.5), if at all possible (4) For each remaining disjunction $Q = Q_{j_1} \vee Q_{j_2} \vee \ldots$, use Eq. (4.3) to choose a separator variable, x, then apply independent project Eq. (4.2), to obtain new queries of the form $Q[a/x]$; if no separator variable exists, apply the attribute-attribute ranking rule for some pairs of attributes, and search again for a separator variable. (5) Each $Q[a/x]$ is expressed in DNF; repeat from step (1). If we ever get stuck, it is technically in the separator variable step, when we cannot find a separator variable. We will show later that, for UCQ queries, the rules are complete (once we replace inclusion-exclusion with Möbius' inversion formula), in the sense that every unsafe query is provably hard; thus, UCQ admits a dichotomy.

4.1.3   EXAMPLES OF UNSAFE (INTRACTABLE) QUERIES

Before we illustrate how the rules work, we will briefly illustrate how they fail. Recall the list of intractable queries from Section 3.2:

$$H_0 = R(x), S(x, y), T(y)$$
$$H_1 = R(x_0), S(x_0, y_0) \vee S(x_1, y_1), T(y_1)$$
$$H_2 = R(x_0), S_1(x_0, y_0) \vee S_1(x_1, y_1), S_2(x_1, y_1) \vee S_2(x_2, y_2), T(y_2)$$
$$H_3 = R(x_0), S_1(x_0, y_0) \vee S_1(x_1, y_1), S_2(x_1, y_1) \vee S_2(x_2, y_2), S_3(x_2, y_2) \vee S_3(x_3, y_3), T(y_3)$$
$$\cdots$$

We have already seen in Chapter 3 that these queries are intractable; hence, they cannot be safe (unless $P = \#P$). However, it is useful to understand how the rules fail to apply in each case, so we briefly discuss why each of them is unsafe.

Consider H_0. We cannot apply an independent-project because no variable is a root variable: x does not occur in the atom $T(y)$ and y does not occur in $R(x)$. We cannot apply the independent join because we cannot write $H_0 = Q_1 \wedge Q_2$ where both Q_1 and Q_2 are Boolean queries; for example, if we write it as $R(x) \wedge (S(x, y) \wedge T(y))$, then $R(x)$ and $S(x, y) \wedge T(y)$ must share the variable x; hence, they are not Boolean queries. For the same reason, we cannot apply the inclusion-exclusion rule. We could rank $S(x, y)$ by its two attributes, and split it into $S_1 = \sigma_{x<y}(S(x, y)), S_2 = \Pi_x(\sigma_{x=y}(S(x, y))), S_3 = \Pi_{yx}(\sigma_{x>y}(S(x, y)))$, but this doesn't help; we obtain $H_0 = R(x), S_1(x, y), T(y) \vee R(x), S_2(x), T(x) \vee R(x), S_3(y, x), T(y)$, and we are stuck because this query has no separator variable (neither the first nor the last query have a root variable). Thus, the rules fail on H_0.

The rules also fail on H_1. While it is the disjunction of two Boolean queries, they are not independent (both contain S). If we tried to apply the independent-project rule by substituting $z = x_0 = x_1$ (as we did in Eq. (4.3)), $H_1 \equiv \exists z.(\exists y_0.R(z), S(z, y_0) \vee \exists y_1.S(z, y_1), T(y_1))$ then z occurs in the same position in both atoms $S(z, y_0)$ and $S(z, y_1)$, but it is not a root variable because it does not occur in $T(y_1)$. If we tried $z = x_0 = y_1$ instead, then $H_1 \equiv \exists z.(R(z) \wedge \exists y_0.S(z, y_0) \vee T(z) \wedge \exists x_1.S(x_1, z))$; now z is a root variable, but it is not a separator variable because it occurs on different positions in $S(z, y_0)$ and in $S(x_1, z)$. The reader can check that none of the rules applies to any H_k, for any $k \geq 0$.

4.1.4   EXAMPLES OF SAFE (TRACTABLE) QUERIES

We now illustrate how to use the rules in Subsection 4.1.2 to evaluate query probabilities. Whenever this is possible, the query is tractable.

Example 4.6   A Really Simple Query   We start with a simple Boolean query:

$$Q = R(x), S(x, y)$$

Write it as $Q = \exists x.(R(x) \wedge \exists y.S(x, y))$, and we evaluate it as follows:

$$P(Q) = 1 - \prod_{a \in ADom(D)} (1 - P(R(a) \wedge \exists y.S(a, y))) \qquad \text{by Eq. (4.2)}$$

$$= 1 - \prod_{a \in ADom(D)} (1 - P(R(a)) \cdot P(\exists y.S(a, y))) \qquad \text{by Eq. (4.1)}$$

$$= 1 - \prod_{a \in ADom(D)} \left(1 - P(R(a)) \cdot (1 - \prod_{b \in ADom(D)} (1 - P(S(a, b)))) \right) \qquad \text{by Eq. (4.2)}$$

The last line is an expression of size $O(n^2)$, where n is the size of the active domain $ADom(D)$ of the database.

Example 4.7   A Query With Self-Joins   Consider the Boolean query:

$$Q_J = R(x_1), S(x_1, y_1), T(x_2), S(x_2, y_2)$$

Note that Q_J is the conjunction of two Boolean queries $Q_1 \wedge Q_2$, where $Q_1 = \exists x_1.\exists y_1.R(x_1), S(x_1, y_1)$ and $Q_2 = \exists x_2.\exists y_2.T(x_2), S(x_2, y_2)$. However, we cannot apply an independent-join because the two queries are dependent (they share the S symbol), but we can apply the inclusion-exclusion formula and obtain:

$$P(Q_J) = P(Q_1) + P(Q_2) - P(Q_1 \vee Q_2) \qquad \text{by Eq. (4.7)}$$

where $Q_U = Q_1 \vee Q_2$ is the same query as that given in Eq. (4.4). Thus, $P(Q_J)$ is expressed in terms of the probability of three other queries: the first two can be computed as in the previous example, the third is Q_U and, as we have seen, has a separator variable, therefore:

$$P(Q_U) = 1 - \prod_{a \in ADom(D)} (1 - P(\exists.y_1.R(a) \wedge S(a, y_1) \vee \exists y_2.T(a) \wedge S(a, y_2))) \quad \text{by Eq. (4.2)}$$

$$= 1 - \prod_{a \in ADom(D)} (1 - P((R(a) \vee T(a)) \wedge \exists.y.S(a, y)))$$

$$= 1 - \prod_{a \in ADom(D)} (1 - P((R(a) \vee T(a))) \cdot P(\exists.y.S(a, y))) \qquad \text{by Eq. (4.1)}$$

The probability $P(R(a) \vee T(a))$ is simply $1 - (1 - P(R(a))) \cdot (1 - P(T(a)))$ while the probability $P(\exists y.S(a, y))$ is $1 - \prod_{b \in ADom(D)}(1 - P(S(a, b)))$.

What is remarkable about Q_J is the following fact. Q_J is a conjunctive query (with self-joins), but in order to evaluate it, we needed to use Q_U, which is a union of conjunctive queries. In other words, CQ is not a natural class to consider in isolation for studying query evaluation on probabilistic databases: UCQ is a natural class.

Example 4.8   A Tractable Query With An Intractable Subquery   Our next example is interesting because it contains H_1 as a subquery, yet the query is tractable:

$$Q_V = R(x_1), S(x_1, y_1) \vee S(x_2, y_2), T(y_2) \vee R(x_3), T(y_3)$$

The first two union terms represents H_1, which is hard. On the other hand, the third union term is the conjunction of $R(x_3)$ and $T(y_3)$ that do not share any variables. Therefore, we can apply distributivity and rewrite Q_V from DNF to CNF:

$$\begin{aligned}
Q_V &= [R(x_1), S(x_1, y_1) \vee S(x_2, y_2), T(y_2) \vee R(x_3)] \wedge \\
&\quad [R(x_1), S(x_1, y_1) \vee S(x_2, y_2), T(y_2) \vee T(y_3)] \\
&= [S(x_2, y_2), T(y_2) \vee R(x_3)] \wedge [R(x_1), S(x_1, y_1) \vee T(y_3)]
\end{aligned}$$

We applied the logical equivalence $R(x_1), S(x_1, y_1) \vee R(x_3) \equiv R(x_3)$. Now we use the inclusion-exclusion formula and obtain:

$$\begin{aligned}
P(Q_V) &= P(S(x_2, y_2), T(y_2) \vee R(x_3)) + P(R(x_1), S(x_1, y_1) \vee T(y_3)) \\
&\quad - P(S(x_2, y_2), T(y_2) \vee R(x_3) \vee R(x_1), S(x_1, y_1) \vee T(y_3)) \\
&= P(S(x_2, y_2), T(y_2) \vee R(x_3)) + P(R(x_1), S(x_1, y_1) \vee T(y_3)) - P(R(x_3) \vee T(y_3))
\end{aligned}$$

Each of the three probabilities on the last line can be computed easily, by first applying the independent-union rule. For example, the first probability becomes:

$$P(S(x_2, y_2), T(y_2) \vee R(x_3)) = 1 - (1 - P(S(x_2, y_2), T(y_2))) \cdot (1 - P(R(x_3)))$$

Example 4.9   Ranking   We give here three examples of ranking. First, lets revisit the Boolean conjunctive query

$$Q_1 = R(x, y), R(y, x)$$

which we already illustrated in the context of ranking in Subsection 4.1.2. There is no separator variable: x is a root variable, but no separator variable because it occurs in different positions in the two atoms, and therefore we cannot apply independent project on x^2. Instead, we rank the two attributes of the relation R; in other words, we partition it into three relations:

$$R_1 = \Pi_{x,y}(\sigma_{x<y}(R(x, y)))$$
$$R_2 = \Pi_x(\sigma_{x=y}(R(x, y)))$$
$$R_3 = \Pi_{y,x}(\sigma_{x>y}(R(x, y)))$$

Then, rewrite Q_1 as: $Q_1^r = R_1(x, y), R_3(x, y) \vee R_2(z)$. Note that the relations R_1, R_2 and R_3 have no common tuples; hence, the database $\langle R_1, R_2, R_3 \rangle$ is a tuple-independent database. It is easy to see that $P(Q_1^r)$ can be computed using the rules in Subsection 4.1.2: first, apply an independent-union, $P(Q_1^r) = 1 - (1 - P(R_1(x, y), R_3(x, y))) \cdot (1 - P(R_2(z)))$, then use x is a separator variable in $P(R_1(x, y), R_3(x, y))$, etc. Notice that the lineages Φ_{Q_1} and $\Phi_{Q_1^r}$ are the same:

$$\Phi_{Q_1} = \bigvee_{i,j} X_{ij} X_{ji} = \bigvee_{i<j} X_{ij} X_{ji} \vee \bigvee_{i} X_{ii} = \Phi_{Q^r}$$

All $n(n-1)/2 + n$ conjuncts in the expression above are independent, which is another way to see why $P(Q_1)$ can be computed in polynomial time.

Second, consider

$$Q_2 = R(x, a), R(a, x)$$

where a is a constant. Here, too, we cannot apply any rule because x is not a separator variable. After we rank both attributs of R w.r.t. the constant a, we obtain four relations:

$$R_1(x_1) = \Pi_{x_1}(\sigma_{x_1 \neq a \wedge x_2 = a}(R(x_1, x_2)))$$
$$R_2(x_2) = \Pi_{x_2}(\sigma_{x_1 = a \wedge x_2 \neq a}(R(x_1, x_2)))$$
$$R_3() = \Pi_\emptyset(\sigma_{x_1 = x_2 = a}(R))$$
$$R_4(x_1, x_2) = \sigma_{x_1 \neq a \wedge x_2 \neq a}(R(x_1, x_2))$$

Then we rewrite the query as $Q_2^r = R_1(x), R_2(x) \vee R_3()$. This is an independent union of two queries, the first has the separator variable x, while the second is a ground tuple; hence, we simply lookup its probability in the database.

Finally, consider $Q_3 = R(x, y), S(x, y) \vee R(u, v), S(v, u)$. Even though none of the two conjunctive queries suggests that ranking is needed, the entire query has no separator, and we must rank, first on R then on S, which partitions both R and S into three sets: $R_1(x, y) = \sigma_{x<y}(R(x, y))$, $R_2(x) = \Pi_x(\sigma_{x=y}(R(x, y)))$, $R_3 = \Pi_{yx}(\sigma_{x>y}(R(x, y)))$, and similarly S is partitioned into S_1, S_2, S_3. After simplifications, the ranked query is:

$$Q_3^r = R_1(x_1, y_1), S_1(x_1, y_1) \vee R_3(y_2, x_2), S_3(y_2, x_2)$$
$$\vee R_1(x_3, y_3), S_3(x_3, y_3) \vee R_3(y_4, x_4), S_1(y_4, x_4)$$
$$\vee R_2(x_5), S_2(x_5)$$

---

[2]The queries $R(a, y), R(y, a)$ and $R(b, y), R(y, b)$ are dependent because they both depend on both $R(a, b)$ and $R(b, a)$, which shows that an independent project is not possible.

The first two lines are independent from the third line, so we can apply an independent union; the first two lines have the separator $z = x_1 = y_2 = x_3 = y_4$, while the third line has the separator x_5: continuing this way one can compute $P(Q_3^r)$ in polynomial time.

4.1.5   THE MÖBIUS FUNCTION

We need to improve the inclusion-exclusion formula in a simple, yet very interesting way, by using Möbius' inversion function. This is necessary in order to ensure that the rules are "complete" for UCQ queries, meaning that they are sufficient to compute the probability of any tractable query. We illustrate with an example.

Example 4.10   Consider the following Boolean query Q_W:

$$Q_W = (\exists x_0.\exists y_0.R(x_0), S_1(x_0, y_0) \vee \exists x_2.\exists y_2.S_2(x_2, y_2), S_3(x_2, y_2))$$
$$\wedge (\exists x_0.\exists y_0.R(x_0), S_1(x_0, y_0) \vee \exists x_3.\exists y_3.S_3(x_3, y_3), T(y_3))$$
$$\wedge (\exists x_1.\exists y_1.S_1(x_1, y_1), S_2(x_1, y_1) \vee \exists x_3.\exists y_3.S_3(x_3, y_3), T(y_3))$$

The query is easier to read if we make the following notations:

$$h_{30} = \exists x_0.\exists y_0.R(x_0), S_1(x_0, y_0)$$
$$h_{31} = \exists x_1.\exists y_1.S_1(x_1, y_1), S_2(x_1, y_1)$$
$$h_{32} = \exists x_2.\exists y_2.S_2(x_2, y_2), S_3(x_2, y_2)$$
$$h_{33} = \exists x_3.\exists y_3.S_3(x_3, y_3), T(y_3)$$

Then Q_W becomes:

$$Q_W = (h_{30} \vee h_{32}) \wedge (h_{30} \vee h_{33}) \wedge (h_{31} \vee h_{33})$$

The union $h_{30} \vee h_{31} \vee h_{32} \vee h_{33}$ is H_3, which we have shown to be hard in Theorem 3.2. On the other hand, the union of any subset of $h_{30}, h_{31}, h_{32}, h_{33}$ is tractable. For example, $h_{30} \vee h_{31} \vee h_{33}$ splits into the union of two independent queries, $h_{30} \vee h_{31}$ and h_{33}; in the former, we obtain a separator variable by substituting $z = x_0 = x_1$, and in the latter, we use y_3 as separator variable.

To compute Q_W, we apply the inclusion-exclusion formula and obtain seven terms:

$$P(Q_W) = P(h_{30} \vee h_{32}) + P(h_{30} \vee h_{33}) + P(h_{31} \vee h_{33})$$
$$- P(h_{30} \vee h_{32} \vee h_{33}) - P(h_{30} \vee h_{31} \vee h_{32} \vee h_{33}) - P(h_{30} \vee h_{31} \vee h_{33})$$
$$+ P(h_{30} \vee h_{31} \vee h_{32} \vee h_{33})$$

Thus, the hard query $h_{30} \vee h_{31} \vee h_{32} \vee h_{33} \equiv H_3$ occurs twice, and it cancels out, leading to:

$$P(Q_W) = P(h_{30} \vee h_{32}) + P(h_{30} \vee h_{33}) + P(h_{31} \vee h_{33})$$
$$- P(h_{30} \vee h_{32} \vee h_{33}) - P(h_{30} \vee h_{31} \vee h_{33})$$

Each of the five expressions above can be computed using the rules. Thus, we can compute $P(Q_W)$ using the rules *provided* we are careful to cancel out terms in the inclusion-exclusion formula; otherwise, we will get stuck trying to compute $P(H_3)$ (twice !).

The coefficients of the inclusion-exclusion formula are given by the *Möbius function in a lattice*; we review it here, and also refer to Figure 4.2 for a short primer.

A *lattice* is a partially ordered set $(L, \leq)$ where any two elements $x, y \in L$ have a least upper bound $x \vee y$ and a greatest lower bound $x \wedge y$. We will consider only finite lattices in this book. It follows that every subset $U \subseteq L$ has a least upper bound $\bigvee U$ and a greatest lower bound $\bigwedge U$; in particular, L has a minimum element $\hat{0} = \bigwedge L$ and a maximum element $\hat{1} = \bigvee L$. A finite lattice admits an alternative, equivalent definition, as an algebraic structure $(L, \vee, \wedge, \hat{0}, \hat{1})$, where $\vee, \wedge$ are binary operators that are associative, commutative, satisfy the absorption laws ($x \vee (x \wedge y) = x$ and $x \wedge (x \vee y) = x$), and have neutral elements $\hat{0}$ and $\hat{1}$ respectively. The operations $\vee$ and $\wedge$ are called *join* and *meet* respectively.

We define the Möbius function next:

Definition 4.11   The Möbius function $\mu_L : L \times L \to \mathbf{int}$ is defined as follows:

$$\mu_L(u, u) = 1$$
$$\mu_L(u, v) = - \sum_{w : u < w \leq v} \mu_L(w, v)$$

We drop the subscript L when it is clear from the context and write simply $\mu(u, v)$. By definition, if $u \not\leq v$, then $\mu(u, v) = 0$. For the most part of this book, the second argument of the Möbius function is $\hat{1}$, and we refer to $\mu(u, \hat{1})$ as "the Möbius value at u". For a simple illustration, consider the lattice in Figure 4.1, with 7 nodes. We compute $\mu(u, \hat{1})$, for every node u in the lattice, starting from the top node $\hat{1}$. By definition $\mu(\hat{1}, \hat{1}) = 1$. Next, $\mu(u_1, \hat{1}) = -\mu(\hat{1}, \hat{1}) = -1$, and similarly $\mu(u_2, \hat{1}) = \mu(u_3, \hat{1}) = -1$. Next, $\mu(u_4, \hat{1}) = -(1 - 1 - 1) = 1$, and similarly $\mu(u_5, \hat{1}) = 1$. Finally, $\mu(\hat{0}, \hat{1}) = -(1 - 1 - 1 - 1 + 1 + 1) = 0$.

The Möbius function in a lattice generalizes the classical Möbius function on numbers and has an elegant interpretation as the inverse of the zeta function in the incidence algebra defined by the lattice L: we refer the reader to Stanley [1997] for background on the Möbius function. For our purpose, we will simply use the definition above as given.

Let $Q_1, \ldots, Q_k$ be k queries, and let $Q = \bigwedge_{i=1,k} Q_i$. For every subset $s \subseteq [k]$, we denote by $Q_s = \bigvee_{i \in s} Q_i$. Notice that, with these notations, the inclusion-exclusion formula becomes $P(Q) = -\sum_{s \neq \emptyset}(-1)^{|s|} P(Q_s)$.

Definition 4.12   The CNF-lattice of the query $Q = Q_1 \wedge \ldots \wedge Q_k$ is the lattice $(L, \leq)$, where:

- The elements of L are queries Q_s, for $s \subseteq [k]$, up to logical equivalence.

- The order relation $\leq$ is defined as follows: $Q_{s_1} \leq Q_{s_2}$ iff the logical implication $Q_{s_2} \Rightarrow Q_{s_1}$ holds.

Thus, when constructing the CNF lattice, we start by forming all 2^k queries Q_s for $s \subseteq [k]$, but we eliminate duplicates: whenever two queries are logically equivalent $Q_{s_1} \equiv Q_{s_2}$, we only keep one of them. The lattice L consists of all such queries, up to logical equivalence; in general, $|L| \leq 2^k$. Note that k depends only on the query, not the database instance: thus, we can afford to compute Q_s for all the 2^k possible sets s; we do not consider the database instance at all at this point. The minimal element of the lattice corresponds to $s = [k]$ and is $\hat{0} \equiv Q_1 \vee Q_2 \vee \ldots \vee Q_k$. The maximal element of the lattice corresponds to $s = \emptyset$ and is denoted $\hat{1}$. We note that the lattice meet operation $\wedge$ corresponds to query union $\vee$: in this book, $\vee$ refers to query union (hence lattice-meet) unless otherwise stated.

Given a lattice element $u \in L$, we write Q_u for the query associated with u, for example, $Q_{\hat{0}} = Q_1 \vee \ldots \vee Q_k$, where $\hat{0}$ is the minimal element of the lattice. The following is a classic application of the Möbius function.

Proposition 4.13 Möbius inversion formula   *Let $Q = Q_1 \wedge Q_2 \wedge \ldots \wedge Q_k$ and let $(L, \leq)$ be its CNF lattice. Then:*

$$P(Q) = -\sum_{u < \hat{1}} \mu(u, \hat{1}) P(Q_u)$$

We use formula to replace the earlier inclusion-exclusion formula Eq. (4.7):

4.1.5.1   Rule 5: Möbius Inversion Formula (Replaces the Inclusion/Exlusion rule)
Suppose a query can be written as $Q = Q_1 \wedge \ldots \wedge Q_k$. Then its probability is:

$$\textbf{Möbius} \qquad P(Q_1 \wedge Q_2 \wedge \ldots \wedge Q_k) = -\sum_{u < \hat{1} : \mu(u, \hat{1}) \neq 0} \mu(u, \hat{1}) \cdot P(Q_u) \qquad (4.9)$$

Notice that we explicitly remove from the sum those terms where $\mu(u, \hat{1}) = 0$ because as we have seen, there are cases when $P(Q_u)$ is hard to compute, yet $\mu(u, \hat{1}) = 0$.

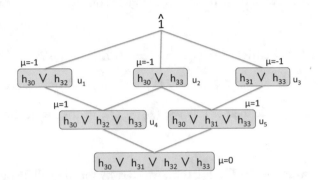

Figure 4.1: The CNF lattices for Q_W. Note that the bottom of the lattice is the intractable query H_3, but the Möbius function at that point is $\mu = 0$, and since all other queries in the lattice are in polynomial time, Q_W is in polynomial time.

Example 4.14   (Example 4.10 continued) We revisit now the query $Q_W = Q_1 \wedge Q_2 \wedge Q_3$. Its CNF lattice consists of the following elements:

$$Q_{u_1} = h_{30} \vee h_{32} \qquad\qquad Q_{u_2} = h_{30} \vee h_{33} \qquad\qquad Q_{u_3} = h_{31} \vee h_{33}$$
$$Q_{u_4} = h_{30} \vee h_{32} \vee h_{33} \qquad Q_{u_5} = h_{30} \vee h_{31} \vee h_{33}$$
$$Q_{\hat{0}} = h_{30} \vee h_{31} \vee h_{32} \vee h_{33}$$

The lattice and its associated Möbius function is shown in Figure 4.1. Notice that the Möbius function for $\hat{0}$ is $\mu(\hat{0}, \hat{1}) = 0$: thus we do not need the bottom query in the Möbius inversion rule. The probability now becomes:

$$P(Q) = P(Q_{u_1}) + P(Q_{u_2}) + P(Q_{u_3}) - P(Q_{u_4}) - P(Q_{u_5})$$

Thus, Q_W is tractable, and can be computed using the Möbius rule. It's lineage, however, is quite complex; we will return to it in Section 5.4.

Note that in order to construct the CNF lattice we need to be able to check if two queries are equivalent (to eliminate duplicates). For UCQ queries, this problem is decidable, see Figure 4.2. The CNF lattice is not unique because it depends on the representation $Q = Q_1 \wedge \ldots \wedge Q_k$ of the UCQ query; however, the co-atomic elements of the lattice are uniquely defined, and so is the set of lattice elements u for which $\mu(u, \hat{1}) \neq 0$; hence, application of the Möbius' inversion formula is independent of the representation of the query (Figure 4.2). The "magic" in Möbius inversion formula only works if all hard queries Q_u in the lattice have $\mu(u, \hat{1}) = 0$. If at least one Q_u is hard *and* $\mu(u, \hat{1}) \neq 0$, then we get stuck. However, the inversion formula is complete: if at least one query Q_u with $\mu(u, \hat{1}) \neq 0$ is hard for #P, then Q is hard as well; we will discuss this in Theorem 4.23.

For arbitrary queries in the Relational Calculus, the equivalence problem between two queries is undecidable. We can still construct a CNF lattice for a query $Q_1 \wedge \ldots \wedge Q_k$, by using sound but not necessarily complete query containment and query equivalence relationships. Implicit in the Definition 4.12 is the requirement "$u \leq v$ iff $Q_v \Rightarrow Q_u$": now, we relax it to "$u \leq v$ implies $Q_v \Rightarrow Q_u$".

One question is whether we could evaluate queries differently, by avoiding to use the Möbius inversion formula. The following result proves that this is not the case.

Theorem 4.22 Let L be any finite lattice. Then there exists a UCQ query Q such that (a) its CNF lattice is isomorphic to L, $L(Q) \simeq L$, (b) the query $Q_{\hat{0}}$ is hard for #P, and (c) for any other lattice element $u \neq \hat{0}$, Q_u is a safe query.

This implies that the query Q is safe iff $\mu(\hat{0}, \hat{1}) = 0$. In other words, any algorithm that figures out whether Q is computable in polynomial time or is hard for #P must, in effect, determine whether $\mu(\hat{0}, \hat{1}) = 0$, in some arbitrary lattice L.

Proof. Let L be a lattice, and $\wedge$ and $\vee$ its meet and join operator. An element $r \in L$ is called *join irreducible* if $r \neq \hat{0}$, and whenever $v_1 \vee v_2 = r$, then either $v_1 = r$ or $v_2 = r$. All atoms[3] are join-irreducible, but the converse is not true, in general. Let $R = \{r_0, r_1, \ldots, r_k\}$ be all join irreducible elements. For every $u \in L$ denote $R_u = \{r \mid r \in R, r \not\leq u\}$. The following properties follow immediately. (1) $u \leq v$ iff $R_u \supseteq R_v$; (2) $R_u = R$ iff $u = \hat{0}$; (3) $R_{u \vee v} = R_u \cup R_v$.

Consider the query H_k defined in Section 3.2, and denote h_{ki} its components: that is, $H_k = h_{k0} \vee \ldots \vee h_{kk}$ (here $\vee$ refers to query union), where:

$$
\begin{aligned}
h_{k0} &= R(x_0), S_1(x_0, y_0) \\
h_{ki} &= S_i(x_i, y_i), S_{i+1}(x_i, y_i) \quad i = 1, k-1 \\
h_{kk} &= S_k(x_k, y_k), T(y_k)
\end{aligned}
$$

For every $u \in L$ define $Q_u = \bigvee_{r_i \in R_u} h_{ki}$ (here, too $\bigvee$ refers to query union). The following are easy to check: the CNF lattice of Q is isomorphic to L; $Q_{\hat{0}} = H_k$; for any other element $u \neq \hat{0}$, Q_u is the union of a strict subset of $h_{k0}, \ldots, h_{kk}$, and therefore is a safe query. This proves the claim. $\square$

4.1.6 COMPLETENESS

Recall that a query Q is *safe* if it is possible to compute $P(Q)$ on any database by applying the six rules in Subsection 4.1.2. To be more precise, we denote those six rules $\mathbf{R}_6$, and we we say that Q is $\mathbf{R}_6$-safe, emphasizing that the safety definition is relative to the six rules. Clearly, every safe query is tractable. But what about the converse? Safety is a syntactic property because it is defined in terms

---

[3]An atom is an element that covers $\hat{0}$.

Primer on Lattices   We follow [Stanley, 1997]. Fix a finite lattice $(L, \leq)$.

Definition 4.15 x *covers* y if $y < x$ and there is no $z \in L$ such that $y < z < x$; x is an *atom* if it covers $\hat{0}$; it is a *co-atom* if it is covered by $\hat{1}$. L^* denotes the set of co-atoms.

Denote $N_k(z) = |\{T \mid T \subseteq L^*, |T| = k, z = \bigwedge T\}|$. Then[a] $\mu_L(z, \hat{1}) = \sum_k (-1)^k N_k(z)$.

Definition 4.16   The *meet closure* of $S \subseteq L$ is $\bar{S} = \{\bigwedge T \mid T \subseteq S\}$. $\bar{S}$ is a lattice[b]. $z \in L$ is called *co-atomic* if $z \in \overline{L^*}$. L is called a *co-atomic lattice* if all elements are co-atomic.

Since $N_k(z)$ is the same in L and in $\overline{L^*}$, it follows:

Corollary 4.17   *(a) If* $z \notin \overline{L^*}$ *then* $\mu_L(z, \hat{1}) = 0$. *(b) If* $z \in \overline{L^*}$ *then* $\mu_L(z, \hat{1}) = \mu_{\overline{L^*}}(z, \hat{1})$.

Primer on Unions of Conjunctive Queries   All queries are Boolean.

Definition 4.18   A CQ query Q is *disconnected* if $Q \equiv Q_1 \wedge Q_2$, where $Q_1 \not\equiv$ *true* and $Q_2 \not\equiv$ *true*; otherwise, Q is called *connected*.

Definition 4.19   A UCQ query can be written in either DNF or CNF:
- A UCQ query is in DNF if $Q = \bigvee Q_i$ where each Q_i is a CQ.
- A *Disjunctive Query* (DQ), is $\bigvee Q_i$ where each Q_i is a connected CQ.
- A UCQ query is in CNF if $Q = \bigwedge_i Q_i$ where each Q_i is a DQ.

Proposition 4.20   *[Abiteboul et al., 1995]*
- *Given CQs* Q, Q': $Q \Rightarrow Q'$ *iff there exists a homomorphism* $h : Q' \to Q$.
- *Given DNFs* $Q = \bigvee Q_i, Q' = \bigvee Q'_j$: $Q \Rightarrow Q'$ *iff* $\forall i. \exists j$ *such that* $Q_i \Rightarrow Q'_j$.
- *Every UCQ query has a unique minimal DNF representation up to isomorphism.*

Proposition 4.21   *[Dalvi and Suciu, 2010] Assume all queries are without constants[c].*
- *Given CNFs* $Q = \bigwedge Q_i, Q' = \bigwedge Q'_j$: $Q \Rightarrow Q'$ *iff* $\forall j. \exists i$ *such that* $Q_i \Rightarrow Q'_j$.
- *Every UCQ* Q *has a unique minimal CNF representation* Q_0 *up to isomorphism. Let* $L = L(Q)$ *and* $L_0 = L(Q_0)$ *be their CNF lattices. Then* $L(Q_0) = \overline{L^*}$.

By Corollary 4.17, we obtain the same result if we apply Möbius' inversion formula to a CNF Q or to its minimized CNF Q_0.

[a]Stanley [1997, Corollary 3.9.4]; $N_k(x)$ is the number of k-sets of co-atoms whose meet is z.
[b]Because it is a meet-lattice with a maximal element: $\hat{1} \in \bar{S}$, by taking $T = \emptyset$.
[c]If Q has constants, then the first bullet fails: $Q_1 = R(a)$, $Q_2 = S(a)$, $Q' = \exists x. R(x), S(x)$, then $Q_1 \wedge Q_2 \Rightarrow Q'$, yet $Q_i \not\Rightarrow Q'$ for $i = 1, 2$.

Figure 4.2: Primer on Lattice Theory and UCQ Queries in CNF.

of the rules and the query expression, while tractability is a semantic property, and the question whether the two notions coincide is not easy. The converse also holds, but only for certain query languages $\mathcal{L}$.

For a query language $\mathcal{L}$, we denote $\mathcal{L}(P)$ the class of tractable queries in $\mathcal{L}$. Thus, $RC(P)$ denotes all tractable relational queries, $UCQ(P)$ denotes all tractable unions of conjunctive queries, and $CQ(P)$ denotes all tractable conjunctive queries. We say that the rules $\mathbf{R}_6$ are complete for $\mathcal{L}$ if every query in $\mathcal{L}(P)$ is $\mathbf{R}_6$-safe.

4.1.6.1   The Dichotomy Theorem for UCQ

When the query language under discussion is UCQ, then the rules $\mathbf{R}_6$ are complete: every query on which they fail is provably hard for #P.

Theorem 4.23   For any Union of Conjunctive Queries Q, one of the following holds:

- Q is $\mathbf{R}_6$-safe, or

- The data complexity of Q is hard for $\#P$.

The proof is quite difficult, and can be found in [Dalvi and Suciu, 2010]. The result means that the queries in UCQ admit a dichotomy: they are either computable in polynomial time, or they are provably hard for #P. The classification into safe or unsafe queries is based only on the syntax of the query Q: if the rules $\mathbf{R}_6$ apply, then Q is safe; otherwise, it is unsafe. Here "syntax" is used in a very loose sense; for example, it includes the Möbius function on the query's CNF lattice.

The theorem tells us *exactly* which UCQ queries are hard and which are easy although the criteria used to decide safety is somewhat unsatisfactory. Given Q, apply the rules: if we do not get stuck, then Q is safe (and tractable); otherwise, it is unsafe. One of the rules, *independent-project*, depends on the active domain of the database: $P(\exists x.Q) = 1 - \prod_{a \in ADom}(1 - P(Q[a/x]))$, but in order to check safety, we can simply consider an active domain of size 1: check if $P(Q[a/x])$ is safe for every constant a that occurs in Q and check if $P(Q[a/x])$ is safe for one single constant a that does not occur in Q. Thus, one can naively apply repeatedly the rules $\mathbf{R}_6$ and check if Q is safe: this requires two exponential steps at each application of the Möbius function because we need to rewrite the UCQ query from DNF to CNF, then we need to enumerate all subsets of the CNF expression, and therefore one can check safety in time super-exponential in the size of the query Q. Currently, it is unknown if there is a simpler criteria for checking safety; in particular, the query complexity for safety is unknown.

4.1.6.2   Hierarchical Queries and Non-Repeating Queries

For the entire relational calculus, it is unknown whether the rules $\mathbf{R}_6$ are complete, or whether RC admits a dichotomy. However, we know a necessary condition and a sufficient condition for tractability. We discuss these two conditions here.

Definition 4.24   A query expression given by Eq. (2.1) is called *hierarchical* if for every subexpression $\exists x.Q$, the variable x occurs in all atoms of Q (i.e., x is a root variable in Q). A query is called *hierarchical* if it is equivalent to a hierarchical expression. For a query language $\mathcal{L}$, we denote the class of hierarchical queries in $\mathcal{L}$ by $\mathcal{L}^H$; in particular, RC^H denotes the class of hierarchical, relational queries.

For a simple illustration, consider $Q = R(x), S(x, y)$. This query is in RC^H because it can be expressed as $\exists x.R(x) \wedge \exists y.S(x, y)$: the variable x is a root variable in the expression $R(x) \wedge \exists y.S(x, y)$, and the variable y is a root variable in the expression $S(x, y)$. Notice that the notion of a hierarchical query is a semantic notion: A query expression is hierarchical if *there exists* an expression equivalent to the query where each variable is a root variable. For example, the query $R(x), S(x, y), S(z, y)$ is in RC^H: while this expression is not hierarchical, the query is equivalent to $R(x), S(x, y)$, which is hierarchical. On the other hand, the query $H_0 = R(x), S(x, y), T(y)$ is not in RC^H. We will prove below that there exists no hierarchical expression equivalent to H_0.

We have:

Proposition 4.25   *If a query Q is $\mathbf{R}_6$-safe then it is hierarchical (i.e., $Q \in RC^H$).*

Proof. We prove the following, for each of the six rules expressing $P(Q)$ in terms of the probabilities of several subqueries $P(Q')$: if all subqueries Q' on the right-hand-side of the rule are hierarchical, then Q is also hierarchical. We illustrate a few cases. In the case of an independent join, $Q = Q_1 \wedge Q_2$: if both subqueries Q_1 and Q_2 are hierarchical, then obviously Q is hierarchical too. In the case of an independent project, $Q = \exists x.Q'$: if $Q'[a/x]$ is hierarchical for some arbitrary constant a, then so is Q because x is a root variable. Finally, for the inclusion exclusion formula $Q = Q_1 \wedge \ldots \wedge Q_k$: if all subqueries $\bigvee_{i \in s} Q_i$ for $s \subseteq [k]$ are hierarchical, then each Q_i is hierarchical, by setting $s = \{i\}$, hence $Q = \wedge_i Q_i$ is also hierarchical.   □

In general, the converse fails. For example, all queries $H_1, H_2, H_3, \ldots$ shown in Subsection 4.1.3 are hierarchical, yet they are all unsafe (and intractable). One can even find a conjunctive query that is hierarchical and unsafe; for example, $H_1' = R(x_0), S(x_0, y_0), S(x_1, y_1), T(y_1)$. After applying the inclusion-exclusion formula, $P(Q) = P(R(x_0), S(x_0, y_0)) + P(S(x_1, y_1), T(y_1)) - P(R(x_0), S(x_0, y_0) \vee S(x_1, y_1), T(y_1))$, and the third query is H_1, proving that H_1' is unsafe (we get stuck at H_1), and therefore it is hard for #P (by Theorem 4.23).

However, if a query is both hierarchical and non-repeating, then it is safe.

Definition 4.26   A query expression given by Eq. (2.1) is called *non-repeating* if every relation symbol occurs at most once. A query is called non-repeating if it is equivalent to a non-repeating expression. We denote $\mathcal{L}^{NR}$ the class of non-repeating queries in the language $\mathcal{L}$; in particular, RC^{NR} is the class of non-repeating relational queries.

An expression is called *hierarchical-non-repeating* if it is both hierarchical and non-repeating, and a query is called hierarchical-non-repeating if it is equivalent to such an expression. We denote $\mathcal{L}^{H,NR}$ the class of hierarchical-non-repeating queries.

Proposition 4.27   *Every query $Q \in RC^{H,NR}$ is $\mathbf{R}_6$-safe. In particular, Q is tractable.*

Proof. By induction on the structure of the non-repeating, hierarchical expression. If $Q = Q_1 \wedge Q_2$ then Q_1 and Q_2 are syntactically independent (because Q is non-repeating), similarly for $Q = Q_1 \vee Q_2$. In these cases, we apply an independent join or an independent union. If $Q = \exists x.Q'$, then x is a root variable, and, since no relational symbol is repeated, x is also a separator variable; hence, we can apply an independent project. Finally, if $Q = \neg Q'$, then we apply the negation. $\square$

One needs to use care when applying Proposition 4.27 because the class $RC^{H,NR}$ is *not* the same as $RC^H \cap RC^{NR}$. To be in $RC^{H,NR}$, a query must be given by an expression that is *both* hierarchical and non-repeating, and this corresponds to a strictly smaller class of queries than $RC^H \cap RC^{NR}$. For example, consider the query $H_1 = R(x_0), S(x_0, y_0) \vee S(x_1, y_1), T(y_1)$, which clearly is a hierarchical query. It can also be written as $\exists x.\exists y.(S(x, y) \wedge (R(x) \vee T(y)))$, which is a non-repeating expression. Hence, $H_1 \in RC^H \cap RC^{NR}$, but H_1 cannot be written as an expression that is both hierarchical and non-repeating, so it is not in $RC^{H,NR}$.

4.1.6.3 Conjunctive Queries Without Self-Joins

A non-repeating conjunctive query is called a *conjunctive query without self-joins*. Thus, CQ^{NR} denotes the set of conjunctive queries without self-joins. We show that, when restricted to this class, the converse to Proposition 4.27 also holds. In other words, a conjunctive query without self-joins is safe if and only if it is hierarchical.

We start by giving a simple criteria for a conjunctive query to be hierarchical. Let Q be a conjunctive query expression, and let $L_1, L_2, \ldots, L_k$ be its atoms. For each variable x, denote $at(x)$ the set of atoms L_i that contain x. If Q is hierarchical, then the following condition holds:

Hierarchy Condition For any two variables x, y, either $at(x) \cap at(y) = \emptyset$, or $at(x) \subseteq at(y)$, or $at(x) \supseteq at(y)$.

Conversely, if the condition above holds, then we can transform Q into a hierarchical expression by "pushing existential quantifiers" down, for example, rewriting $\exists x.\exists y.R(x) \wedge S(x, y)$ to $\exists x.R(x) \wedge \exists y.S(x, y)$. Notice that the hierarchy-condition is a syntactic condition, i.e., it depends on the query expression. Given an arbitrary conjunctive query Q, if Q is hierarchical then, by definition, there exists an equivalent expression Q' that is hierarchical. Minimize Q': this means remove redundant atoms, until one obtains an equivalent query expression Q'' where no atom can be further removed. Q'' also satisfies the hierarchy condition because it consists of a subset of the atoms of Q', which satisfied the hierarchy condition. This observation gives us a simple syntactic test for checking whether Q is hierarchical: minimize it first, then check the hierarchy condition. For example, consider $H_0 = R(x), S(x, y), T(y)$. It is already minimized, and the hierarchy condition fails because $at(x) = \{R, S\}$, $at(y) = \{S, T\}$; thus, H_0 is not hierarchical. For another example, consider $Q = R(x), S(x, y), S(z, y)$. The expression is not hierarchical, but the query minimizes to $R(x), S(x, y)$, which is hierarchical.

Therefore, unlike general relational queries, for conjunctive queries, we have:

Lemma 4.28 $CQ^{H,NR} = CQ^H \cap CQ^{NR}$

The proof follows immediately from the observation that both properties H and NR are preserved under query minimization, and the minimal expression is unique up to isomorphism.

Theorem 4.29 [**Dalvi and Suciu, 2004**]   Let Q be a non-repeating conjunctive query, $Q \in CQ^{NR}$. Then one of the following holds:

- If Q is hierarchical, then it is tractable and can be evaluated using two rules: independent-join, and independent-project.

- If Q is not hierarchical, then its data complexity is hard for $\#P$.

Proof. If Q is hierarchical, then $Q \in CQ^{H,NR}$ and therefore is tractable by Proposition 4.27. If Q is not hierarchical, then we prove hardness by reduction from H_0, whose hardness we proved in Theorem 3.2. Consider a minimal expression for Q, and let $R_1 \in at(x) - at(y)$, $S_1 \in at(x) \cap at(y)$, $T_1 \in at(y) - at(x)$. Thus, the three atoms look like this: $R_1(\ldots, x, \ldots)$, $S_1(\ldots, x, \ldots, y, \ldots)$, and $T_1(\ldots, y, \ldots)$. Consider any tuple-independent probabilistic database instance $\mathbf{D}$ for the query $H_0 = R(x), S(x, y), T(y)$. Define the following tuple-independent probabilistic database instance $\mathbf{D}_1$ for Q. Each tuple $R_1(\ldots, x, \ldots)$ is derived from a tuple in $R(x)$ by padding all extra attributes with a fixed constant a; similarly, each tuple $S_1(\ldots, x, \ldots, y, \ldots)$ is derived from a tuple $S(x, y)$, and each tuple $T_1(\ldots, y, \ldots)$ is derived from $T(y)$: padding is always done with the same constant a. The probabilities of the tuples in R_1, S_1, T_1 are the same as those in R, S, T. All relations other than R_1, S_1, T_1 are filled with all possible tuples from the active domain of R_1, S_1, T_1, and their probabilities are 1.0. It is easy to see that the probability of Q on $\mathbf{D}_1$ is equal to the probability of H_0 on $\mathbf{D}$. $\square$

4.2   QUERY EVALUATION USING EXTENSIONAL PLANS

An *extensional operator* is a standard relational algebra operator that is extended to manipulate tuple probabilities explicitly. For example, a join will multiply the probabilities, a projection with duplicate elimination may treat tuples as either independent and compute the output probability as $1 - (1 - p_1) \cdot (1 - p_2) \cdots$, or it may treat tuples as disjoint and compute $p_1 + p_2 + \ldots$ An *extensional plan* for a query Q is a relational plan with extensional operators. In general, the plan may not compute the output tuple probabilities correctly; when it computes them correctly for any input tuple-independent (or BID) database, then the plan is called a *safe plan*. For example, the plan on the left of Figure 4.3 is an extensional, but unsafe plan, while the plan on the right is safe.

In this section, we describe several extensional operators and show that every safe query Q can translated into a safe plan. This is very important for practical purposes because it means that one can evaluate Q by using existing query evaluation engines and take advantage of indexes, different join implementations, cost-based query optimization, or parallelism. If a query is safe, then it scales to large probabilistic databases like queries on regular databases. If the query is unsafe, then one can still use an extensional plan to evaluate Q on a probabilistic database: it still scales, but the output probabilities are incorrect. We also discuss briefly in this section how extensional plans can be used to approximate queries that are unsafe.

In this section, we no longer restrict the queries to Boolean queries; instead, we allow a query to have arbitrary head variables. We continue to assume that all input relations are tuple-independent, and we will discuss extensions to BID tables in Section 4.3.

The extensional plans will manipulate relations with an explicit probability attribute. That is, every relation R has schema of the form $R(\bar{A}, P)$, where $\bar{A}$ are the regular attributes and P is the probability. We refer to $\Pi_{\bar{A}}(R)$ as the *deterministic* part of R. If $u \in R$ is a tuple, then $u.\bar{A}$ is a regular tuple, and $u.P$ is its probability. Given an $\bar{A}$-tuple $\bar{a}$, we write $P_R(\bar{a})$ for the probability of $\bar{a}$ in R: That is, if $\bar{a} = u.\bar{A}$ for some tuple $u \in R$ then $P_R(\bar{a}) = u.P$; otherwise, $P_R(\bar{a}) = 0$. We assume w.l.o.g. that every tuple $\bar{a}$ occurs at most once in R; in other words, $\bar{A}$ is a key in $R(\bar{A}, P)$.

4.2.1   EXTENSIONAL OPERATORS

We now describe each of the extensional operators that are used in safe plans.

4.2.1.1   Independent Join

The independent join of two relations $R(\bar{A}, P), S(\bar{B}, P)$, in notation $R \bowtie_C^i S$, is the regular join of their deterministic parts, $\Pi_{\bar{A}}(R) \bowtie_C \Pi_{\bar{B}}(S)$, augmented with the product of the two probabilities, from R and from S:

$$R \bowtie_C^i S = \{(\bar{a}, \bar{b}, P_R(\bar{a}) \cdot P_S(\bar{b})) \mid \bar{a} \in \Pi_{\bar{A}}(R), \bar{b} \in \Pi_{\bar{B}}(S), (\bar{a}, \bar{b}) \in \Pi_{\bar{A}}(R) \bowtie_C \Pi_{\bar{B}}(S)\}$$

Here C is the join condition, expressed over the attributes $\bar{A}$ and $\bar{B}$.

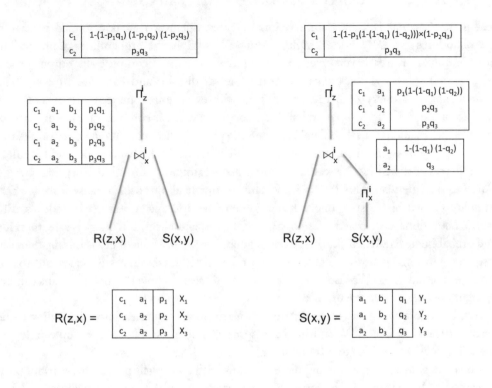

$$\Phi_{Q[c_1/z]} = X_1Y_1 \vee X_1Y_2 \vee X_2Y_3$$
$$P(c_1 \in Q) = P(\Phi_{c_1}) = 1 - [1 - p_1 \cdot (1 - (1 - q_1) \cdot (1 - q_2))] \cdot (1 - p_2 \cdot q_3)$$

Figure 4.3: An extensional plan (left) and a safe plan (right). On the given database the query returns two tuples, c_1, c_2. The plan on the left computes the probabilities incorrectly; the plan on the right computes them correctly. We show the lineage of the output c_1, and its probability: one can see that it is equal to the probability returned by the safe plan.

4.2.1.2 Independent Project

The independent projection $\Pi^i_{\bar{A}}(R)$ of a relation R on a set of attributes $\bar{A}$ is the regular projection $\Pi_{\bar{A}}(R)$ extended with a probability attribute computed as follows. If $u_1, u_2, \ldots, u_k$ are all the tuples in R that have a common value $\bar{a}$ of the $\bar{A}$ attribute, then the probability of $\bar{a}$ is set to

$$1 - (1 - u_1.P) \cdot (1 - u_2.P) \cdots (1 - u_k.P):$$

$$\Pi^i_{\bar{A}}(R) = \{(\bar{a}, 1 - \prod_{u \in R: u.\bar{A} = \bar{a}} (1 - u.P)) \mid \bar{a} \in \Pi_{\bar{A}}(R)\}$$

4.2.1.3 Independent Union

The independent union, in notation $R \cup^i_{\bar{A}} S$, takes as input two relations $R(\bar{A}_1, P)$, $S(\bar{A}_2, P)$ and returns a relation $T(\bar{A}, P)$, where $\bar{A} = \bar{A}_1 \cup \bar{A}_2$. The deterministic part of T is the set of tuples $\bar{a} \in (ADom)^k$ such that $\bar{a}.\bar{A}_1 \in \Pi_{\bar{A}_1}(R)$ or $\bar{a}.\bar{A}_2 \in \Pi_{\bar{A}_2}(R)$. If a tuple occurs in both R and S, with probabilities p_1 and p_2, respectively, then we set its probability in the union to $1 - (1 - p_1)(1 - p_2)$; if it occurs only in R, then we set its probability to p_1, and similarly if it occurs only in S:

$$R \cup^i_{\bar{A}} S = \{(\bar{a}, 1 - (1 - P_R(\bar{a}.\bar{A}_1)) \cdot (1 - P_S(\bar{a}.\bar{A}_2))) \mid \bar{a}.\bar{A}_1 \in \Pi_{\bar{A}_1}(R) \vee \bar{a}.\bar{A}_2 \in \Pi_{\bar{A}_2}(R)\}$$

By convention, $P_T(t) = 0$ if the tuple does not appear in the table T. We usually subscript the union on the common attributes $\bar{A}$, to indicate the schema. To get the intuition behind the union, consider first the typical case when the two relations have the same set of attributes $\bar{A} = \bar{A}_1 = \bar{A}_2$, then the deterministic part of $R \cup^i_{\bar{A}} S$ is the regular union of R and S.

In general, however, we may have to compute the union of two subexpression with different sets of attributes, which is a domain-dependent query[4]. This is a consequence of applying Möbius inversion rule to non-Boolean queries: for example, if $q(x, y) = R(x), S(x), S(y), T(y)$, then Möbius inversion rule requires us to compute the probability of three queries, one being $q_3(x, y) = R(x), S(x) \vee S(y), T(y)$. This is no longer a domain-independent query: the answer consists of all pairs (a, b) where either $R(a), S(a)$ is true and b is *any* value in the domain, or where $S(b), T(b)$ is true and a is any value. Thus, we must define the independent union $R \cup^i_{\bar{A}} S$ in a domain-dependent way, when $A_1 \neq A_2$. We start by extending each tuple in R with attributes $\bar{A}_2 - \bar{A}_1$, and we fill these with all possible values from the active domain, adding all resulting tuples to the union, similarly for S. In practice, the initial query Q was domain-independent, and then one can replace this domain-dependent union with a simple outer-join, $\Pi_{\bar{A}_1}(R) \bowtie \Pi_{\bar{A}_2}(S)$: in other words, we pad the extra attributes with NULLs instead of all values in the domain. This will not affect the semantics of the query because the query is assumed to be domain independent.

4.2.1.4 Weighted Sum

The weighted sum is an operation parameterized by k integers $\mu_1, \ldots, \mu_k$. It takes as input k relations $R_1(\bar{A}_1, P), \ldots, R_k(\bar{A}_k, P)$; it computes natural join of their deterministic part and sets the probability of every tuple $\bar{a}$ in the result to $\mu_1 p_1 + \ldots + \mu_k p_k$, where $p_1, \ldots, p_k$ are the

---

[4]A relational query is called *domain independent* if its semantics does not depend on the domain of the database, but it only depends on the active domain, i.e., the set of constants occurring in the database; otherwise, it is called *domain dependent*. Classical examples of domain dependent queries are $q(x, y) = R(x) \vee S(y)$, and $q'(x) = \neg R(x)$. Practical query languages like SQL or Relational Algebra can express only domain independent queries, by design; in datalog, domain dependence is ensured by requiring that every head variable occurs in at least one positive atom.

probabilities of $\bar{a}.\bar{A}_1, \ldots, \bar{a}.\bar{A}_k$ in relations $R_1, \ldots, R_k$, respectively. We will apply the weighted sum only as an instance of Möbius inversion formula, and in that case, the sum $\mu_1 p_1 + \ldots + \mu_k p_k$ is guaranteed to be a number in $[0, 1]$. We superscript the weighted sum with the weights and subscript it with the attribute names $\bar{A}$:

$$\Sigma_{\bar{A}}^{\mu_1,\ldots,\mu_k}(R_1, \ldots, R_k) = \{(\bar{a}, \sum_{i=1,k} \mu_i P_{R_i}(\bar{a}.\bar{A}_i)) \mid \bar{a} \in \Pi_{\bar{A}_1}(R_1) \bowtie \ldots \bowtie \Pi_{\bar{A}_k}(R_k)\}$$

For example, consider the query $q(x, y) = R(x), S(x), S(y), T(y)$. We apply the weighted sum to three subqueries: $q_1(x) = R(x), S(x)$, $q_2(y) = S(y), T(y)$ and $q_3(x, y) = R(x), S(x) \vee S(y), T(y)$, in notation $q(x, y) = \Sigma_{x,y}^{1,1,-1}(q_1(x), q_2(y), q_3(x, y))$. If we compute $q_3(x, y)$ naively, using the entire active domain, then the weighted sum is simply the natural join of the three subqueries. If we compute $q_3(x, y)$ as an outerjoin, then we need to interpret a NULL in the x or in the y position as standing for all values in the active domain: the result of the weighted sum consists of all tuples (a, b) such that a is in $q_1(x)$, b is in $q_2(y)$, and either (a, b), or $(a, NULL)$, or $(NULL, b)$ is in $q_3(x, y)$.

4.2.1.5 Complementation
The complement of a probabilistic relation $R(\bar{A}, P)$ with k deterministic attributes is:

$$C_{\bar{A}}(R) = \{(\bar{a}, 1 - P_R(\bar{a})) \mid \bar{a} \in (ADom(D))^k\}$$

In practice, since the query is domain independent, we never need to compute the complement w.r.t. to the entire active domain, but only w.r.t. to some other relation. In that case, every complement operation can be replaced with the difference of two relations $R(\bar{A}, P)$ and $S(\bar{A}, P)$, which is $R -^i S = R \bowtie_{\bar{A}}^i C_{\bar{A}}(S)$.

4.2.1.6 Selection
The selection operator is the same as on deterministic tables:

$$\sigma_C(R) = \{(\bar{a}, P_R(\bar{a})) \mid C \models \bar{a}\}$$

It is needed both to compute selections that occur naturally in the query and to implement attribute ranking. For example, if we rank the attributes A, B of R, then we split R into three tables, by using selection: $R_1 = \sigma_{A<B}(R)$, $R_2 = \sigma_{A=B}(R)$, and $R_3 = \sigma_{A>B}(R)$.

Example 4.30   We illustrate the query plans for several (non-Boolean) queries in Figure 4.3, Figure 4.4, Figure 4.5, and Figure 4.6. The figures make the following conventions. All leaves show the regular attribute names, omitting the probability attribute: for example, the relation $S(x, y)$ in

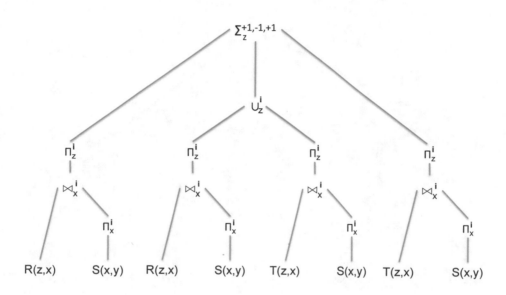

$$Q_J(z) : -R(z, x_1), S(x_1, y_1), T(z, x_2), S(x_2, y_2)$$

Figure 4.4: A safe plan for a conjunctive query with self-joins.

Figure 4.3 denotes a table with three attributes $S(x, y, P)$, but we omit the probability P. All joins are natural joins; thus, $R(x) \bowtie_x S(x, y)$ means the natural join on the x-attribute, and we follow standard practice of including the common attributes only once in the output relation.

For any non-Boolean query, its head variables are treated as constants for the purpose of attribute-constant ranking. For example, consider the query $Q(u) = R(x, u), R(u, x)$ This query is identical to Q_2 in Example 4.9 except that it uses a head variable u instead of a constant. The ranked query is $Q^r(u) = (R(x, u), x \neq u), (R(u, x), x \neq u) \vee (R(x, u), x = u)$ hence a safe plan is:

$$Q = \Pi_u^i[\sigma_{x \neq u}(R(x, u)) \bowtie_{x,u}^i \sigma_{x \neq u}(R(u, x))] \cup_u^i \Pi_u^i[\sigma_{x=u}(R(x, u))]$$

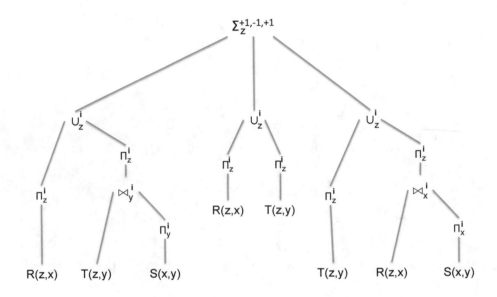

$$Q_V(z) : -R(z, x_1), S(x_1, y_1)$$
$$Q_V(z) : -S(x_2, y_2), T(z, y_2)$$
$$Q_V(z) : -R(z, x_3), T(z, y_3)$$

Figure 4.5: A safe plan for a union of conjunctive queries. The query is shown in datalog notation, and it is equivalent to $(\exists x_3.R(z, x_3) \vee \exists x_2.\exists y_2.S(x_2, y_2), T(z, y_2)) \wedge (\exists x_1.\exists y_1.R(z, x_1), S(x_1, y_1) \vee \exists y_3.T(z, y_3))$.

4.2.2   AN ALGORITHM FOR SAFE PLANS

We now give an algorithm that computes a safe plan for a query Q, or indicates that none exists. The algorithm adapts the six rules in Subsection 4.1.2 to compute operators rather than probabilities, and it is shown in Algorithm 1. The algorithms assumes that the ranking rule has already been applied. That means that some of the relations used in the query Q are actually selections applied

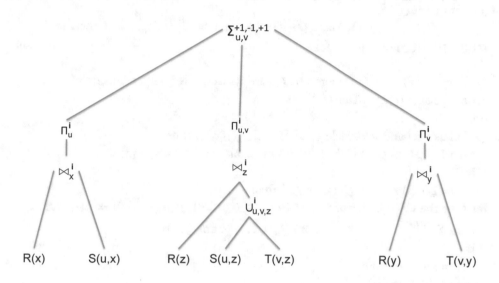

$$Q(u, v) : -R(x), S(u, x), R(y), T(v, y)$$

Figure 4.6: A safe plan illustrating the need for outer joins. The expression $S(u, z) \cup^i_{u,v,z} T(v, z)$ is domain-dependent and computes $A(u, v, z) = S(u, z) \vee T(v, z)$; it can be replaced with the outerjoin $S(u, z)_{\text{d}\rightarrow><-\text{d}} T(v, z)$.

to base relations, as in the last query in Example 4.30; if we do not apply all required ranking rules before invoking the algorithm, then it may fail to find a safe plan.

4.2.3 EXTENSIONAL PLANS FOR UNSAFE QUERIES

If Q is unsafe, then it does not have a safe plan. But we can still use an extensional to compute it, with the understanding that the output probabilities are incorrect. In some cases, these probabilities are approximations of the correct probabilities in a precise sense, allowing us to use the extensional plan to approximate the output probabilities.

Algorithm 1 Input: A query $Q(\bar{x})$, with head variables $\bar{x}$.

Output: A safe query plan for $Q(\bar{x})$, or `fail` if none exists.

Assumption We assume that the attributes in the query have already been attribute-ranked; thus, some of the tables R occurring in the query are actually selections over base tables.

```
 1: algorithm plan(Q(x̄)).
 2: if Q(x̄) = Q₁(x̄) ∧ Q₂(x̄), where Q₁, Q₂ are syntactically independent then
 3:     return plan(Q₁) ⋈ᵢx̄ plan(Q₂)
 4: end if
 5: if Q(x̄) = Q₁(x̄) ∨ Q₂(x̄) where Q₁, Q₂ are syntactically independent then
 6:     return plan(Q₁) ∪ᵢx̄ plan(Q₂)
 7: end if
 8: if Q(x̄) has a separator variable z: Q(x̄) = ∃z.Q₁(x̄, z) then
 9:     return Πᵢx̄(plan(Q₁)) /* the new head variables of Q₁ are x̄ ∪ {z} */
10: end if
11: if Q(x̄) = Q₁(x̄) ∧ ... ∧ Qₖ(x̄), k ≥ 2 then
12:     let L be the CNF lattice of Q, and {u | u ∈ L, u ≠ 1̂, μ(u, 1̂) ≠ 0} = {u₁, ..., uₘ}
13:     return Σ⁻μ(u₁,1̂),...,⁻μ(uₘ,1̂)x̄ (plan(Qᵤ₁), ..., plan(Qᵤₘ))
14: end if
15: if Q(x̄) = ¬Q₁(x̄) then
16:     return Cx̄(plan(Q₁))
17: end if
18: if Q(x̄) = a base table R(x̄) (possibly ranked by attributes and/or constants) then
19:     return R(x̄).
20: end if
21: otherwise FAIL /* no safe plan exists */
```

Consider the unsafe plan on the left of Figure 4.3. The query is safe, but the plan on the left is "unsafe". We claim that the unsafe plan computes an upper bound of the correct probabilities. In particular, the probability for c_1 returned by the plan on the right is $\leq$ that returned by the plan on the left, in other words $1 - [1 - p_1 \cdot (1 - (1 - q_1) \cdot (1 - q_2))] \cdot (1 - p_2 \cdot q_3) \leq 1 - (1 - p_1 q_1) \cdot (1 - p_1 q_2) \cdot (1 - p_2 q_3)$. Instead of showing this directly (which is possible but tedious), we give the general statement, which is much easier to understand. To give the intuition, let Φ denote the correct lineage for the output c_1, and let Φ^d be the lineage of the same output computed by the unsafe plan. Then:

$$\Phi = X_1 Y_1 \vee X_1 Y_2 \vee X_2 Y_3$$
$$\Phi^d = X_1' Y_1 \vee X_1'' Y_2 \vee X_2 Y_3$$

where X_1' and X_1'' are two *clones* of X_1. In other words, the reason why the plan on the left is unsafe is because it fails to recognize that two occurrences of X_1 are the same variable, but instead treats them as independent variables, with the same probability as X_1. This is captured by Φ^d, where we have replaced the two occurrences of X_1 with two distinct variables X_1' and X_1'', with the same probability p_1 as X_1. The following proposition shows that $P(\Phi) \leq P(\Phi^d)$:

Proposition 4.31   *Consider two propositional formulas:*

$$\Phi^d = \Phi_0 \vee \Phi_1 X_1 \vee \ldots \vee \Phi_k X_k$$
$$\Phi = \Phi_0 \vee \Phi_1 X \vee \ldots \vee \Phi_k X$$

such that $P(X) = P(X_1) = \ldots = P(X_k)$ and none of the formulas Φ_i, $i = 0, k$ contains any of the variables $X, X_1, \ldots, X_k$. Then $P(\Phi) \leq P(\Phi^d)$.

Intuitively, the proposition says this. We have a formula Φ that has multiple occurrences of some variable X: all these occurrences are positive (i.e., non-negated), and separated by $\vee$. If we "clone" each occurrence into a new variable X_i, such that all the clones are independent and have the same probability as X, then the probability can only increase. This cloning is called *dissociation* [Gatterbauer et al., 2010, Gatterbauer and Suciu, 2011] and is related to *relaxation* [Darwiche, 2010] but differs from the latter in that it gives an upper bound guarantee.

Proof. We claim that $P(\Psi) \leq P(\Psi^d)$, where

$$\Psi^d = \Psi_1 X_1 \vee \Psi_2 X_2$$
$$\Psi = \Psi_1 X \vee \Psi_2 X$$

and $x = P(X) = P(X_1) = P(X_2)$. The claim follows from the inclusion-exclusion formula:

$$P(\Psi) = x P(\Psi_1) + x P(\Psi_2) - x P(\Psi_1 \Psi_2) \leq P(\Psi^d) = x P(\Psi_1) + x P(\Psi_2) - x^2 P(\Psi_1 \Psi_2)$$

thus $P(\Psi) \leq P(\Psi^d)$ because $x^2 \leq x$.

We prove now the proposition by induction on k. For the base case, $k = 2$, denote $\Psi_i = (\neg\Phi_0) \wedge \Phi_i$, for $i = 1, 2$, then we have:

$$\Phi^d = \Phi_0 \vee (\neg\Phi_0)\Phi_1 X_1 \vee (\neg\Phi_0)\Phi_2 X_2 = \Phi_0 \vee \Psi^d$$
$$\Phi = \Phi_0 \vee (\neg\Phi_0)\Phi_1 X \vee (\neg\Phi_0)\Phi_2 X = \Phi_0 \vee \Psi$$

The base case follows from $P(\Phi_0 \vee \Psi) = P(\Phi_0) + P(\Psi) \leq P(\Phi_0) + P(\Psi^d) = P(\Phi_0 \vee \Psi^d)$. We prove now the inductive step. Consider:

$$\Phi^d = \Phi_0 \vee \Phi_1 X_1 \vee \ldots \vee \Phi_{k-2} X_{k-2} \vee \Phi_{k-1} X_{k-1} \vee \Phi_k X_k$$
$$\Phi' = \Phi_0 \vee \Phi_1 X_1 \vee \ldots \vee \Phi_{k-2} X_{k-2} \vee (\Phi_{k-1} \vee \Phi_k) Y$$
$$\Phi = \Phi_0 \vee \Phi_1 X \vee \ldots \vee \Phi_{k-2} X \vee (\Phi_{k-1} \vee \Phi_k) X$$

Then $P(\Phi) \leq P(\Phi')$ follows by induction (for $k - 1$), and $P(\Phi') \leq P(\Phi^d)$ follows from the base case ($k = 2$). $\qquad\square$

The proposition implies immediately.

Corollary 4.32 *Let $Q = Q_1 \vee Q_2 \vee \ldots \vee Q_m$ be a UCQ query where each conjunctive query Q_i is without self-joins. Then any extensional plan for Q that uses the operators independent join, independent project, independent union, and selection, computes an upper bound for the probabilities of Q.*

For example, the plan on the left in Figure 4.3 is guaranteed to return an upper bound of the correct probabilities of the query in the figure. However, the corollary is much more interesting when applied to an unsafe query. Consider, for example, $Q(z) = R(z, x), S(x, y), T(y)$, which, for a fixed output value z, is equivalent H_0 in Subsection 4.1.3; in other words, Q is provably hard for #P. There are three extensional plans for Q:

$$P_1 = \Pi_z^i[\Pi_{z,x}^i(R(z, x) \bowtie_x^i S(x, y)) \bowtie_y^i T(y)]$$
$$P_2 = \Pi_z^i[R(z, x) \bowtie_x^i \Pi_x^i(S(x, y) \bowtie_y^i T(y))]$$
$$P_3 = \Pi_z^i[R(z, x) \bowtie_x^i S(x, y) \bowtie_y^i T(y)]$$

Each of them is guaranteed to return an upper bound on the true probability for Q. Therefore, if we evaluate all three plans and take the minimum probability for each output tuple, we get a tighter upper bound. Moreover, it is possible to show that the probabilities returned by P_3 are always an upper bound of those returned by either P_1 and P_2 (because the lineage that P_3 computes is a dissociation of the lineage by P_1, and also a dissociation of the lineage computed by P_2). Thus, P_3 does not provide any additional information, and it suffices to evaluate only P_1 and P_2. We can generalize this example to any query without self-joins[5] and therefore compute approximate answers quite efficiently. The disadvantage, however, is that there is no guarantee on how tight the upper bound is.

4.3 EXTENSIONS

We discuss here several extensions to query evaluation.

4.3.1 BID TABLES

So far, in this chapter, we have considered only tuple-independent tables. In a BID table, the tuples are partitioned into blocks, such that tuples from different blocks are independent, and tuples within a block are disjoint (Section 2.7). The query evaluation techniques discussed in this chapter extend with minor modifications to BID tables. Recall that a BID table has a schema of the form $R(\underline{A_1, \ldots, A_k}, B_1, \ldots, B_m)$, where the attributes $A_1, \ldots, A_k$ uniquely identify a block; in other words, they are a key in any possible world. For example, we write $T(\underline{z}, y)$ to say that z is a key attribute; in any possible world, there cannot be two distinct tuples $T(b, c_1)$ and $T(b, c_2)$. But the

---
[5]The dissociation inequality no longer holds for self-joins.

representation of the BID table has schema $T(z, y, P)$, and there may be several tuples with $z = b$, and the sum of their probabilities is ≤ 1. A tuple-independent table is a special case of a BID table, where all attributes are key attributes: thus, $S(\underline{x}, \underline{y})$ is a tuple-independent table, and in that case, we simply write it as $S(x, y)$ when no confusion arises.

The six query evaluation rules discussed in Section 4.1 extend to BID tables, with the following changes.

- A *root variable* is a a variables x occurs in every atom *in a key position*. A *separator variable* is a root variable such that for any two unifiable atoms it occurs on a common key position. Thus, non-key positions do not matter when determining whether a variable is a root or a separator variable.

- All six rules in Section 4.1 remain unchanged. The *independent-project* applies to any separator variable, with the adjustment mentioned here.

- There is one new rule, called *disjoint project*. It comes in two variants. First, suppose Q is a Boolean conjunctive query that has an atom $R(\ldots)$ where (a) all attributes in key positions contain constants (i.e., there are no variables in key positions), and (b) x is a variable occurring on a non-key attribute of R. Then:

$$P(Q) = \sum_{a \in ADom} P(Q[a/x])$$

Second, suppose Q is a UCQ query of the form $Q = Q_1 \vee Q'$ where Q_1 is a conjunctive query having an atom where all key attribute are constants, and Q' is any other UCQ query. Then we write $P(Q) = P(Q_1) + P(Q') - P(Q_1 \wedge Q')$, then apply the disjoint-project rule both to Q_1 and to $Q_1 \wedge Q'$.

- It is known that for the class of conjunctive queries without self-joins, CQ^{NR}, the rules extended with disjoint project are sufficient to compute all polynomial-time queries. Thus, these queries admit a dichotomy over BID tables. The hard queries in CQ^{NR} over BID tables can be described by three types of queries: $H_0 = R(\underline{x}), S(\underline{x}, \underline{y}), T(\underline{y})$ (here all three tables are tuple-independent), and two more queries, $R(\underline{x}, y), S(\underline{y})$ and $R(\underline{x}, y), S(x, \underline{y})$ [Dalvi and Suciu, 2007c]. It is not known whether a similar dichotomy holds for UCQ.

- Finally, the disjoint-project rule above corresponds to a simple relational operator, called *disjoint project*, Π_A^d: during duplicate elimination, it computes the output probability as $p_1 + p_2 + \ldots$

Example 4.33 Let $R(x)$, $S(x, y)$ be tuple-independent tables, and $T(\underline{z}, y), U(\underline{w}, z)$ be BID-tables. Consider the Boolean query $Q = R(x), S(x, y), T(\underline{z}, y), U(\underline{a}, z)$, where a is a constant. Then we have:

$$P(Q) = \sum_b P(R(x), S(x, y), T(\underline{b}, y), U(\underline{a}, b))$$

$$= \sum_b P(R(x), S(x, y), T(\underline{b}, y)) \cdot P(U(\underline{a}, b))$$

$$= \sum_b \sum_c P(R(x), S(x, c), T(\underline{b}, c)) \cdot P(U(\underline{a}, b))$$

$$= \sum_b \sum_c P(R(x), S(x, c)) \cdot P(T(\underline{b}, c)) \cdot P(U(\underline{a}, b))$$

$$= \sum_b \sum_c (1 - \prod_d (1 - P(R(d), S(d, c)))) \cdot P(T(\underline{b}, c)) \cdot P(U(\underline{a}, b))$$

Now consider the non-Boolean variant of the query: $Q(w) = R(x), S(x, y), T(\underline{z}, y), U(\underline{w}, z)$. It can be computed by the following safe plan:

$$P = \Pi^d_w [\Pi^i_y (R(x) \bowtie^i_x S(x, y)) \bowtie^i_y T(\underline{z}, y) \bowtie^i_z U(\underline{w}, z)$$

4.3.2   DETERMINISTIC TABLES

In many applications of probabilistic databases, several of the tables are deterministic. Typically, one starts with a standard database and extends it with new probabilistic tables that contain the uncertain data. Queries are therefore expressed over a mixed schema where some tables are probabilistic and others are deterministic. So far, we have assumed that *all* tables occurring in a query are probabilistic. Deterministic tables could be treated simply as probabilistic tables where all tuples have probability 1.0, but this approach is too pessimistic: by recognizing that some tables are deterministic, we can often transform a hard query into a tractable query. For example, consider the Boolean query $Q = R(x), S(x, y), T(y)$: if all three tables are tuple-independent tables, then this query is exactly H_0, which we have shown in Subsection 4.1.3 to be intractable. However, assume now that T is a deterministic table. Then the query can be computed by the following safe plan: $\Pi^i_\emptyset (R(x) \bowtie^i_x (S(x, y) \bowtie_y T(y))$. The last join is between a probabilistic table and a deterministic table. Thus, the query becomes tractable, if T is known to be deterministic.

Consider a probabilistic database, where each relation name is labeled as being either deterministic or probabilistic. To take advantage of the deterministic tables, we make the following change to the independent-project rule: we require the variable x to occur in all key positions of all *probabilistic tables* only. For example, in $R(x), S(x, y), T(y)$, if T is deterministic, then we call x a root variable since it occurs in all probabilistic tables (and it is also a separator variable since the query is without self-joins). The modified rule is still sound. It is not known whether the rules $\mathbf{R}_6$ are complete over probabilistic databases with mixed schemas, except for conjunctive queries without self-joins: here is known that the rules are complete [Dalvi and Suciu, 2007c].

4.3.3   KEYS IN THE REPRESENTATION

It is common to have a key attribute in the representation of a tuple-independent or a BID table. For example, consider a tuple-independent relation $S(x, y)$, and assume that in its representation the attribute x is a key. This means that the tuples continue to be independent, but that the x attribute is distinct among all possible tuples.

In general, if x is a key in the representation of a table, then it is also a key in all possible worlds since a possible world is just some subset of the representation; the table is like a BID table where every block is uniquely identified by x and contains a single tuple. But the converse does not hold: if x is key in every possible world, then it means that $S(\underline{x}, y)$ is a BID-table, and it does not imply that x is a key in the representation.

If we know which attributes are keys in the representation, then we may be able to find safe plans for queries that otherwise would be intractable. More generally, assume an arbitrary set of functional dependencies. For any conjunctive query without self-joins, one can check if it is tractable using the following process, similar to a chase. We repeat until no more change is possible: if a functional dependency $X \rightarrow y$ holds, where X is a set of variables, then add the variable y to all other atoms that contain all variables in X. Once the chase terminates, check if the resulting query is safe: the original query is tractable iff the chased query is tractable.

For example, assume that $x \rightarrow y$ holds in $S(x, y)$, and consider the Boolean query $Q = R(x), S(x, y), T(y)$: this is the same as H_0, but we denote it differently to emphasize that it is over a table $S(x, y)$ where x is a key attribute. Then the chase process described above rewrites Q to $Q' = R(x, y), S(x, y), T(y)$, which is a safe query. In other words, if we know that x is a key in the representation of S, then the query becomes tractable. It is known that the chase procedure is complete for conjunctive queries without self-joins: it is unknown whether it is complete, or even how to extend it to a richer class of queries.

4.4   BIBLIOGRAPHIC AND HISTORICAL NOTES

Safe queries and safe query plans are introduced by Dalvi and Suciu [2004]. They also prove a dichotomy into polynomial time and #P-hard for conjunctive queries without self-joins over tuple-independent tables. The evaluation algorithm for UCQ queries that we discussed in Section 4.1 was first introduced by Dalvi et al. [2010]. They introduced the inclusion-exclusion rule and its extension to Möbius inversion formula, and also announced the dichotomy result in Theorem 4.23. The complete proof of this theorem is in [Dalvi and Suciu, 2010].

The safe plans discussed in Section 4.2 have an important practical limitation: they restrict severely the choices of the query optimizers. Olteanu et al. [2009] address this problem, by decoupling the data processing part of the query plan from the probabilistic inference part. They introduce a new type of plan that allows the optimizer to choose the best plan for the data processing part, yet allowing the probabilistic inference to take advantage of the query's safety. In that framework, a safe plan is an *eager* plan, where all probabilistic computations are performed as early as possible; *lazy* plans are at the other extreme as they compute the probabilities after the result tuples are computed.

Depending on the selectivities of join conditions, probability computation can be pushed past joins in the query plans. Olteanu et al. [2009] also extend relational plans with a new aggregation operator that is optimized using the query structure and schema information in the form of keys and functional dependencies to minimize the number of table scans needed for probability computation. This operator computes the query probability while factorizing the query lineage into read-once formulas in polynomial time. Olteanu and Huang [2009] extend this idea to a class of tractable conjunctive queries with inequalities. Gatterbauer et al. [2010] introduced the dissociation technique described in Subsection 4.2.3; they define an order between query plans and thus approximate the query probabilities with best possible upper bounds in a database independent way.

Section 4.3 is based on several references. Query evaluation on BID tables was first discussed by Andritsos et al. [2006] and Ré et al. [2006]; the extended algorithm described in Subsection 4.3.1 and the dichotomy for conjunctive queries without self-joins was given by [Dalvi and Suciu, 2007a]. Safe plans for BID tables are discussed by Ré et al. [2006]. Only conjunctive queries without self-joins have been studied over BID tables; the evaluation of UCQ, or arbitrary Relational Calculus queries over BID tables has not been studied yet. The second rule that we give in Subsection 4.3.1, which pushes the disjoint-project past unions, was communicated to us by Abhay Jha. Extensions to queries over deterministic tables (Subsection 4.3.2) and functional dependencies in the representation (Subsection 4.3.3) are discussed by Dalvi and Suciu [2007b], who also establish a dichotomy for conjunctive queries without self-joins. The chase-like criteria for checking safety over tables with functional dependencies that we described in Subsection 4.3.3 is much simpler than the criteria given by Dalvi and Suciu [2007b], and it was first introduced by Olteanu et al. [2009].

Several extensions of the query evaluation problem for richer probabilistic models have been considered in the literature.

Sen and Deshpande [2007] discuss query evaluation over probabilistic databases represented by a graphical model. An optimization to query processing over such probabilistic databases is described by Sen et al. [2008]. The optimization finds common subgraphs in the GM and applies a technique similar to *lifted inference* [Poole, 2003]; this can be very effective over large probabilistic databases, because they tend to have a large number of similar, repeated subgraphs.

Twig queries over probabilistic XML data are discussed by Senellart and Abiteboul [2007], Cohen et al. [2009], Kimelfeld et al. [2008], and Kimelfeld et al. [2009]: They give a polynomial-time algorithm for computing any twig pattern over an XML document in the *PrXML^{exp}* model. Furthermore, it is shown that if the model is extended to *PrXML^{cie}*, then *every* non-trivial twig pattern has #P-hard data complexity. Later, Benedikt et al. [2010] consider more expressive and exponentially more succinct models that are restrictions of recursive Markov Chains (RMCs, cf. [Etessami and Yannakakis, 2009]). RMCs are extensions of the standard Markov chains, i.e., of graphs whose edges are labeled with probabilities and that define processes evolving via independent choices at nodes. The extension consists of a notion of subroutine or recursive call and, consequently, the runs of RMCs have a natural hierarchical structure, and it can thus be seen as nested words or trees. These new models capture probabilistic versions of schemas of XML documents, can define infinite probability distributions, and can be exponentially more succinct than the $PrXML^{exp}$ model, while still preserving tractability for Monadic Second-Order Logic. In particular, it is shown that the so-called hierarchical Markov chains are tractable under fixed-cost arithmetic, and so-called tree-like Markov chains are tractable in the usual bit-cost arithmetic. The yardstick particularly useful to differentiate among these models is the ability to represent succinctly trees of arbitrary width or depth, and probability spaces with worlds that have probabilities double-exponentially close to 1. Deutch et al. [2010a] discuss the query evaluation problem for datalog with a stochastic extension that determines the execution of a datalog program to be a Markov Chain. They show that the query evaluation problem is hard in general and describe approximation algorithms for special cases.

CHAPTER 5

Intensional Query Evaluation

In this chapter we discuss *intensional query evaluation*, which is based on the query's lineage. Intensional query evaluation reduces the query evaluation problem to computing the probability of a propositional formula, $P(\Phi)$.

Given a pc-database $\mathbf{D}$ (i.e., a set of pc-tables, cf. Section 2.7), a query $Q(\bar{x})$, and a possible tuple $\bar{a}$, intensional evaluation computes $P(Q)$ in two conceptual steps: first, compute the lineage $\Phi = \Phi^{\mathbf{D}}_{Q[\bar{a}/\bar{x}]}$, then compute the probability $P(\Phi)$. In practice, these steps are often intertwined. The size of the lineage expression $\Phi^{\mathbf{D}}_Q$ depends both on the query and on the database. This dependency is polynomial in $\mathbf{D}$ and exponential in Q. More precisely, the size of the lineage formula is $|\Phi^{\mathbf{D}}_Q| = O(|ADom|^m)$, where m is the number of variables in Q, and $ADom$ is the active domain of the database, i.e., the set of all constants occurring in the database.

The data complexity for the first step is in polynomial time, meaning that for any fixed query Q, one can compute $\Phi^{\mathbf{D}}_Q$ in polynomial time in the size of the database. The main complexity in intensional query evaluation comes from the second step. Here we need to compute $P(\Phi)$, where Φ is a propositional formula, whose size depends on the input database. This is a key difference to extensional query evaluation; for example, we cannot apply the inclusion-exclusion rule on Φ because its complexity would be exponential in the size of Φ and thus in the size of the input database.

The probability computation problem for propositional formulas has been studied both in the verification and in the AI communities. We start by reviewing the most basic approaches for computing $P(\Phi)$ in Section 5.1. These can be best explained in terms of a set of rules, which compute $P(\Phi)$ as a function of simpler propositional formulas $P(\Phi_1), \ldots, P(\Phi_n)$. The rules either exploit independence between formulas, or disjointness, or apply Shannon's expansion on one Boolean variable X. The complexity of evaluating $P(\Phi)$ depends significantly on the order in which the rules are applied, and on the order in which variables are eliminated during the Shannon expansion step.

Formula compilation refers to the translation of a propositional formula Φ into a circuit for computing Φ. The circuit is required to have certain properties that ensure that one can compute $P(\Phi)$ in linear time in the size of the circuit. We discuss in Section 5.2 four well-known types of circuits, also called *compilation targets*: read-once formulas, OBDD, FBDD, and d-DNNF. One approach to computing $P(\Phi)$ is thus to first compile Φ and then compute its probability. The advantage of this approach is that the compiled circuit can also be used for other applications, besides the probability computation [Darwiche and Marquis, 2002]. Most evaluation algorithms for $P(\Phi)$ can be converted into an algorithm for constructing a circuit for Φ [Darwiche, 2006].

Since computing $P(\Phi)$ is #P-hard, in general, several approximation techniques have been developed in the literature. We review in Section 5.3 two approximation techniques, which have been used in probabilistic databases. The first approximation technique keeps the same flexible, rule-based evaluation algorithm, but it stops it at any time and returns a lower and upper bound for the true probability. The second approximation technique is a well known Monte Carlo simulation algorithm due to Karp and Luby [1983] and Karp et al. [1989], which is an FPTRAS (Fully Polynomial-Time Randomized Approximation Scheme). This algorithm has the advantage that it runs in polynomial time in the desired precision; the disadvantage is that it must always pay a relatively high price, even if Φ is rather simple, and that it requires the input formula to be in disjunctive normal form.

Finally, in Section 5.4, we discuss the connection between a query's expression and the tractability of its compilation into various compilation targets. More precisely: given a query Q, can one compile the lineage Φ_Q into an efficient circuit in a given target? For two targets (read-once formulas and OBDD), this problem can be completely decided by examining the expression Q. For the other two targets (FBDD and d-DNNF), we give only partial answers.

5.1   PROBABILITY COMPUTATION USING RULES

Let $\mathbf{X}$ be a set of independent random variables, where each variable X takes values from a finite domain Dom_X. The probability of the atomic event $X = a$ is given by a number $P(X = a) \in [0, 1]$, such that $\sum_{a \in Dom_X} P(X = a) = 1$. If Φ is a propositional formula over atomic events of the form $X = a$, then we denote by $P(\Phi)$ the probability that Φ is true. More precisely, writing $\omega(\Phi) = \{\theta \mid \Phi[\theta] = true\}$, the probability is given by $P(\Phi) = \sum_{\theta \in \omega(\Phi)} P(\theta)$, see Eq. (2.3).

A special role in our discussion will be played by DNF formulas. A conjunction of atomic events $(X_1 = a_1) \wedge \cdots \wedge (X_n = a_n)$ is called a *conjunct*, and a *DNF formula* is a disjunction of conjuncts. A formula Φ is *consistent*, or *satisfiable* if there exists at least one assignment θ of the random variables that makes the formula true, $\Phi[\theta] = true$. DNF formulas are easy to test for consistency: a single conjunct is consistent iff it does not contain two atomic formulas $X = a$ and $X = b$ where $a \neq b$, and a DNF formula is consistent if at least one of its conjuncts is consistent. For example, $X = a \wedge Y = b \wedge Z = c$ is consistent, while $X = a \wedge Y = b \wedge X = c$ is not.

5.1.1   FIVE SIMPLE RULES FOR $P(\Phi)$

We give here five simple rules for computing $P(\Phi)$. These rules can be used to compute the probability of any propositional formula Φ. In some cases, they can be quite effective, but, in general, they lead to an exponential time algorithm.

5.1.1.1   Rules 1 and 2: Independent AND and OR
Consider the following example: $\Phi = XY \vee XZ$. Re-write Φ as $X \wedge (Y \vee Z)$ and obtain $P(\Phi) = P(X) \cdot P(Y \vee Z)$ because the two formulas X and $Y \vee Z$ are independent events. Furthermore,

$P(Y \vee Z) = 1 - (1 - P(Y)) \cdot (1 - P(Z))$, also because of independence, which leads to:

$$P(\Phi) = P(X) \cdot (1 - (1 - P(Y)) \cdot (1 - P(Z)))$$

For the general approach, we need a definition.

Definition 5.1   For a propositional formula Φ denote by $Var(\Phi)$ the set of propositional variables on which Φ depends. More precisely, $Var(\Phi)$ consists of all variables X such that there exists an assignment θ to the other $n - 1$ variables, and two values $a, b \in Dom_X$ such that $\Phi[\theta \cup \{X \mapsto a\}] \neq \Phi[\theta \cup \{X \mapsto b\}]$.

Intuitively, $Var(\Phi)$ consists of all the variables used in Φ, and it is called the *support* of Φ. One needs to be careful when computing the support $Var(\Phi)$ because not all variables that occur syntactically in Φ are part of the support. Instead, one needs to simplify Φ first, then $Var(\Phi)$ consists of all variables that still occur in Φ. For example, if $\Phi = Y \vee XY$ then Φ does not depend on X because the absorption law simplifies it to $\Phi = Y$ and therefore $Var(\Phi) = \{Y\}$. The definition above takes care of this by requiring that $\Phi[\theta]$ actually depend on X.

Definition 5.2   Two propositional formulas Φ_1, Φ_2 are called *syntactically independent* if $Var(\Phi_1) \cap Var(\Phi_2) = \emptyset$.

The following is easy to check:

Proposition 5.3   *If $\Phi_1, \Phi_2, \ldots, \Phi_k$ are pairwise syntactically independent, then the probabilistic events $\Phi_1, \Phi_2, \ldots, \Phi_k$ are independent.*

Our first two rules for computing $P(\Phi)$ are *independent-and* and the *independent-or* rules and are defined as follows. If Φ_1, Φ_2 are syntactically independent, then:

Independent-and:	$P(\Phi_1 \wedge \Phi_2) = P(\Phi_1) \cdot P(\Phi_2)$	(5.1)
Independent-or:	$P(\Phi_1 \vee \Phi_2) = 1 - (1 - P(\Phi_1)) \cdot (1 - P(\Phi_2))$	(5.2)

Checking if two formulas are syntactically independent is co-NP-complete in general, because SAT can be reduced to syntactic dependence: if Φ is a formula and X a variable that does not occur in Φ, then X and $X \wedge \Phi$ are syntactically dependent iff Φ is satisfiable. In practice, however, it suffices to use a sufficient condition for syntactical independence. Given a propositional formula *expression* Φ, denote $V(\Phi)$ the set of variables that occur in Φ. Obviously, $V(\Phi)$ can be computed in polynomial time, and $Var(\Phi) \subseteq V(\Phi)$. For example, for the expression $\Phi = Y \vee XY$, we have $Var(\Phi) = \{Y\}$ and $V(\Phi) = \{X, Y\}$. Then, for any two formulas Φ_1, Φ_2, if $V(\Phi_1) \cap V(\Phi_2) = \emptyset$, then Φ_1 and Φ_2 are syntactically independent: the condition $V(\Phi_1) \cap V(\Phi_2) = \emptyset$ can be computed in polynomial time. Thus, in the rest of this chapter, we will assume that we may use $V(\Phi)$ instead $Var(\Phi)$, in order to compute it efficiently.

Proposition 5.3 is somewhat surprising in the sense that it states that *pairwise* syntactic independence implies independence. This shows that syntactic independence is a stronger notion than independence because, in general, pairwise independent events are *not* necessarily syntactically independent. For example, consider:

$$\Phi_1 = X \qquad\qquad \Phi_2 = Y \qquad\qquad \Phi_3 = (\neg X \wedge \neg Y) \vee (X \wedge Y)$$

Assuming $P(X) = P(Y) = P(Z) = 1/2$, we have $P(\Phi_1) = P(\Phi_2) = P(\Phi_3) = 1/2$. Also, $\Phi_1 \wedge \Phi_2 = \Phi_1 \wedge \Phi_3 = \Phi_2 \wedge \Phi_3 = XY$, hence their probabilities are $1/4$. Therefore, the three events Φ_1, Φ_2, Φ_3 are pairwise independent, $P(\Phi_i \wedge \Phi_j) = P(\Phi_i) \cdot P(\Phi_j)$, for $i \neq j$. On the other hand, $P(\Phi_1 \wedge \Phi_2 \wedge \Phi_3) = P(XY) = 1/4 \neq P(\Phi_1) \cdot P(\Phi_2) \cdot P(\Phi_3) = 1/8$, meaning that the three events are not independent.

It is interesting to note that a converse to Proposition 5.3 also holds:

Proposition 5.4   *If Φ_1, Φ_2 are independent probabilistic events, i.e., $P(\Phi_1 \wedge \Phi_2) = P(\Phi_1) \cdot P(\Phi_2)$, for any choice of the probabilities $P(X = a)$ of the atomic events, then Φ_1, Φ_2 are syntactically independent.*

Proof. For each random variable X_i, with domain $Dom_{X_i} = \{a_0, a_1, \ldots, a_{m_i}\}$, we introduce m_i real variables $x_{i,1}, x_{i,2}, \ldots, x_{i,m_i}$ representing the probabilities of the atomic events $x_{i,1} = P(X = a_1), \ldots, x_{i,m_i} = P(X = a_{m_i})$: we do not need a variable for $P(X = a_0)$ since this value is uniquely defined as $1 - x_{i,1} - x_{i,2} - \ldots - x_{i,m_i}$. We claim that the probability $P(\Phi)$ of any propositional formula Φ is a multi-variate polynomial in the variables $x_{i,j}$ with the following properties: (a) it is a multi-linear, i.e., the degree of each variable $x_{i,j}$ is a most 1, and (b) if two variables x_{i_1,j_1} and x_{i_2,j_2} occur in the same monomial, then $i_1 \neq i_2$. Indeed, the claim follows from the fact that for each assignment θ, the probability $P(\theta)$ given by Eq. (2.2) obviously satisfies these two properties, and the fact $P(\Phi)$ is a sum of such polynomials (Eq. (2.3)).

Using this claim, we prove the proposition. Let Ψ be any propositional formula and θ an assignment to some of its variables, i.e., $\theta(X_i) = a_j$, for some subset of variables X_i. Then, the polynomial $P(\Psi[\theta])$ is obtained from $P(\Psi)$ by performing the following substitution on the variables $x_{i,j}$ for which $\theta(X_i)$ is defined, $\theta(X_i) = a_j$: if $j > 0$ then substitute $x_{i,j} = 1$ and set all other $x_{i,k} = 0$, and if $j = 0$ then set substitute all variables $x_{i,1} = x_{i,2} = \ldots = 0$.

Suppose now Eq. (5.1) holds as an identity. Assume that $X_i \in Var(\Phi_1) \cap Var(\Phi_2)$: we will derive a contradiction. Since $X_i \in Var(\Phi_1)$, there exists some substitution θ of all variables other than X_i, and two values a_{j_1} and a_{j_2} such that $\Phi_1[\theta, X_i \mapsto a_{j_1}] \neq \Phi_1[\theta, X_i \mapsto a_{j_2}]$; that means that one of the two expressions is *true* and the other *false*, implying $P(\Phi_1[\theta, X_i \mapsto a_{j_1}]) \neq P(\Phi_1[\theta, X_i \mapsto a_{j_2}])$ (one is 0 the other is 1). The polynomial $P(\Phi_1[\theta])$ can only depend on the variables $x_{i,1}, x_{i,2}, \ldots$, since all variables other than X_i are substituted with constants. Since it cannot be a constant polynomial, it must depend on at least one of these variables, say x_{i,j_1}. Then the polynomial $P(\Phi_1)$ must also depend on x_{i,j_1}. Similarly, the polynomial $P(\Phi_2)$ must depend on some variable x_{i,j_2}, with the same index i. Then, the identity $P(\Phi_1) \cdot P(\Phi_2) = P(\Phi_1 \wedge \Phi_2)$ implies that the latter polynomial contains the product $x_{i,j_1} \cdot x_{i,j_2}$, violating either condition (a) (when $j_1 = j_2$) or condition (b) (when $j_1 \neq j_2$), which is a contradiction. This proves the claim. □

5.1.1.2 Rule 3: Disjoint OR

To motivate the next heuristics, consider the formula $\Phi_3 = \neg X \wedge \neg Y \vee X \wedge Y$ above. Since the two events $\neg X \wedge \neg Y$ and $X \wedge Y$ are disjoint probabilistic events, we have:

$$P(\Phi_3) = P(\neg X \wedge \neg Y) + P(X \wedge Y) = (1 - P(X)) \cdot (1 - P(Y)) + P(X) \cdot P(Y)$$

Definition 5.5 Two propositional formulas Φ_1, Φ_2 are called *disjoint* if the formula $\Phi_1 \wedge \Phi_2$ is not satisfiable.

The *disjoint-or* rule is the following. If Φ_1, Φ_2 are disjoint formulas, then:

$$\textbf{Disjoint-or:} \qquad P(\Phi_1 \vee \Phi_2) = P(\Phi_1) + P(\Phi_2) \qquad (5.3)$$

5.1.1.3 Rule 4: Negation

It is easy to push the probability operator past negation:

$$\textbf{Negation:} \qquad P(\neg \Phi) = 1 - P(\Phi) \qquad (5.4)$$

5.1.1.4 Rule 5: Shannon Expansion

We illustrate Shannon's expansion using the following example: $\Phi = XY \vee XZ \vee YZ$. None of our prior rules apply immediately here. Instead, we write it as a disjoint-or: $\Phi = (\Phi \wedge X) \vee (\Phi \wedge \neg X)$; hence, $P(\Phi) = P(\Phi \wedge X) + P(\Phi \wedge \neg X)$. Denote $\Phi |_X = Y \vee Z \vee YZ \equiv Y \vee Z$ the formula obtained from Φ by substituting X with *true*. Similarly, $\Phi |_{\neg X} = YZ$. Then, we have $P(\Phi) = P(\Phi |_X \wedge X) + P(\Phi |_{\neg X} \wedge \neg X) = P(Y \vee Z) \cdot P(X) + P(YZ) \cdot (1 - P(X)) = (1 - (1 - P(Y)) \cdot (1 - P(Z))) \cdot P(X) + P(Y) \cdot P(Z) \cdot (1 - P(X))$.

In general, given a propositional formula Φ, a random variable X, and a value $a \in Dom_X$, denote $\Phi |_{X=a}$ the formula obtained from Φ by substituting all occurrences of X with a. Note that the formula $\Phi |_{X=a}$ does not depend on the variable X: $X \notin Var(\Phi |_{X=a})$.

Definition 5.6 Let $Dom_X = \{a_0, a_1, \ldots, a_m\}$. Then the Shannon expansion of a propositional formula Φ is:

$$\Phi \equiv \Phi |_{X=a_0} \wedge (X = a_0) \vee \Phi |_{X=a_1} \wedge (X = a_1) \vee \ldots \vee \Phi |_{X=a_m} \wedge (X = a_m)$$

Obviously, every $\wedge$ is an independent-and, and every $\vee$ is a disjoint-or, and therefore we obtain the following rule, which is called the *Shannon-expansion rule*:

$$\text{Shannon expansion:} \qquad P(\Phi) = \sum_{i=0,m} P(\Phi \mid_{X=a_i}) \cdot P(X = a_i) \qquad (5.5)$$

In contrast to the rules of independent-and, independent-or, and disjoint-or, Shannon expansion can always be applied.

We note that the disjoint-or rule has a natural dual, which is the following. If $\Phi_1 \vee \Phi_2 \equiv true$, then $P(\Phi_1 \wedge \Phi_2) = P(\Phi_1) + P(\Phi_2) - 1$. Traditionally, this rule does not seem to have been used in practice, so we do not include it in our discussion.

5.1.2   AN ALGORITHM FOR $P(\Phi)$

The five rules can be combined into a simple non-deterministic algorithm for computing $P(\Phi)$, shown in Algorithm 2. It proceeds recursively on the structure of the propositional formula Φ, applying the rules described earlier, until it reaches an atomic formula $X = a$, when it simply looks up its probability in a table.

We describe briefly how the algorithm works. Consider any propositional formula Φ. If Φ is a conjunction $\Psi_1 \wedge \Psi_2 \wedge \ldots$, then the algorithms tries to partition the conjuncts into independent sets. For that, construct a graph whose nodes $V = \{1, 2, \ldots\}$ correspond to the conjuncts $\Psi_1, \Psi_2, \ldots$, and whose edges (i, j) correspond to pairs of conjuncts Ψ_i, Ψ_j such that $Var(\Psi_i) \cap Var(\Psi_j) \neq \emptyset$. Compute the connected components of this graph, $C_1, C_2 \ldots$, and define $\Phi_i = \bigwedge_{j \in C_i} \Psi_j$ the conjunction of all conjuncts in the component C_i. Then $\Phi = \Phi_1 \wedge \Phi_2 \wedge \ldots$ and, moreover, the formulas $\Phi_1, \Phi_2, \ldots$ are independent. This explains the *independent AND* rule (Algorithm 2 shows the rule for only a conjunction of two formulas: it generalizes obviously to $m \geq 2$ formulas). Notice that this rule can be applied only if there are ≥ 2 connected components: otherwise, the algorithm makes no progress. If Φ is a disjunction, then we proceed similarly and use the *independent OR* rule. Alternatively, we can check whether Φ is disjunction of disjoint formulas and apply disjoint-or. If Φ is a negation, then we apply the negation rule. If everything else fails, then we can always apply the Shannon expansion rule.

The algorithm is non-deterministic: the Shannon expansion step can always be applied even if one of the other rules applies, and there are several choices for the order in which to eliminate variables during the Shannon expansion steps.

Example 5.7   Consider the formula $\Phi = (X \vee Y) \wedge ((Z \wedge U) \vee (\neg Z \wedge V))$. We can apply the independent-and rule and obtain

$$P(\Phi) = P(\Phi_1) \cdot P(\Phi_2), \text{ where } \Phi_1 = X \vee Y, \text{ and } \Phi_2 = (Z \wedge U) \vee (\neg Z \wedge V).$$

Algorithm 2 Algorithm for Computing $P(\Phi)$. The *Independent AND* and *Independent OR* rules apply only if $Var(\Phi_1) \cap Var(\Phi_2) = \emptyset$ holds; these rules generalize from 2 subformulas to $m \geq 2$ subformulas. The *Disjoint OR* rule applies only if $\Phi_1 \wedge \Phi_2 \equiv false$. As a special case, the Shannon expansion rule gives us a rule for atomic formulas: if $\Phi = (X = a)$, then return the probability of the atomic predicate $P(X = a)$.

1: **if** $\Phi \equiv \Phi_1 \wedge \Phi_2$ **then** $P(\Phi_1) \cdot P(\Phi_2)$	/* Independent AND */
2: **if** $\Phi \equiv \Phi_1 \vee \Phi_2$ **then** $1 - (1 - P(\Phi_1)) \cdot (1 - P(\Phi_2))$	/* Independent OR */
3: **if** $\Phi \equiv \Phi_1 \vee \Phi_2$ **then** $P(\Phi_1) + P(\Phi_2)$	/* Disjoint OR */
4: **if** $\Phi \equiv \neg\Phi_1$ **then** $1 - P(\Phi_1)$	/* Negation */
5: **choose** $X \in Var(\Phi)$ **then** $\sum_{a \in Dom_X} P(\Phi \mid_{X=a}) P(X = a)$	/* Shannon expansion */

Now, we recurse into Φ_1 and Φ_2. For Φ_1, we apply the independent-or rule and obtain

$$P(\Phi_1) = 1 - (1 - P(X)) \cdot (1 - P(Y)).$$

For Φ_2, we cannot apply the independent-and or independent-or rules since the two conjuncts are not independent. The first applicable rule is the disjoint-or rule:

$$P(\Phi_2) = P(\Phi_3) + P(\Phi_4), \text{ where } \Phi_3 = Z \wedge U, \text{ and } \Phi_4 = \neg Z \wedge V.$$

We continue with Φ_3 and Φ_4: both can be decomposed into atomic formulas using the independent-and rule.

The running time of the algorithm can vary from linear time, to exponential time in the size of the formula Φ. It depends dramatically on the number and order of Shannon expansion steps; we return to this topic in Section 5.2. At an extreme case, if the algorithm can be executed by applying only the independent-and and independent-or rules, then it runs in linear time in the size of the expression Φ. On the other hand, if it needs to apply Shannon's expansion n times, then it runs in exponential time in n.

The algorithm should be implemented using dynamic programming instead of recursive calls, in order to avoid processing the same expression repeatedly. For example, consider the simple propositional formula $\Phi_n = X_1 Y_1 \vee X_2 Y_2 \vee \ldots \vee X_n Y_n$, and suppose we decide to use only Shannon expansion. Assume we eliminate the variables in the order $X_n, Y_n, X_{n-1}, Y_{n-1}, \ldots$ After eliminating X_n then Y_n, we obtain:

$$\begin{aligned} P(\Phi_n) =& P(X_n) \cdot P(Y_n) + P(\Phi_{n-1}) \cdot P(X_n) \cdot (1 - P(Y_n)) \\ &+ P(\Phi_{n-1}) \cdot (1 - P(X_n)) \cdot P(Y_n) + P(\Phi_{n-1}) \cdot (1 - P(X_n)) \cdot (1 - P(Y_n)) \end{aligned}$$

Here $P(\Phi_{n-1})$ occurs three times, and a naïve recursive evaluation of the algorithm has a running time $O(3^n)$. With dynamic programming, we store the values $P(\Phi_k)$ for every $k = 1, 2, \ldots, n$, and the running time is $O(n)$.

5.1.3   READ-ONCE FORMULAS

An important class of propositional formulas that play a special role in probabilistic databases are read-once formulas. We restrict our discussion to the case when all random variables X are Boolean variables.

Φ is called *read-once* if there is a formula Φ' equivalent to Φ such that every variable occurs at most once in Φ'. For example:

$$\Phi = X_1 Y_1 \vee X_1 Y_2 \vee X_2 Y_3 \vee X_2 Y_4 \vee X_2 Y_5$$

is read-once because it is equivalent to the following formula:

$$\Phi' = X_1 (Y_1 \vee Y_2) \vee X_2 (Y_3 \vee Y_4 \vee Y_5)$$

Read-once formulas admit an elegant characterization, which we describe next.

A formula Φ is called *unate* if every propositional variable X occurs either only positively (X), or only negatively $(\neg X)$ in Φ. Let Φ be written in DNF and assume each conjunct is a minterm; that is, no other conjunct is a strict subset (otherwise, absorption rule applies, and we can further simplify Φ in polynomial time). The *primal graph* of Φ is $G_P = (V, E)$ where V is the set of propositional variables in Φ, and for every pair of variables X, Y that occur together in some conjunct, there is an edge (X, Y) in E. Thus, every conjunct in Φ becomes a clique in G_P.

Let P_4 denote the following graph with 4 vertices: $u - v - w - z$; that is, P_4 consists of a path of length 4 and no other edges. We say that Φ is P_4-*free* if no subgraph induced by 4 vertices in G_P is isomorphic to P_4. Finally, we say that Φ is *normal* if for every clique in G_P, there exists a conjunct in Φ containing all variables in the clique. The following characterization of unate read-once formulas is due to Gurvich [1991].

Theorem 5.8   A unate formula Φ is read-once iff it is P_4-free and normal.

For example, the primal graph of $XU \vee XV \vee YU \vee YV$ is the complete bipartite graph with vertices $\{X, Y\}$ and $\{U, V\}$; thus, it is P_4-free and normal: sure enough, the formula can be written as $(X \vee Y) \wedge (U \vee V)$, which is read-once. On the other hand, the primal graph of $XY \vee YZ \vee ZU$ is precisely P_4; hence, it is not read-once. The primal graph of $XY \vee XZ \vee YZ$ contains the clique $\{X, Y, Z\}$ but there is no minterm XYZ, hence the formula is not normal and, therefore, not read-once. If Φ is given as a read-once expression, then $P(\Phi)$ can be computed in linear time, by simply running Algorithm 2, and applying only the independent-and, independent-or, and negation rules. Moreover, if a unate DNF formula Φ admits a read-once equivalent Φ', then Φ' can be computed from Φ in polynomial time [Golumbic et al., 2005]. Thus, read-once formulas can be evaluated very efficiently, and this justifies our special interest in this class of formulas.

5.2 COMPILING $P(\Phi)$

Compiling a propositional formula Φ means converting the formula into a Boolean circuit that has some nice properties, ensuring that we can compute $P(\Phi)$ in linear time in the size of the circuit. Several types of circuits have been discussed in the verification and in the AI communities, which trade off representation power with ease of construction. Whenever a tractable compilation is possible, then $P(\Phi)$ is computable in polynomial time, but the converse is not necessarily true. We review here four compilation targets: read once formulas, OBDDs, FBDDs, and d-DNNFs.

Throughout this section, we assume that all discrete variables X are Boolean variables, i.e., their domain is {*false, true*}. A circuit for a formula Φ is a rooted, labeled DAG computing Φ, with the following types of gates and restrictions:

Independent AND Such a gate has $n \geq 0$ children, representing formulas $\Phi_1, \ldots, \Phi_n$; the gate represents the formula $\Phi_1 \wedge \cdots \wedge \Phi_n$. The following property is required to hold: for all $i \neq j$, $Var(\Phi_i) \cap Var(\Phi_j) = \emptyset$.

Independent OR Such a gate has $n \geq 0$ children, representing formulas $\Phi_1, \ldots, \Phi_n$; the gate represents the formula $\Phi_1 \vee \cdots \vee \Phi_n$. The following property is required to hold: for all $i \neq j$, $Var(\Phi_i) \cap Var(\Phi_j) = \emptyset$.

Disjoint OR Such a gate has $n \geq 0$ children, representing formulas $\Phi_1, \ldots, \Phi_n$; the gate represents the formula $\Phi_1 \vee \cdots \vee \Phi_n$. The following property is required to hold: for all $i \neq j$, $\Phi_i \wedge \Phi_j \equiv false$.

NOT Has a single child; if the child represents Φ, then the gate represents $\neg \Phi$.

Conditional gate The gate is labeled with a Boolean variable X and has two children. The edges leading to the children are labeled with $X = 0$ and $X = 1$, respectively. The node computes the formula $(\neg X \wedge \Phi_0) \vee (X \wedge \Phi_1)$, where Φ_0 and Φ_1 are the formulas represented by the two children. The following property must hold $X \notin Var(\Phi_0)$ and $X \notin Var(\Phi_1)$.

Leaf Node The gate is labeled either with 0 or 1 representing either *false* or *true*, respectively, or with a variable X.

Algorithm 2 can be modified easily to compute a circuit for Φ instead of computing the probability $P(\Phi)$ directly: each rule in the algorithm will construct a gate of the corresponding type. Moreover, given any circuit for Φ, one can compute the probability $P(\Phi)$ in linear time in the size of the circuit, by traversing the nodes in topological order, and computing the probability at each node from the probabilities of the children.

The goal of compilation is to find a circuit for Φ satisfying the restrictions above, and whose size is polynomial in the size of Φ.

We consider four compilation targets: read-once formulas, OBDD, FBDD, and d-DNNF$^{\neg}$. We review them here, in decreasing order of their expressive power.

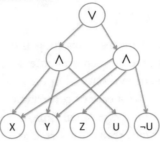

Figure 5.1: A d-DNNF for the propositional formula $XYU \vee XYZ(\neg U)$.

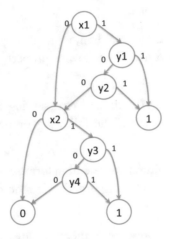

Figure 5.2: An OBDD (which is also an FBDD) for the propositional formula $X_1Y_1 \vee X_1Y_2 \vee X_2Y_3 \vee X_2Y_4$.

5.2.1   D-DNNF¬

A d-DNNF is a circuit restricted to *independent-AND*, to *disjoint-OR*, and to *NOT* gates. All variables are on the leaf nodes. The independent-AND gates are called *decomposable* (D) and the disjoint-OR gates are called *deterministic* (d). Furthermore, all the NOT gates are restricted to be applied only to variables (which can be achieved by applying repeatedly de Morgan's laws), which is also called a *Negation Normal Form* (NNF): this gives the name, d-DNNF [Darwiche and Marquis, 2002]. Figure 5.1 illustrates a simple d-DNNF.

The restriction that the NOT gates be applied only to variables has an undesirable consequence: it is not known whether one can represent the negation of a d-DNNF without increasing the size by more than a polynomial amount. However, for our purpose, we do not need to restrict the application of NOT gates, and we will allow them to occur anywhere in the circuit: we denote d-DNNF¬ such a circuit. Thus, a d-DNNF¬ consists of independent-AND, of independent-OR, and of NOT gates, which are allowed to combined in any order. The family d-DNNF⁻ is closed under negation: to compute $\neg\Phi$, simply add a new root node, labeled NOT, to the d-DNNF⁻ for Φ. Given an d-DNNF⁻-circuit representing a formula Φ, one can compute the probability $P(\Phi)$ in linear time in the size of the circuit.

5.2.2   FBDD

A *Free Binary Decision Diagram* is a circuit where every internal node is a conditional gate on some variable X, and where every leaf gate is either 0 or 1 [Wegener, 2004]. They are called Binary Decision Diagrams because each internal node makes a decision based on one variable X; they are called free because of the restriction that every path from the root to a leaf checks every variable X at most once. Figure 5.2 shows an FBDD. d-DNNF's are at least as powerful as FBDD's in the following sense. Any *FBDD* of size n can be converted to an d-DNNF of size at most $5n$ [Darwiche and Marquis, 2002], as follows. For every node in the *FBDD* that tests a variable X, write its formula as $(\neg X) \wedge \Phi_0 \vee X \wedge \Phi_1$, where Φ_0, Φ_1 are the two formulas of its 0-child and 1-child, respectively: obviously, the $\vee$ is "deterministic", and the $\wedge$'s are "decomposable". We have thus replaced one node in the FBDD with 5 nodes in the d-DNNF: $\vee$, $\wedge$, $\wedge$, X, and $\neg X$.

5.2.3   OBDD

An *Ordered Binary Decision Diagram* is an FBDD with the property that every path from the root to a leaf node inspects the Boolean variables in the same order. Thus, every OBDD is also an FBDD, but the converse is not true. The FBDD shown in Figure 5.2 is actually an OBDD because all paths inspect the variables in the same order, $X_1, Y_1, Y_2, X_2, Y_3, Y_4$. We review here two important properties of OBDDs. The first is that every read-once formula Φ has an OBDD of linear size. The proof is by induction, as follows: if $\Phi = \Phi_1 \wedge \Phi_2$, then one first constructs inductively an OBDD for Φ_1 and for Φ_2. Then, redirect all 1-leaves of Φ_1, to the root of the OBDD for Φ_2. The result is still an OBDD because Φ is read-once, meaning that Φ_1 and Φ_2 use disjoint sets of Boolean variables; hence, any path, starting in Φ_1 and continuing in Φ_2, inspects every variable only once. The case $\Phi = \Phi_1 \vee \Phi_2$ is similar. Thus, by induction, a read-once expression Φ has an OBDD of linear size. The second property is that OBDDs can be *synthesized*, inductively on the structure of a formula. To describe the synthesis process, we will assume that every path in an OBDD from the root to a leaf node contains all variables: this can be ensured by inserting new nodes for the missing variables, with both edges leading to the same child. Call the *width* of an OBDD at level i, the number of conditional gates for the variable X_i; the *width* of the OBDD is the largest width at any level. Clearly, an OBDD of width w has size $\leq wn$, where n is the number of Boolean variables. The synthesis property is the following. Suppose we are given two OBDDs for Φ_1, Φ_2, respectively, of width w_1 and w_2, and that they use the same variable order. Then one can construct an OBDD for $\Phi_1 \wedge \Phi_2$ (or for $\Phi_1 \vee \Phi_2$, respectively) of width at most $w_1 \cdot w_2$. The reader is invited to check the proof: the synthesized OBDD simply keeps track, at leach level i, of all nodes in both OBDDs, and for that it needs at most $w_1 \cdot w_2$ gates; a leaf node returns a 1 if both OBDDs returned 1 (for $\Phi_1 \wedge \Phi_2$) or if at least one of the two OBDDs returned 1 (for $\Phi_1 \vee \Phi_2$).

5.2.4   READ-ONCE FORMULAS

We consider read-once formulas as a simple case of a circuit, where all non-leaf gates are either *independent-AND*, *independent-OR*, or *NOT* gates, and all variables are on the leaf nodes. Read-once are different from the other compilation targets in that some formulas are not read-once, but every formula can be compiled into any of the other three targets.

5.3   APPROXIMATING $P(\Phi)$

The rules in Subsection 5.1.1 are good heuristics for computing $P(\Phi)$, but we should expect them to run in exponential time on some formulas Φ because computing $P(\Phi)$ is provably hard (Theorem 3.1). In probabilistic databases, however, we often do not need to compute $P(\Phi)$ exactly. In many applications we need probabilities only to rank the answers to a query, and approximate values of the probabilities are often sufficient for ranking (as we discuss in Section 6.1). Even when probability values need to be returned to the user, it is often desirable to improve performance by sacrificing precision.

   We next present two approximation algorithms, a deterministic algorithm that works on any propositional formula but cannot guarantee polynomial running time as a function of the desired precision and a randomized algorithm that works on DNF formulas and can guarantee polynomial time in the desired precision. Both these algorithms can becomes quite effective in probabilistic databases when combined with the top-k evaluation technique discussed in Section 6.1.

5.3.1   A DETERMINISTIC APPROXIMATION ALGORITHM

Olteanu et al. [2010] describe an approach by which instead of computing the exact probability $p = P(\Phi)$ of a formula Φ, one returns an interval $[L, U]$ such that $L \le p \le U$. We start with the following two simple approximations rules:

$$\max(P(\Phi_1), P(\Phi_2)) \le P(\Phi_1 \vee \Phi_2) \le \min(P(\Phi_1) + P(\Phi_2), 1) \tag{5.6}$$
$$\max(0, P(\Phi_1) + P(\Phi_2) - 1) \le P(\Phi_1 \wedge \Phi_2) \le \min(P(\Phi_1), P(\Phi_2)) \tag{5.7}$$

   By applying the rules repeatedly, together with $P(\neg\Phi) = 1 - \Phi$, we can obtain a lower and upper bound for every formula Φ, $P(\Phi) \in [L, U]$. Importantly, the bounds $[L, U]$ can be computed in linear time in the size of Φ. In the special case of a DNF formula Φ, we only need Eq. (5.6) for the approximation: once we reach conjuncts, we can compute their probabilities exactly, by multiplying the probabilities of their atomic events.

   We will modify Algorithm 2 such that it can stop at any time and return an approximate value of $P(\Phi)$; in other words, we modify it to trade off performance for accuracy. We start by

Algorithm 3 Approximation Algorithm for $P(\Phi)$. It improves Algorithm 2 by updating continuously the bounds $[L, U]$ for $P(\Phi)$: therefore, one can stop the algorithm at any time and use the bounds $[L, U]$ instead of the exact probability. As in Algorithm 2, the rules for independent AND, independent OR, and disjoint OR generalize from 2 subformulas to $m \geq 2$ subformulas.

1: Choose a non-atomic leaf node, expand it using one of the five rules in Algorithm 2.
2: For each child Φ_i of Φ, compute $[L_i, U_i]$ by applying repeatedly Eq. (5.7) and Eq. (5.6).
3: **for all** non-leaf nodes Φ in the circuit, update its bounds $[L, U]$: **do**
4:      /* Independent-AND */
       if $\Phi \equiv \Phi_1 \wedge \Phi_2$ **then** $[L, U] = [L_1 \cdot L_2, U_1 \cdot U_2]$
5:      /* Independent-OR */
       if $\Phi \equiv \Phi_1 \vee \Phi_2$ **then** $[L, U] = [1 - (1 - L_1) \cdot (1 - L_2), 1 - (1 - U_1) \cdot (1 - U_2)]$
6:      /* Disjoint-OR */
       if $\Phi \equiv \Phi_1 \vee \Phi_2$ **then** $[L, U] = [L_1 + L_2, \min(U_1 + U_2, 1)]$
7:      /* Negation */
       if $\Phi \equiv \neg \Phi_1$ **then** $[L, U] = [1 - U_1, 1 - L_1]$
8:      /* Shannon expansion */
       if $\Phi = \bigvee \Phi_i \wedge (X = a_i)$ **then** $[L, U] = [\sum L_i \cdot P(X = a_i), \sum U_i \cdot P(X = a_i)]$
9: **end for**

---

modifying it such that it computes a circuit for Φ, rather than returning $P(\Phi)$ directly, as we described in Section 5.2. That is, each node of the circuit corresponds to some subformula, and each non-leaf node is labeled with an an independent-AND, independent-OR, disjoint-OR, negation, or Shannon-expansion. The algorithm starts with a circuit consisting of a single node, labeled Φ, and no children. At each step, it chooses (using some heuristics) a leaf node that is not an atomic formula; if Φ is the formula labeling the node, then the algorithm expands it by using one of the five rules in Subsection 5.1.1. The algorithm terminates when all leaves in the circuit are labeled with atomic formulas: the probabilities $P(\Phi)$ can now be computed in linear time, by traversing the circuit in topological order, from the leaves to the root node Φ.

Algorithm 3 shows the modified algorithm that can stop at any time an return some bound $[L, U]$ for the probability $P(\Phi)$ of a circuit node Φ. Whenever it expands a formula by applying some rule, the bounds for the new leaf nodes are computed by applying repeatedly the rules Eq. (5.6) and Eq. (5.7): after that, the algorithm updates the lower/upper bounds for all nodes in the circuit, as shown in Algorithm 3. This update step can be optimized since only the nodes that are ancestors of the node Φ need to be updated. Thus, at each moment, the algorithm has a pair of bounds $[L, U]$ for the root node Φ, which improve over time. If the algorithm needs to be stopped early, one can use the current bound. If the algorithm reaches atomic formulas for all leaf nodes in the circuit, then $L = U = P(\Phi)$ and the algorithm returns the exact probability.

Absolute or relative approximations can be obtained for any given error ε: a value $\hat{p}$ is an absolute ε-approximation of a probability p if $p - \varepsilon \leq \hat{p} \leq p + \varepsilon$, and it is a relative ε-approximation of a probability p if $(1 - \varepsilon) \cdot p \leq \hat{p} \leq (1 + \varepsilon) \cdot p$. In case $U - \varepsilon \leq L + \varepsilon$, then any value in $[U - \varepsilon, L + \varepsilon]$ is an absolute ε-approximation of $P(\Phi)$. In case $(1 - \varepsilon) \cdot U \leq (1 + \varepsilon) \cdot L$, then any value in $[(1 - \varepsilon) \cdot U, (1 + \varepsilon) \cdot L]$ is a relative ε-approximation of $P(\Phi)$.

This algorithm can be further improved by employing a different strategy on computing bounds for the subformulas Φ_i obtained by any of the five decomposition rules. The idea is as follows. Given a formula Φ, we would like to efficiently derive two formulas Φ_L and Φ_U such that the satisfying assignments of Φ_L are also satisfying assignments of Φ and that the satisfying assignments of Φ are also satisfying assignments of Φ_U; that is, $\omega(\Phi_L) \subseteq \omega(\Phi) \subseteq \omega(\Phi_U)$. We call Φ_L and Φ_U a lower bound and respectively an upper bound of Φ. These model-based bounds imply probability bounds; that is, if $\omega(\Phi_L) \subseteq \omega(\Phi) \subseteq \omega(\Phi_U)$, then $P(\Phi_L) \leq P(\Phi) \leq P(\Phi_U)$. We can make effective use of these bounds if $P(\Phi_L)$ and $P(\Phi_U)$ can be computed efficiently, such as when Φ_L and Φ_U are read-once formulas.

Example 5.9   Consider the formula $\Phi = X_1 Y_1 \vee X_1 Y_2 \vee X_2 Y_2$. This is not read-once. Examples of read-once lower and upper bound formulas would be $\Phi_L = X_1(Y_1 \vee Y_2)$ and, respectively, $\Phi_U = X_1 \vee X_2 Y_2$. Note that these bounds are also optimal in the following sense: there are no read-once formulas Φ'_L and Φ'_U that are lower and upper bounds of Φ, respectively, such that $\omega(\Phi_L) \subset \omega(\Phi'_L)$ and $\omega(\Phi'_U) \subset \omega(\Phi_U)$.

5.3.2   MONTE CARLO APPROXIMATION

Karp et al. [1989] gave a fully polynomial-time randomized approximation scheme (FPTRAS) for model counting of DNF formulas based on Monte Carlo simulation. We refer the reader to [Vazirani, 2001] for an in-depth treatment of this approach, we only sketch here how this approach can be modified to compute the probability of a DNF over independent discrete random variables.

The restriction to DNF formulas is important for the Karp-Luby approximation algorithm, so in this section, we will make the following two restrictions: the input database $\mathbf{D}$ is a tuple-independent database or a BID database, and the query Q is a UCQ: then, one can compute a DNF formula for the lineage $\Phi^{\mathbf{D}}_Q$ in polynomial time in the size of the database.

We start by describing the naïve Monte Carlo algorithm for a propositional formula Φ over Boolean variables. (Here we do not need to restrict Φ to be in DNF.). Recall that Θ represents the space of all 2^n possible valuations of the n Boolean variables.

Definition 5.10   Naïve Estimator   The Naïve Estimator for the probability of propositional formula Φ over independent Boolean random variables is:

1. Choose a valuation $\theta \in \Theta$, with probability $P(\theta)$. This means the following: every variable X occurring in Φ is set to true with probability $P(X)$.

2. If $\Phi[\theta]$ is true, then return $Z = 1$; otherwise, return $Z = 0$.

The Naïve Monte Carlo Algorithm proceeds by computing the Naïve Estimator N times and returning their mean; thus, instead of the exact probability $p = P(\Phi)$, the algorithm returns an approximate value $\hat{p}$. If we use 0-1-random variable Z_k to represent the outcome of the k-th call of the Naïve Estimator, the result of the algorithm can be modeled by a random variable

$$\hat{p} = \frac{\sum_{k=1}^{N} Z_k}{N}$$

The expected value of Z_k is $\mathbf{E}[Z_k] = P(\Phi)$, which implies that Z_k is an unbiased estimator for $P(\Phi)$, and, hence, so is $\hat{p}$: $\mathbf{E}[\hat{p}] = p$. The question is, how well does $\hat{p}$ approximate p. This depends on the number of steps N, as follows. Fix $\varepsilon > 0$ and $\delta > 0$. We say that the algorithm is an (ε, δ)-approximation, if:

$$\mathbf{Pr}(|\hat{p} - p| > \varepsilon \cdot p) \leq \delta$$

The probability above, $\mathbf{Pr}$, is taken over the random choices of the algorithm, and should not be confused with the probability $p = P(\Phi)$ that we are trying to compute. In other words, the algorithm is an (ε, δ)-approximation, if the probability that it makes an error worse than ε is smaller than δ. By choosing

$$N = \left\lceil \frac{4 \cdot \log \frac{2}{\delta}}{p\varepsilon^2} \right\rceil \tag{5.8}$$

We obtain

$$\mathbf{Pr}(|\hat{p} - p| > \varepsilon \cdot p) \leq \delta$$

In other words: if we want to compute a (ε, δ)-approximation of $p = P(\Phi)$, then we must run the Naïve Monte Carlo algorithm for N steps, where N is given by the formula above.

A better way to look at the formula above is to see it as giving us an approximation interval $[L, U]$ for p, which improves with N. Fix the desired confidence $1 - \delta$ (a typical confidence value of 0.9 would require $\delta = 0.1$). Then, after N steps of the algorithm, we can compute from the formula above the value

$$\varepsilon = \sqrt{\frac{4}{pN} \cdot \log \frac{2}{\delta}}$$

Then, we are guaranteed (with confidence $1 - \delta$) that $p \in [L, U] = [\hat{p} - \varepsilon/2, \hat{p} + \varepsilon/2]$.

Notice that the relationship between N and ε depends on p, which is, of course, unknown. Worse, p may be as small as $1/2^n$, where n is the number of variables, and therefore, in theory, N

may be exponential in the size of the formula Φ. For example, if $\Phi = X_1 X_2 \ldots X_n$ (a conjunction of n independent variables), assuming $P(X_1) = \ldots = P(X_n) = 1/2$, then $P(\Phi) = 1/2^n$, and we have to sample about 2^n random assignments θ to have a chance to hit the unique assignment that makes Φ true.

Karp and Luby [1983] and Karp et al. [1989] gave two improved algorithms that are guaranteed to run in polynomial time in $1/\varepsilon$ and the size of Φ. We study one such algorithm next. The algorithm estimates the probability p of a DNF $\Phi = \phi_1 \vee \phi_2 \vee \cdots \vee \phi_n$, over independent Boolean random variables. The clauses ϕ_i are assumed to be in some order that will be made use of but is arbitrary. We use n to denote the *number* of clauses in the DNF.

Let $M = \sum_i P(\phi_i)$. Here, $P(\phi_i)$ is, of course, the product of the probabilities of the literals (i.e., random variables or their negations) occurring in ϕ_i. Recall that $\omega(\phi_i)$ denotes the set of assignments θ that make ϕ_i true; θ denote complete assignments, including assignments to variables that do not occur in ϕ_i.

Definition 5.11 Karp-Luby Estimator The Karp-Luby estimator for the probability of DNF Φ over independent Boolean random variables is:

1. Choose a number $i \in [n]$ with probability $P(\phi_i)/M$.

2. Choose a valuation $\theta \in \omega(\phi_i)$, with probability $P(\theta)/P(\phi_i)$. This means the following: every variable X occurring in ϕ_i is set deterministically to what is required by ϕ_i, and every variable Y of Φ which does not occur in ϕ_i is set to true with probability $P(Y)$.

3. Consider the indexes of the conjunctions of Φ that are consistent with θ, i.e., the indexes j such that $\theta \in \omega(\phi_j)$. If i is the smallest among these, return $Z = 1$; otherwise, return $Z = 0$. In other words, return 1 iff $\phi_1[\theta] = \ldots \phi_{i-1}[\theta] = \mathit{false}$ (and note that $\phi_i[\theta] = \mathit{true}$ by construction).

The algorithm proceeds by computing the Karp-Luby estimator N times and returning their mean times M. If we use 0-1-random variable Z_k to represent the outcome of the k-th call of the Karp-Luby estimator, the result of the algorithm can be modeled by the random variable $\hat{p}$, where:

$$Z = \sum_{k=1}^{N} Z_k, \qquad \hat{p} = \frac{Z \cdot M}{N}$$

The expected value of Z_k is

$$
\begin{aligned}
\mathbf{E}[Z_k] &= \sum_i \frac{P(\phi_i)}{M} \cdot \sum_{\theta \in \omega(\phi_i)} \frac{P(\theta)}{P(\phi_i)} \cdot \frac{1}{|\{\phi_j \mid \theta \in \omega(\phi_j)\}|} \\
&= \sum_{\theta:\, \exists\phi_i\, \theta\in\omega(\phi_i)} \frac{P(\theta) \cdot |\{\phi_i \mid \theta \in \omega(\phi_i)\}|}{M \cdot |\{\phi_j \mid \theta \in \omega(\phi_j)\}|} \\
&= \frac{1}{M} \cdot \underbrace{\sum_{\theta:\, \exists\phi_i\, \theta\in\omega(\phi_i)} P(\theta)}_{P(\Phi)} \\
&= \frac{p}{M},
\end{aligned}
$$

so Z_k is an unbiased estimator for p/M and $\mathbf{E}[Z] = N \cdot p/M$. We approximate p thus by $\hat{p} = Z \cdot M/N$, and its expected value is $\mathbf{E}[\hat{p}] = \mathbf{E}[Z] \cdot M/N = p$.

Computing Z consists of summing up the outcome of N Bernoulli trials. For such a scenario, we can use the Chernoff bound

$$
\mathbf{Pr}\big[|Z - \mathbf{E}[Z]| \geq \varepsilon \cdot \mathbf{E}[Z]\big] \leq 2 \cdot e^{-\varepsilon^2 \cdot \mathbf{E}[Z]/3}
$$

(cf., e.g., [Mitzenmacher and Upfal, 2005], Eq. 4.6). By substitution, we get

$$
\mathbf{Pr}\big[|\hat{p} - p| \geq \varepsilon \cdot p\big] = \mathbf{Pr}\Big[\frac{N}{M} \cdot |\hat{p} - p| \geq \varepsilon \cdot \frac{N \cdot p}{M}\Big] \leq 2 \cdot e^{-\frac{N \cdot p \cdot \varepsilon^2}{3 \cdot M}}
$$

and thus since $p/M \geq 1/n$,

$$
\mathbf{Pr}\big[|\hat{p} - p| \geq \varepsilon \cdot p\big] \leq 2 \cdot e^{-\frac{N \cdot \varepsilon^2}{3 \cdot n}} = \delta
$$

By choosing

$$
N = \left\lceil \frac{3 \cdot n \cdot \log \frac{2}{\delta}}{\varepsilon^2} \right\rceil \tag{5.9}
$$

we get an (ε, δ) fully polynomial-time randomized approximation scheme (FPTRAS) for computing the probability of a DNF over independent Boolean random variables.

Thus, we have two algorithms, the naïve Monte Carlo, and Karp-Luby, for approximating the probability of a DNF expression. The question whether one is preferable over the other depends on whether queries usually compute only large probabilities or not. Consider the two bounds on N, for the naïve and the Karp-Luby algorithm, given by Eq. (5.8) and Eq. (5.9), respectively. The first is of the form $N = C(\varepsilon, \delta)/p$ while the second is of the form $N = C(\varepsilon, \delta) * n$, where $C(\varepsilon, \delta)$ is $O(\log(2/\delta)/\varepsilon^2)$. Recall that $p = P(\Phi)$ is the probability of the formula, while n is the number of conjuncts in Φ. This suggests a trade-off between the two algorithms; the naïve MC is preferable if the DNFs are very large and the Karp-Luby MC is preferable if its probability is small. In a DNF that was created as the lineage of a conjunctive query, the number of variables in each clause is the number of joins in the query plus one. So, even if we assume that probabilities of base tuples in tuple-independent or BID tables are lower-bounded by 0.1, a query with three joins may still produce probabilities on the order of 1/10000. Taking the above bounds at face value, very large DNFs – as a product of projections that map large numbers of tuples together – are required for the naïve algorithm to be competitive with the Karp-Luby algorithm. Note, though, that these bounds on the number of required iterations are far from tight, and sequential analysis techniques such as those of Dagum et al. [2000] can be used to detect when a Monte Carlo algorithm can be stopped much earlier. The technique of Dagum et al. [2000] puts the more sophisticated algorithm at advantage over the naïve one – in experiments performed in [Koch and Olteanu, 2008, Olteanu et al., 2009, 2010], the optimal approximation scheme of Dagum et al. [2000] usually led to two orders of magnitude fewer Monte Carlo iterations than the above bound on the required iterations of the Karp-Luby algorithm suggested.

While the absolute values of the output probabilities are often of little significance to the user, the system needs good approximations of these probabilities for several purposes: in order to rank the output answers, cf. Section 6.1, when approximate probabilities are used in range predicates [Koch, 2008b], or when conditional probabilities are computed as ratios of approximated probabilities [Koch, 2008b, Koch and Olteanu, 2008].

5.4   QUERY COMPILATION

In this section, we restrict the input database D to be a tuple-independent database, meaning that every tuple t is annotated with a unique Boolean variable X_t. We study the following problem. Fix a Boolean query Q, which determines a family of propositional formulas, Φ_Q^D, one formula for every database D. Consider one of the four compilation targets discussed in Section 5.2. *Query compilation* is a function that maps every database D into a circuit for Φ_Q^D in that target. We say that the query admits an *efficient compilation*, if the size of this circuit is bounded by a polynomial in the size of the database D. In this section, we ask the following question: which queries admit an *efficient compilation* into a given target?

Denote $\mathcal{C}$ one of the four compilation targets: RO (read once), OBDD, FBDD, and d-DNNF⁻. We consider three query languages: the entire Relational Calculus (RC), Unions of Conjunctive Queries (UCQ), and Conjunctive Queries (CQ), see Section 2.1. Thus, queries are built from atomic predicates using the connectives $\wedge, \vee, \exists, \neg$. For each query language $\mathcal{L}$, we denote $\mathcal{L}(\mathcal{C})$ the class of queries in $\mathcal{L}$ that admit an "efficient compilation" to $\mathcal{C}$. Formally:

Definition 5.12   Let $\mathcal{L}$ be a query language.

- $\mathcal{L}(RO)$ represents the set of queries $Q \in \mathcal{L}$ with the following property: for every database instance D, the lineage Φ_Q^D is a read-once propositional formula.

- $\mathcal{L}(OBDD) = \bigcup_{k \geq 1} \mathcal{L}(OBDD, k)$, where $\mathcal{L}(OBDD, k)$ is the set of queries $Q \in L$ with the following property: for every database instance D with n tuples, the lineage Φ_Q^D has an OBDD of size $\leq O(n^k)$. In other words, $\mathcal{L}(OBDD)$ is the class of queries that have a polynomial-size OBDD.

- $\mathcal{L}(FBDD)$ is the class of queries $Q \in \mathcal{L}$ that have a polynomial-size FBDD (defined similarly to $\mathcal{L}(OBDD)$).

- $\mathcal{L}(d\text{-}DNNF^\neg)$ is the class of queries that have a polynomial-size d-DNNF$^\neg$.

- $\mathcal{L}(P)$ is the class of tractable queries.

The compilation target RO differs from the others, in that $\mathcal{L}(RO)$ is the set of queries that have *some* read-once circuit. In other words, queries that are not $\mathcal{L}(RO)$ do not have a read-once circuit at all. In contrast, for any other target $\mathcal{C}$, every query can be compiled into the target $\mathcal{C}$, and $\mathcal{L}(\mathcal{C})$ denotes the class of queries for which the compilation is *efficient*. In all cases however, $\mathcal{L}(\mathcal{C})$ denotes the class of queries that have an efficient compilation into $\mathcal{C}$ because, even in the case of read-once formulas, the read-once circuit is linear in the size of the input database.

We have immediately:

$$\mathcal{L}(RO) \subseteq \mathcal{L}(OBDD) \subseteq \mathcal{L}(FBDD) \subseteq \mathcal{L}(d\text{-}DNNF^\neg) \subseteq \mathcal{L}(P) \tag{5.10}$$

5.4.1   CONJUNCTIVE QUERIES WITHOUT SELF-JOINS

For conjunctive queries without self-join, these classes collapse:

Theorem 5.13   [Olteanu and Huang, 2008]   Let $\mathcal{L} = CQ^{NR}$ be the language of non-repeating conjunctive queries (a.k.a. conjunctive queries without self-joins). Then, $\mathcal{L}(RO) = \mathcal{L}(P)$. In particular, all inclusions in Eq. (5.10) become equalities.

In other words, a conjunctive query with self-joins is either very easy (read-once), or it is very hard (hard for #P): there is no middle ground. The proof follows immediately from Theorem 4.29. Indeed, let $Q \in CQ^{NR}(P)$ be a tractable conjunctive query without self-joins. By Theorem 4.29, the query is hierarchical and non-repeating. Therefore, by Proposition 4.27 (see comment after the proof) the query's lineage is read-once.

5.4.2 UNIONS OF CONJUNCTIVE QUERIES

On the contrary, for unions of conjunctive queries, $\mathcal{L} = UCQ$, these classes can be shown to form a strict hierarchy, except for the inclusion $UCQ(d\text{-}DNNF)^{\neg} \subsetneq UCQ(P)$, for which it is still open whether it is strict.

Theorem 5.14 **[Jha and Suciu, 2011]** Let $\mathcal{L} = UCQ$ be the language of unions of conjunctive queries. Then

$$\mathcal{L}(RO) \subsetneq \mathcal{L}(OBDD) \subsetneq \mathcal{L}(FBDD) \subsetneq \mathcal{L}(d\text{-}DNNF^{\neg}).$$

We explain the theorem by illustrating each separation result: also refer to Figure 5.5 and to Figure 5.4.

5.4.2.1 $UCQ(RO)$

This class admits a simple syntactic characterization.

Proposition 5.15 $UCQ(RO) = UCQ^{H,NR}$

The inclusion $UCQ^{H,NR} \subseteq UCQ(RO)$ follows from the proof of Proposition 4.27: that proof actually shows that if a query is in $RC^{H,NR}$, then its lineage on any probabilistic database is a read-once propositional formula. The proof of the opposite inclusion is given in [Jha and Suciu, 2011].

In other words, we can check whether a query Q has a read-once lineage for all input databases, by examining the query expression: if we can write Q such that it is both hierarchical and non-repeating, then its lineage is always read-once; otherwise, there exists databases for which Q's lineage is not read-once.

We illustrate the proposition with a few examples.

Example 5.16 Consider the Boolean query $Q = R(x), S(x, y)$ (Example 4.6). It is both hierarchical and non-repeating; hence, its lineage is always read-once. To see this, denote $X_1, \ldots, X_n$ the Boolean variables associated with R-tuples, and $Y_{11}, Y_{12}, \ldots, Y_{nn}$ the Boolean variables associated with the S-tuples. Thus, X_i represents the tuple $R(i)$ and Y_{ij} represents the tuple $S(i, j)$. The lineage is:

$$\Phi_Q = X_1 Y_{11} \vee X_1 Y_{12} \ldots X_1 Y_{1n} \vee X_2 Y_{21} \vee \ldots X_n Y_{nn}$$
$$= X_1(Y_{11} \vee Y_{12} \ldots) \vee X_2(Y_{21} \vee Y_{22} \vee \ldots) \vee \ldots$$

For another example, consider $Q_U = R(x_1), S(x_1, y_1) \vee T(x_2), S(x_2, y_2)$ (Example 4.7). If we write it as $\exists x.(R(x) \vee T(x)) \wedge \exists y.S(x, y)$, then it is both hierarchical *and* read-once, and therefore the lineage of Q_U is read-once, on any database instance. Indeed, denoting $Z_1, \ldots Z_n$ the Boolean variables associated with the T-tuples, the query's lineage is:

$$\Phi_{Q_U} = \bigvee_{ij} (X_i Y_{ij} \vee Z_i Y_{ij}) = \bigvee_{ij} [(X_i \vee Z_i) \wedge Y_{ij}]$$

Example 5.17   We show two examples where the lineage is not a read-once formula. First, consider $Q_J = R(x_1), S(x_1, y_1), T(x_2), S(x_2, y_2)$; we have seen in Example 4.7 that $P(Q)$ can be evaluated by applying a few simple rules. Its lineage is not read-once, in general, because the query cannot be written as a hierarchical non-repeating expression[1]. We can also check directly that the lineage is not read once. Denote X_i, Y_{ij}, Z_i the Boolean variables associated with the tuples $R(i), S(i, j), T(i)$ of a database instance. The lineage is:

$$\Phi_{Q_J} = \left(\bigvee_{i,j} X_i Y_{ij} \right) \wedge \left(\bigvee_{k,l} Z_k Y_{k,l} \right) = \bigvee_{i,j,k,l} X_i Z_k Y_{ij} Y_{kl} \tag{5.11}$$

Assume that both R and T contain at least two elements each, say $\{1, 2\} \subseteq R$ and $\{1, 2\} \subseteq T$, and that S contains at least three of the four possible pairs; for example, $\{(1, 1), (1, 2), (2, 1)\} \subseteq S$. Then the primal graph of Φ_{Q_J} is not normal: it contains the edges $(Y_{11}, Y_{12}), (Y_{11}, Y_{21}), (Y_{12}, Y_{21})$, but there is no conjunction containing $Y_{11} Y_{12} Y_{21}$.

Finally, consider the query Q_V, discussed in Example 4.8. Its lineage is not a read-once either because the primal graph contains the edges $(S(1, 1), T(1)), (T(1), R(2)), (R(2), S(2, 2))$, but no other edges between these four nodes; hence, the induced subgraph is P_4.

We end the discussion on queries with read-once lineage expressions by poiting out an important distinction between CQ and UCQ. For CQ, we have seen in Theorem 4.29 that if a query is hierarchical and also non-repeating, then it is simultaneously hierarchical and non-repeating, and, moreover that these queries are precisely the tractable queries:

$$CQ^{H,NR} = CQ^{NR}(P) = CQ^H \cap CQ^{NR}$$

For UCQ queries, however, this property fails. The tractable non-repeating queries, $UCQ^{NR}(P)$, lie strictly between the two classes:

$$UCQ^{H,NR} \subsetneq UCQ^{NR}(P) \subsetneq UCQ^H \cap UCQ^{NR}$$

---

[1]This can be verified by exhaustively trying all unions of conjunctive queries that use each of the relation symbols R, S, T exactly once.

We have already shown at the end of Subsubsection 4.1.6.2 that $H_1 \in UCQ^H \cap UCQ^{NR}$, yet it is clearly not in $UCQ^{NR}(P)$, which proves that the latter two classes are separated. The former two classes are separated by the query:

$$Q = \exists x.\exists y. [A(x) \wedge ((B(x) \wedge C(y)) \vee (D(x) \wedge E(y))) \wedge F(y)]$$
$$= \exists x_1.\exists y_1.A(x_1), B(x_1), C(y_1), F(y_1) \vee \exists x_2.\exists y_2.A(x_2), D(x_2), E(y_2), F(y_2)$$

The expression on the first line is non-repeating; hence, the query is in UCQ^{NR}, and the query is also tractable: in fact, one can check that *any* UCQ query over a unary vocabulary is $\mathbf{R}_6$-safe and, hence, tractable. On the other hand, this query is not in $UCQ^{H,NR}$ because its lineage is not read-once: over an active domain of size ≥ 2 the primal graph of the lineage contains the following edges (this is best seen on the second line above) $(B(1), F(1)), (F(1), A(2)), (A(2), E(2))$. This induces the graph P_4 because there are no edges $(B(1), A(2)), (B(1), E(2))$, or $(F(1), E(2))$.

5.4.2.2 UCQ(OBDD)

This class, too, admits a simple syntactic characterization. Let Q be a query expression, and assume that, for every atom $R(v_1, v_2, \ldots)$, the terms $v_1, v_2, \ldots$ are distinct variables: that is, there are no constants, and every variable occurs at most once. This can be ensured by ranking all attribute-constant, and all attribute-attribute pairs, see the ranking rules in Subsection 4.1.2. For every atom $L(x_1, x_2, \ldots, x_k)$ let π^L be the permutation on $[k]$ representing the nesting order of the quantifiers for $x_1, \ldots, x_k$. That is, the existential quantifiers are introduced in the order $\exists x_{\pi(1)}.\exists x_{\pi(2)} \ldots$ For example, if the expression is $\exists x_2 \ldots \exists x_3 \ldots \exists x_1.R(x_1, x_2, x_3) \ldots$ then $\pi^{R(x_1,x_2,x_3)} = (2, 3, 1)$.

Definition 5.18 A UCQ query expression Q is *inversion-free* if it is hierarchical and for any two unifiable atoms L_1, L_2, the following holds: $\pi^{L_1} = \pi^{L_2}$. A query is called *inversion-free* if it is equivalent to an inversion free expression.

One can check[2] that Q is inversion free iff its minimal representation as a union of conjunctive queries is inversion free. For example, the query $Q_J = R(x_1), S(x_1, y_1), T(x_2), S(x_2, y_2)$ (Example 4.7) is inversion-free because it can be written as $Q_J = \exists x_1.(R(x_1), \exists y_1.S(x_1, y_1)) \wedge \exists x_2.(T(x_2), \exists y_2.S(x_2, y_2))$, and the variables in both S-atoms are introduced in the same order. On the other hand, the query $Q_V = R(x_1), S(x_1, y_1) \vee S(x_2, y_2), T(y_2) \vee R(x_3), T(y_3)$ (defined in Example 4.8) has an inversion: in the hierarchical expression, the variables in $S(x_1, y_1)$ are introduced in the order $\exists x_1.\exists y_1$ while in $S(x_2, y_2)$ they are introduced in the order $\exists y_2.\exists x_2$.

The connection between inversion-free queries and safety is the following. If a query Q is inversion free, then it is $\mathbf{R}_6$-safe. Indeed, write Q as a union of conjunctive queries $Q_1 \vee Q_2 \vee \ldots$ If at least one of Q_i is disconnected, $Q_i = Q_i' \wedge Q_i''$, then apply the distributivity law to write $Q = Q' \wedge Q''$ (where $Q' = Q_1 \vee \ldots \vee Q_i' \vee \ldots$ and $Q'' = Q_1 \vee \ldots \vee Q_i'' \vee \ldots$), then use the

---

[2]If a query expression is inversion free, then, if we rewrite it as a union of conjunctive queries $Q_1 \vee Q_2 \vee \ldots$ by repeatedly apply the distributivity law, the expression remains inversion free. Moreover, by minimizing the latter expression, it continues to be inversion free.

inclusion-exclusion formula: all three queries Q', Q'', and $Q' \vee Q''$ are inversion free, and the claim follows by induction. If, on the other hand, $Q = Q_1 \vee Q_2 \vee \ldots$ and each Q_i is connected, then it must have a root variable x_i. Write $Q = \exists z.(Q_1[z/x_1] \vee Q_2[z/x_2] \vee \ldots)$: clearly z is a root variable, and it is also a separator variable because for any two unifiable atoms L_1, L_2, z occurs on the same position $\pi^{L_1}(1) = \pi^{L_2}(1)$. Thus, inversion free queries are $\mathbf{R}_6$-safe queries and, therefore, in $UCQ(P)$. The following proposition strengthen this observation:

Proposition 5.19   *The following holds: UCQ(OBDD) = UCQ(OBDD,1) = "inversion free queries".*

The proposition says two things. On one hand, every inversion-free query admits an OBDD whose size is linear in the size of the database: in fact, we will show that its width is $2^k = O(1)$, where k is the total number of atoms in the hierarchical, inversion free expression of Q. Thus, the width of the OBDD depends only on the query, not on the database instance, and therefore the size of the OBDD is linear, $O(n)$, meaning that $Q \in UCQ(OBDD,1)$. On the other hand, if a query is not inversion-free, then the size of the smallest OBDD grows exponentially in the size of the database. For example, the proposition implies that the lineage of Q_J (Example 4.7) has an OBDD whose size is linear in that of the input database, while the lineage of Q_V (Example 4.8) does not have polynomial-size OBDDs.

We give here the main intuition behind the positive result, namely that an inversion free query has an OBDD of width 2^k. We illustrate with the example Q_J: the reader can derive the general case from this example. Start by writing $Q_J = Q_1 \wedge Q_2$, where $Q_1 = R(x_1), S(x_1, y_1)$ and $Q_2 = T(x_2), S(x_2, y_2)$. Fix a database instance D. Then, the lineage Φ_{Q_1} is read-once, and therefore it admits an OBDD of width 1. For example, on a database with with four tuples, $R(1), R(2)$ and $S(1, 1), S(1, 2), S(2, 3), S(2, 4)$, its lineage is $X_1Y_1 \vee X_1Y_2 \vee X_2Y_3 \vee X_2Y_4$, and its OBDD is shown in Figure 5.2. In general, the OBDD examines the tuples $S(i, j)$ in row-major order; that is, for some arbitrary data instance D, the variable order of the OBDD is $R(1), S(1, 1), S(1, 2), \ldots, R(2), S(2, 1), S(2, 2), \ldots$ Next, we transform the OBDD such that every path examines all the variables. For that, we must insert on the 0-edge from $R(1)$ dummy nodes $S(1, 1), S(1, 2), \ldots$, and we must insert in the 0-edge from $R(2)$ the dummy nodes $S(2, 1), S(2, 2), \ldots$ Thus, we have a "complete" OBDD for Φ_{Q_1} of width 2. Similarly, we obtain a complete OBDD for Φ_{Q_2} of width 2, which reads the Boolean variables in the *same* order: $T(1), S(1, 1), S(1, 2), \ldots, T(2), S(2, 1), S(2, 2), \ldots$ We insert the missing variables $T(1), T(2), \ldots$ in the first OBDD, and the missing variables $R(1), R(2), \ldots$ in the second OBDD, without increasing the width. Now, we can synthesize an OBDD for $\Phi_Q = \Phi_{Q_1} \wedge \Phi_{Q_2}$ of width 4, by using the property on OBDD synthesis mentioned above (see also [Wegener, 2004]). Thus, Q_J admits an OBDD of size $4n$, where n is the total number of tuples in the database.

In general, we can synthesize the OBDD inductively on the structure of the query Q, provided that the subqueries Q_1, Q_2 used *the same* variable order: this is possible for inversion-free queries because the variable order of the tuples in a relation $R(x_1, x_2, \ldots)$ is the lexicographic order, determined by the attribute-order $\pi^R(1), \pi^R(2), \ldots$ If the query has an inversion, then the synthesis is no longer possible. For a counterexample, consider the query $Q_V = R(x_1), S(x_1, y_1) \vee S(x_2, y_2), T(y_2) \vee R(x_3), T(y_3)$ (Example 4.8). The OBDD for the sub-query $R(x_1), S(x_1, y_1)$ needs to inspect the S-tuples in row-major order $S(1, 1), S(1, 2), \ldots, S(2, 1), S(2, 2), \ldots$, while the OBDD for the sub-query $S(x_2, y_2), T(y_2)$ needs column-major order $S(1, 1), S(2, 1), \ldots, S(1, 2), S(2, 2), \ldots$, and we can no longer synthesize the OBDD for their disjunction (the OBDD for the third subquery $R(x_3), T(y_3)$ could read these variables in any order).

5.4.2.3 *UCQ(FBDD)*

It is open whether this class admits a syntactic characterization. However, the following two properties are known:

Proposition 5.20   *(1) The query Q_V defined in Example 4.8 admits a polynomial-size FBDD. (2) The query Q_W defined in Example 4.14 does not have a polynomial-size FBDD.*

We describe here the FBDD for Q_V. It has a spine inspecting the tuples $R(1), T(1), R(2), T(2), \ldots$, in this order. Each 0-edge from this spine leads to the next tuple in the sequence. Consider the 1-edge from $R(k)$: when $R(k)$ is true, then the query Q_V is equivalent to $Q' = R(x_1), S(x_1, y_1) \vee T(y_3)$. In other words, we can drop the query $S(x_2, y_2), T(y_2)$ because it logically implies $T(y_3)$. But Q' is inversion-free (in fact, it is even non-repeating); hence, it has an OBDD of linear size. Thus, the 1-edge from $R(k)$ leads to a subgraph that is an OBDD for Q', where all tests for $R(1), \ldots, R(k-1)$ have been removed, since they are known to be 0. Similarly, the 1-edge from $T(k)$ leads to an OBDD for $Q'' = R(x_3) \vee S(x_2, y_2), T(y_2)$. Notice that the two subgraphs, for Q' and for Q'', respectively, use *different* orders for $S(i, j)$; in other words, we have constructed an FBDD, not an OBDD. Thus, Q_V is in *UCQ(FBDD)*, which proves *UCQ(OBDD)* $\subsetneq$ *UCQ(FBDD)*.

5.4.2.4 *UCQ(d-DNNF)⁻*

We give here a sufficient syntactic condition for for membership in this class: it is open whether this condition is also necessary. For that, we describe a set of rules, called $\mathbf{R}_d$, which, when applied to a query Q, compute a polynomial size *d-DNNF⁻*, $d(Q)$, for the lineage Φ_Q.

Independent-join	$d(Q_1 \wedge Q_2) = d(Q_1) \wedge d(Q_2)$
Independent-project	$d(\exists x.Q) = \neg(\bigwedge_{a \in ADom} \neg d(Q[a/x]))$
Independent-union	$d(Q_1 \vee Q_2) = \neg(\neg d(Q_1) \wedge \neg d(Q_2))$
Expression-conditioning	$d(Q_1 \wedge Q_2) = \neg(\neg d(Q_1) \vee \neg(\neg d(Q_1 \vee Q_2) \vee d(Q_2)))$
Attribute ranking	$d(Q) = d(Q^r)$

These rules correspond one-to-one to the rules $\mathbf{R}_6$ in Subsection 4.1.2, except that inclusion-exclusion is replaced with *expression-conditioning*. For every rule, we assume the same preconditions as for the corresponding R_6 rule. For example, Q_1, Q_2 must be independent in the *independent-join* and *independent-union* rules, and x must be a separator variable in *independent-project*. As a consequence, all operations used in these rules are permitted by *d-DNNF⁻*'s: all $\wedge$'s are independent, and all $\vee$'s are disjoint.

$\mathbf{R}_d$-safety is a sufficient condition for membership in *UCQ(d-DNNF)⁻*, but it is open whether it is also a necessary condition:

Proposition 5.21   *Let Q be a UCQ query that is $\mathbf{R}_d$-safe (meaning that the rules $\mathbf{R}_d$ terminate on Q). Then $Q \in UCQ(d\text{-}DNNF)^-$.*

We explain now the *expression-conditioning* rule. For a query $Q = Q_1 \wedge Q_2$, we have the following derivation for $\neg Q$, where we write $\vee^d$ to indicate that a $\vee$ operation is disjoint:

$$
\begin{aligned}
\neg(Q_1 \wedge Q_2) &= \neg Q_1 \vee \neg Q_2 \\
&= \neg Q_1 \vee^d [Q_1 \wedge \neg Q_2] \\
&= \neg Q_1 \vee^d \neg[\neg Q_1 \vee Q_2] \\
&= \neg Q_1 \vee^d \neg[(\neg Q_1 \wedge \neg Q_2) \vee^d Q_2] \\
&= \neg Q_1 \vee^d \neg[\neg(Q_1 \vee Q_2) \vee^d Q_2]
\end{aligned}
\tag{5.12}
$$

This justifies the *expression-conditioning* rule. In general, this rule is applied to a query $Q = \bigwedge_i Q_i$, where the $\mathbf{R}_6$ rules would normally apply Möbius' inversion formula on the CNF lattice $L = L(Q)$. The effect of the expression-conditioning rule is that it reduces Q to three subqueries, namely Q_1, Q_2, and $Q_1 \vee Q_2$, whose CNF lattices are meet-sublattices of L, obtained as follows. Let $Q = Q_1 \wedge Q_2$, where $Q_1 = Q_{11} \wedge Q_{12} \wedge \ldots$ and $Q_2 = Q_{21} \wedge Q_{22} \wedge \ldots$, and let L denote the CNF lattice of Q. Denote $v_1, \ldots, v_m, u_1, \ldots, u_k$ the co-atoms of this lattice (see the lattice primer in Figure 4.2), such that $v_1, v_2, \ldots$ are the co-atoms corresponding to $Q_{11}, Q_{12}, \ldots$ and $u_1, u_2, \ldots$ are the coatoms for $Q_{21}, Q_{22}, \ldots$Recall (Figure 4.2) that $\overline{S}$ denotes the meet-closure of a set $S \subseteq L$.

- The CNF lattice of $Q_1 = Q_{11} \wedge \ldots \wedge Q_{1m}$ is $\overline{M}$, where $M = \{v_1, \ldots, v_m\}$.

- The CNF lattice of $Q_2 = Q_{21} \wedge \ldots \wedge Q_{2k}$ is $\overline{K}$, where $K = \{u_1, \ldots, u_k\}$.

- The CNF lattice of $Q_1 \vee Q_2 = \bigwedge_{i,j}(Q_{1i} \vee Q_{2j})$ is $\overline{N}$, where $N = \{v_i \wedge u_j \mid i = 1, m; j = 1, k\}$. Here $v_i \wedge u_j$ denotes the lattice-meet, and corresponds to the query-union.

It follows immediately that the *expression-conditioning* rule terminates because each of the three lattices above, $\overline{M}, \overline{K}, \overline{N}$ is a strict subset of L.

Example 5.22   For a simple illustration of the *expression-conditioning* rule, consider the query Q_W in Figure 4.1. We will refer to the notations introduced in Example 4.14. The lattice elements are denoted u_1, u_2, u_3, u_4, u_5; we write Q_u for the query at each node u. Therefore, $Q_W = Q_{u_1} \wedge Q_{u_2} \wedge Q_{u_3}$. To apply the *expression-conditioning* rule, we group as follows: $Q_W = Q_{u_1} \vee (Q_{u_2} \vee Q_{u_3})$. Then the rule gives:

$$\neg Q_W = \neg Q_{u_1} \vee^d \neg[\neg(Q_{u_1} \vee (Q_{u_2} \wedge Q_{u_3})) \vee^d (Q_{u_2} \wedge Q_{u_3})]$$

Thus, we need to compute the *d-DNNF$^\neg$* recursively for three queries: Q_{u_1}, $Q_{u_2} \wedge Q_{u_3}$, and $Q_{u_1} \vee (Q_{u_2} \wedge Q_{u_3})$. The first query, Q_{u_1}, has a polynomial-size *d-DNNF$^\neg$* because it is both hierarchical and non-repeating. The second query $Q_{u_2} \wedge Q_{u_3}$ is inversion-free query and, therefore, by Proposition 5.19, has a polynomial-size OBDD, and, hence, it also has a polynomial-size *d-DNNF$^\neg$*. It remains to explain how to construct a *d-DNNF$^\neg$* for $Q_{u_1} \vee (Q_{u_2} \wedge Q_{u_3})$ (here $\vee$ is not a disjoint-or):

$$\begin{aligned} Q_{u_1} \vee (Q_{u_2} \wedge Q_{u_3}) &= (Q_{u_1} \vee Q_{u_2}) \wedge (Q_{u_1} \vee Q_{u_3}) \\ &= Q_{u_4} \wedge Q_{\hat{0}} \\ &= Q_{u_4} \end{aligned}$$

This query, too, is inversion-free (see the lattice in Figure 4.1 and the notations in Example 4.10).

It is interesting to examine the CNF lattices of these three queries, which, according to our discussion, are the meet-closures of $M = \{u_1\}$, $K = \{u_2, u_3\}$, and $N = \{u_1 \wedge u_2, u_1 \wedge u_3\} = \{u_4, \hat{0}\}$: $\overline{M} = \{u_1, \hat{1}\}$, $\overline{K} = \{u_5, u_2, u_3, \hat{1}\}$, and $\overline{N} = \{\hat{0}, u_4, \hat{1}\}$. Notice that the co-atomic elements of $\overline{N}$ are $\{u_4, \hat{1}\}$; hence, we have completely eliminated $\hat{0}$. We say that we have "erased $\hat{0}$".

We prove now that $\mathbf{R}_d$-safety implies $\mathbf{R}_6$-safety. Fix a lattice L. Every non-empty subset $S \subseteq L - \{\hat{1}\}$ corresponds to a query, $\bigwedge_{u \in S} Q_u$. We define a nondeterministic function NE that maps a non-empty set $S \subseteq L - \{\hat{1}\}$ to a set of elements $NE(S) \subseteq \overline{S}$, as follows. If $S = \{v\}$ is a singleton set, then $NE(S) = \{v\}$. Otherwise, partition S non-deterministically into two disjoint, non-empty sets $S = M \cup K$, define $N = \{v \wedge u \mid v \in M, u \in K\}$, and define $NE(S) = NE(M) \cup NE(K) \cup NE(N)$. Thus, $NE(S)$ is non-deterministic because it depends on our choice for partitioning S. The intuition the following: in order for the query $\bigwedge_{u \in S} Q_u$ to be $\mathbf{R}_d$-safe, all lattice points in $NE(S)$ must also be $\mathbf{R}_d$-safe: they are "non-erasable".

Call an element $z \in L$ *erasable* if there exists a non-deterministic choice for $NE(L^*)$ that does not contain z. The intuition is that if z is erasable, then there exists a sequence of applications of the expression-conditioning rule, which avoids computing z; in other words, it "erases" z from the list of queries in the lattice for which it needs to compute the *d-DNNF$^\neg$*, and, therefore, Q_z is not required to be $\mathbf{R}_d$ safe. We prove that only queries Q_z where $\mu_L(z, \hat{1}) = 0$ can be erased:

Lemma 5.23 *If z is erasable in L, then $\mu_L(z, \hat{1}) = 0$.*

Proof. We prove the following claim, by induction on the size of the set S: if $z \notin NE(S)$, $z \neq \hat{1}$, then $\mu_{\overline{S}}(z, \hat{1}) = 0$ (if $z \notin \overline{S}$, then we define $\mu_{\overline{S}}(z, \hat{1}) = 0$). The lemma follows by taking $S = L^*$ (the set of all co-atoms in L).

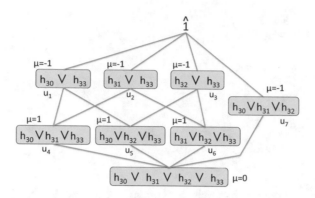

Figure 5.3: The CNF lattices for a query denoted Q_9. The query is the conjunction of the co-atoms in the lattice, $Q_9 = Q_{u_1} \wedge Q_{u_2} \wedge Q_{u_3} \wedge Q_{u_7}$, and each lattice element is indicated; for example, $Q_{u_1} = h_{30} \vee h_{33}$ (the queries h_{3i} were introduced in Subsection 4.1.5). The minimal element of the lattice, $\hat{0}$, represents an intractable query, namely $Q_{\hat{0}} = H_3$, but the Möbius function at that point is $\mu = 0$, and since all other queries in the lattice are in polynomial time, Q_9 is in polynomial time. Unlike the lattice for Q_W, here the bottom element is not "erasable". It is conjectured that Q_9 does not admit a polynomial-size d-DNNF.

If $S = \{v\}$, then $NE(S) = \{v\}$ and $\overline{S} = \{v, \hat{1}\}$: therefore, the claim hold vacuously. Otherwise, let $S = M \cup K$, and define $N = \{v \wedge u \mid v \in M, u \in K\}$. We have $NE(S) = NE(M) \cup NE(K) \cup NE(N)$. If $z \notin NE(S)$, then $z \notin NE(M)$, $z \notin NE(K)$, and $z \notin NE(N)$. By induction hypothesis, $\mu_{\overline{M}}(z, \hat{1}) = \mu_{\overline{K}}(z, \hat{1}) = \mu_{\overline{N}}(z, \hat{1}) = 0$. Next, we notice that (1) $\overline{M}, \overline{K}, \overline{N} \subseteq \overline{S}$, (2) $\overline{S} = \overline{M} \cup \overline{K} \cup \overline{N}$ and (3) $\overline{M} \cap \overline{K} = \overline{N}$. Then, we apply the definition of the Möbius function directly (Definition 4.11), using a simple inclusion-exclusion formula:

$$
\begin{aligned}
\mu_{\overline{S}}(z, \hat{1}) &= - \sum_{u \in \overline{S}, z < u \le \hat{1}} \mu_{\overline{S}}(u, \hat{1}) \\
&= - \left(\sum_{u \in \overline{M}, z < u \le \hat{1}} \mu_{\overline{S}}(u, \hat{1}) + \sum_{u \in \overline{K}, z < u \le \hat{1}} \mu_{\overline{S}}(u, \hat{1}) - \sum_{u \in \overline{N}, z < u \le \hat{1}} \mu_{\overline{S}}(u, \hat{1}) \right) \\
&= \mu_{\overline{M}}(z, \hat{1}) + \mu_{\overline{K}}(z, \hat{1}) - \mu_{\overline{N}}(z, \hat{1}) = -0 - 0 + 0 = 0
\end{aligned}
$$

$\square$

The lemma implies immediately:

Proposition 5.24 *For any UCQ query Q, if Q is $\mathbf{R}_d$-safe, then it is $\mathbf{R}_6$-safe. The converse does not hold in general: query Q_9 Figure 5.3 is $\mathbf{R}_6$-safe but it is not $\mathbf{R}_d$-safe.*

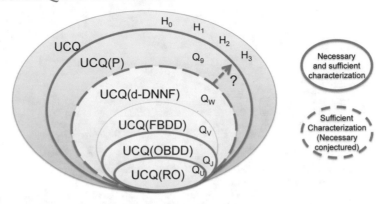

Figure 5.4: The query compilation hierarchy for Unions of Conjunctive Queries (UCQ).

It is conjecture that $Q_9 \notin UCQ(d\text{-}DNNF)^-$. Note that the proposition only states that Q_9 is not $\mathbf{R}_d$-safe, but it is not known whether $\mathbf{R}_d$ is a complete set of rules.

Proof. We prove the statement by induction on Q. We show only the key induction step, which is when $Q = \bigwedge_i Q_i$, and L is its CNF lattice. Let $Z \subseteq L$ denote the nodes corresponding to $\mathbf{R}_d$-unsafe queries: if Q is $\mathbf{R}_d$-safe, then all elements in Z are erasable. This implies that $\forall z \in Z, \mu(z, \hat{1}) = 0$. Hence, we can apply Möbius' inversion formula to the lattice L, and refer only to queries that are $\mathbf{R}_d$-safe; by induction hypothesis, these queries are also $\mathbf{R}_6$-safe, implying that Q is $\mathbf{R}_6$-safe.

We show that Q_9 in Figure 5.3 is $\mathbf{R}_6$-safe, but is not $\mathbf{R}_d$-safe. Indeed, the query at $\hat{0}$ is the only hard query (since it is equivalent to H_3), and $\mu(\hat{0}, \hat{1}) = 0$. On the other hand, we prove that $\hat{0}$ cannot be erased. Indeed, the coatoms of the lattice are $L^* = \{u_1, u_2, u_3, u_7\}$; given the symmetry of u_1, u_2, u_3, there are only three ways to partition the coatoms into two disjoint sets $L^* = M \cup K$:

- $M = \{u_1, u_2, u_3\}$, $K = \{u_7\}$. In this case, the lattice $\overline{M}$ is $\{\hat{0}, u_4, u_5, u_6, u_1, u_2, u_3, \hat{1}\}$, and $\mu_{\overline{M}}(\hat{0}, \hat{1}) = -1$, proving that this query is $\mathbf{R}_6$-unsafe, and, therefore, $\mathbf{R}_d$-unsafe.

- $M = \{u_1, u_2\}$, $K = \{u_3, u_7\}$. In this case the lattice $\overline{K}$ is $\{\hat{0}, u_3, u_7, \hat{1}\}$ and has $\mu_{\overline{K}}(\hat{0}, \hat{1}) = 1$; hence, by the same argument, is $\mathbf{R}_d$-unsafe.

- $M = \{u_1\}$, $K = \{u_2, u_3, u_7\}$. Here, too, $\overline{K} = \{\hat{0}, u_6, u_2, u_3, u_7, \hat{1}\}$, and $\mu_{\overline{K}}(\hat{0}, \hat{1}) = 1$.

□

5.4.2.5 *UCQ(P)*

Finally, this class represents all tractable queries, which, by Theorem 4.23, are precisely the $\mathbf{R}_6$-safe queries. It is easy to see that Q_9 is safe because the Möbius function for the bottom lattice element is 0. Thus, Q_9 is a candidate query for separating *UCQ(d-DNNF)* from *UCQ(P)*.

Query	Syntactic properties	Membership in $UCQ(\mathcal{C})$, where $\mathcal{C}$ is				
		RO	*OBDD*	*FBDD*	*dDNNF$\neg$*	*P*
$Q_U = R(x_1), S(x_1, y_1)$ $\lor\ T(x_2), S(x_2, y_2)$	hierarchical; non-repeating	yes	yes	yes	yes	yes
$Q_J = R(x_1), S(x_1, y_1)$ $\land\ T(x_2), S(x_2, y_2)$	inversion-free	no	yes	yes	yes	yes
$Q_V = R(x_1), S(x_1, y_1)$ $\lor\ S(x_2, y_2), T(y_2)$ $\lor\ R(x_3), T(y_3)$	has inversion; all lattice points have separators	no	no	yes	yes	yes
Q_W (Figure 4.1)	lattice point $\hat{0}$ has no separator; is erasable	no	no	no	yes	yes
Q_9 (Figure 5.3)	lattice point $\hat{0}$ has no separator; has $\mu = 0$; non-erasable	no	no	no	no?	yes
$H_1 = R(x_1), S(x_1, y_1)$ $\lor\ S(x_2, y_2), T(y_2)$	lattice point $\hat{0}$ has no separator; and has $\mu \neq 0$	no	no	no	no	no*

Figure 5.5: Queries used to separate the classes in Figure 5.4. All queries are hierarchical and have some additional syntactic properties indicated in the table. $\hat{0}$ denotes the minimal element of the query's CNF-lattice; μ its Möbius function. *no?* means conjectured. *no** means "assuming $P \neq \#P$".

5.5   DISCUSSION

In summary, intensional query evaluation first constructs the lineage Φ of a query, then computes the probability $P(\Phi)$ of this propositional formula. The advantage of this approach lies in its generality: every query on any database can be evaluated this way, on any pc-database. The disadvantage is that it is impossible to guarantee scalability because computing $P(\Phi)$ is #P-hard, in general. Applying the heuristics discussed in Section 5.1 may work very well in some cases, but it may lead to exponential running times in other cases: thus, the query processor is not predictable.

The approximation methods described in Section 5.3 alleviate this problem to some extent, but they come with their own issues. One approximation method is Monte Carlo (MC) simulation discussed in Subsection 5.3.2. The problem with any MC based approach is that it fails to take advantage of simple formulas. In other words, an MC algorithm is *always* relatively slow, even if the formula is very simple. For example, consider a read-once formula Φ. By applying the rules in Section 5.1, one can compute exactly $P(\Phi)$ in linear time. On the other hand, any MC algorithm needs to run at least a few tens of thousands of iterations, and its running time is a couple of orders of magnitude worse. The expectation that users have from database management systems is that simple queries run fast, and only difficult queries run slower: MC algorithms do not fulfill this expectation because they make no distinction between simple and complex queries. In that regard, the algorithm described in Subsection 5.3.1 is much better because it takes advantage of simple formulas. For example, if Φ is read-once, then the algorithm will quickly reach atomic formulas and return the exact value; only if it is forced to use the Shannon expansion repeatedly will it run out of time and be forced to return an approximation. This is the right behavior that we expect in a probabilistic database system: simple queries should be identified naturally and processed at peak performance, while for more complex queries the performance should degrade smoothly.

Finally, we note that the extensional and intensional query evaluation approaches can be combined. The query evaluation rules discussed in Chapter 4 can be applied as long as possible, and once we get stuck, we can switch to intensional query evaluation.

5.6   BIBLIOGRAPHIC AND HISTORICAL NOTES

The taxonomy of intensional/extensional evaluation is introduced by Pearl [1989]. *Intensional query semantics* was first used in probabilistic databases by Fuhr and Rölleke [1997] and refers essentially to the intensional query evaluation discussed in this chapter.

The evaluation rules for propositional formulas described in Section 5.1 are very well known, and form the basis of a variety of different algorithms and techniques. We followed here mostly the work by Olteanu et al. [2010], and the extension to RC queries on pc-tables by Fink et al. [2011b]. Intensional query evaluation on probabilistic databases was done in the Trio project, by Sarma et al. [2008b] and, more extensively, in the MayBMS and SPROUT projects. Most of the query evaluation techniques developed in these projects are available in open-source prototypes. Jha et al. [2010] extend the notion of tractable conjunctive queries to tractable data-query instances where general hard queries can become tractable on restricted data instances. The query evaluation is separated into two steps: the (possibly large) tractable data-query instance is evaluated first by efficient database techniques using an extensional approach such as that presented in Chapter 4, and then the (usually small) intractable residue is processed using an intensional approach based on inference techniques and treewidth.

The two approximation methods in Section 5.3 have different histories. The simple approximation algorithm presented in Subsection 5.3.1 is based on the recent work by Olteanu et al. [2010] and Fink et al. [2011b]. They also discuss incremental compilation of query lineage into so-called *de-*

composition trees that support linear-time probability computation. Fink and Olteanu [2011] propose a different approach to approximating the probability of propositional formula by giving lower and upper bounds expressed as read-once expressions (mentioned briefly at the end of Subsection 5.3.1).

The FPTRAS algorithms described in Subsection 5.3.2 are much older and well established. They were first introduced by Karp and Luby [1983] and Karp et al. [1989] and started a line of research to derandomize these approximation techniques, eventually leading to a polynomial time deterministic $(\varepsilon, 0)$-approximation algorithm [Trevisan, 2004] for k-DNF formulas. This result seems promising since a k-bound on the size of clauses of DNF formulas is not an unrealistic assumption in the context of probabilistic databases, where k can represent the number of joins in case of DNFs constructed by positive relational algebra queries. However, the constant in this algorithm is astronomical (above 2^{50} for 3-DNF). Another approach to approximating lineage expression is based on Fourier series: one application to probabilistic databases is discussed by Ré and Suciu [2008].

The compilation targets discussed in Section 5.2 have a long history. In a landmark paper, Bryant [1986] introduced Ordered BDDs, which has led to a flurry of study of variants of BDDs. A good survey of the topic can be found in [Wegener, 2004]. In the AI community, Darwiche and Marquis [2002] extended the idea of a circuit from BDDs to more complex circuits, which can represent succinctly a richer class of propositional formulas; d-DNNF's were introduced by Darwiche [2001]. Compilation can be obtained from any probabilistic inference algorithm: Darwiche [2006] describes a general approach for doing that, converting any probabilistic inference algorithm into a circuit construction algorithm. We followed this principle when we argued that Algorithm 2 can be converted from a probability-computation algorithm, into a circuit-construction algorithm.

Section 5.4 on query compilation is based on the work by Olteanu and Huang [2008] and Jha and Suciu [2011]. Olteanu and Huang [2008] first showed that all conjunctive queries without self-joins are either read-once or #P-hard (Theorem 5.13). This is surprising because it says that for conjunctive queries without self-joins, every query is either extremely easy or extremely hard. Jha and Suciu [2011] showed that, for UCQ queries, one obtains a strict hierarchy with respect to different compilation targets (Theorem 5.14). In other words, conjunctive queries without self-joins and UCQ behave very differently with respect to query compilation. These results are summarized in Figure 5.4 and Figure 5.5.

Several researchers have studied techniques for practical query compilation. In two different papers, Sen et al. [2010] and Roy et al. [2011] study query compilation into read-once formulas. They propose two different algorithms for testing whether the lineage of a conjunctive query without self-joins is a read-once formula, by examining both the query and the input database. Olteanu and Huang [2008] and Olteanu and Huang [2009] describe efficient compilation techniques into OBDDs and FBDDs for conjunctive queries extended with disequalities ($\neq$) and inequalities ($<$), respectively, and study which queries can be compiled this way. For conjunctive queries without self-joins, the compilation-based probability computation technique presented by Olteanu et al. [2010] provably finishes in polynomial time if the query is tractable, i.e., hierarchical, or when its lineage has a read-once equivalent.

Compilation has applications beyond the computation of marginal probabilities. Darwiche and Marquis [2002] describe several applications of knowledge compilation for propositional formulas, including probabilistic inference and model counting. For probabilistic databases, Koch and Olteanu [2008] introduce compilation-based techniques for *conditioning* probabilistic databases. The conditioning problem is to transform a probabilistic database of priors into a posterior probabilistic database which is materialized for subsequent query processing or further refinement. Here, the new evidence used for conditioning is in the form of database constraints.

CHAPTER 6

Advanced Techniques

This chapter includes a selection of advanced topics that extend the model discussed in previous chapters in several ways: top-k processing, sequential databases, Monte Carlo databases, and indexes for speeding up query processing. This material is more advanced and treated at a higher level (meaning with less detail) than the material in the previous chapters: the reader is referred to the bibliographic references for more details.

We begin by discussing top-k processing, which is a practical optimization to query processing in probabilistic databases. We then present sequential probabilistic databases that allow us to apply probabilistic database ideas to sophisticated text processing applications or to applications that use sensor data, audio data, or optical character recognition data. We then discuss more sophisticated generalizations that allow us to capture deep analytic applications by us finely capturing statistical correlations and dependencies, such as Markov Network-based Databases and Monte Carlo-based databases. Finally, we discuss some novel techniques for indexing probabilistic databases, with applications both to sequential databases, and databases representing large graphical models.

6.1   TOP-k QUERY ANSWERING

We have discussed so far, in the previous two chapters, how to compute the output probabilities exactly or approximately. We now discuss a way to avoid computing most of the output probabilities, namely when the user asks for the top k highest ranked answers.

The justification for the approach discussed here is that, in many applications of probabilistic databases, the probabilities are mere degrees of uncertainty in the data, and do not have any otherwise semantics that is meaningful to the user. Instead, users care only about ranking the query answers and want to retrieve only the top k answers: if the outputs are $(t_1, p_1), \ldots, (t_n, p_n)$, and $p_1 \geq \ldots \geq p_n$, then the system should display only the top k answers, in decreasing order of their probabilities. In Section 1.1, we showed a SQL query on the NELL probabilistic database: its answers are ranked[1] in decreasing order of their probabilities. The actual probabilities may, or may not be printed: the ranking is the most important information for the user. Also, usually $k \ll n$: for example, $k = 10$ while n can be in the thousands. It seems a waste of resources to compute all n probabilities, only to return the top k.

When the probabilities can be computed exactly and efficiently, then one should just compute all n output probabilities, sort them, and return the top k. We assume in this section that the probabilities are expensive to compute exactly; instead, we approximate them, through some iterative

---

[1]Ranking output tuples should not be confused with ranking attributes, in Subsection 4.1.2.

process, like Monte Carlo simulation. We show how to concentrate most of the iterations on the top k probabilities and compute for the others only a very coarse approximation, just the necessary approximation to ensure that they are not in the top k.

Consider the following problem. There are n possible tuples, $t_1, t_2, \ldots, t_n$, each has a probability, $p_1, \ldots, p_n$, and our task is to rank the tuples in decreasing order of their probabilities and return only the top k tuples: in other words, compute $Top_k = (t_{i_1}, t_{i_2}, \ldots, t_{i_k})$, where $i_1, i_2, \ldots, i_n$ is a permutation such that $p_{i_1} \geq p_{i_2} \geq \ldots \geq p_{i_n}$. Assume that we have no easy method to compute these probabilities exactly, but, instead, we have a lower bound and an upper bound, $p_i \in [L_i, U_i]$, for $i = 1, n$. These bounds may be obtained by one of the approximation methods in Section 5.3. Through an iterative process we can improve each interval, i.e., at each iteration we narrow the bound to $[L_i', U_i'] \subset [L_i, U_i]$: we call such an iteration a *simulation step*; in other words, a simulation step for the tuple t_i improves its bound from $[L_i, U_i]$ to $[L_i', U_i']$. The *Multisimulation* problem is to decide in which order to apply the simulation steps to all the intervals $[L_1, U_1], \ldots, [L_n, U_n]$, in order to quickly find Top_k. This is a catch-22 problem: if we knew the set Top_k, then we could focus all simulation steps only on the k tuples in this set, but in order to compute this set, we need to know the probabilities of all n tuples. In general, n is large (say, 1000 or more) while k is small (say, 10).

To simplify our discussion, we will assume that the probabilities $p_1, \ldots, p_n$ are distinct, $p_i \neq p_j$ for $i \neq j$, which implies that Top_k is uniquely defined. We discuss below how to relax this assumption.

In order to be able to make incremental progress on each interval $[L_i, U_i]$, we need to maintain some additional data structures for each tuple t_i, which we denote generically by $G_i, i = 1, n$. For example, consider the two approximation algorithms discussed in Section 5.3. For Algorithm 3, we need to maintain for each tuple t_i the currently expanded circuit for its lineage expression and the lower/upper bound for each gate in the circuit; for the Monte Carlo approximation algorithms in Subsection 5.3.2, we need to maintain the total number of trials N and the number of successful trials c, for each t_i.

We split the multisimulation problem into two parts. First, compute the *set* $Top_k = \{t_1, \ldots, t_k\}$, then rank this set.

6.1.1 COMPUTING THE SET Top_k

Given a n positive numbers $a_1, \ldots, a_n$ denote $\max_k(a_1, \ldots, a_n)$ the k's largest number in the sequence. In other words, given any ordered permutation $a_{i_1} \geq a_{i_2} \geq \ldots \geq a_{i_n}$, $\max_k(A) = a_{i_k}$. If $k > n$ then, by convention, $\max_k(a_1, \ldots, a_n) = 0$. The *critical region* for a set of n intervals $[L_i, U_i]$ is the interval (L^c, U^c) where:

$$L^c = \max_k(L_1, \ldots, L_n) \qquad\qquad U^c = \max_{k+1}(U_1, \ldots, U_n)$$

Figure 6.1 illustrates the critical region for the case when $n = 5$ and $k = 2$. The critical region plays a key role in guiding the algorithm that simulates the tuples $t_1, \ldots, t_n$ in an optimal order.

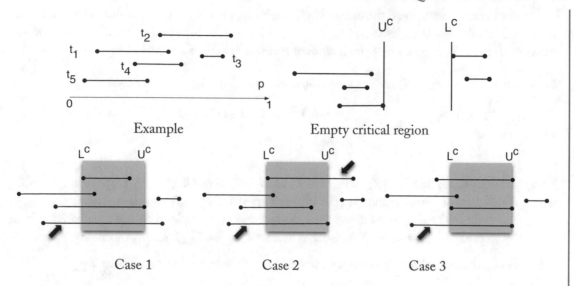

Figure 6.1: Illustration of the multi-simulation technique. The goal is to retrieve the top $k = 2$ highest probabilities. Intervals represent uncertainty about the value of a tuple's probability score.

We assume that during any simulation step, no lower bound L_i decreases, and no upper bound U_i increases. It is easy to check that this holds for Algorithm 3; for the Monte Carlo approximation algorithms in Subsection 5.3.2, while it fails if we define a simulation step to consists of one single Monte Carlo trial, the assumption still holds with high probability is we perform $\sqrt{N}$ trials during any simulation step [Ré et al., 2007]. This assumption implies immediately that L^c never decreases, and U^c never increases. Thus, the critical region (L^c, U^c) will only shrink after a simulation step, or stay the same.

Next, we define four sets of tuples as follows:

$$B_k = \{i \mid U_i \le L^c\} \qquad\qquad T_k = \{i \mid U^c \le L_i\}$$
$$\bar{B}_k = \{i \mid U_i \le U^c\} \qquad\qquad \bar{T}_k = \{i \mid L^c \le L_i\}$$

If the critical region is non-empty $(L^c < U^c)$, then $T_k \subseteq \bar{T}_k$ and $B_k \subseteq \bar{B}_k$; if the critical region is empty, then the opposite inclusions hold.

It is always the case that $|\bar{T}_k| \ge k$ because, by the definition of $L^c = \max_k(L_1, \ldots, L_n)$, there exists k lower bounds L_i such that $L_i \ge L^c$. By duality, it follows that $|\bar{B}_k| \ge n - k$ since $U^c = \max_{k+1}(U_1, \ldots, U_n) = \min_{n-k}(U_1, \ldots, U_n)$.

For the next lemma and the discussion following it, we will assume without loss of generality that all intervals $[L_i, U_i]$ are strict, i.e., $L_i < U_i$ for $i = 1, n$. To ensure that this holds, we can increase all upper bounds U_i by a small amount $\varepsilon > 0$. Then, the following holds:

Lemma 6.1 *Denoting $c(S)$ the complement of a set S, the following properties hold:*

$$B_k \cap \bar{T}_k = \emptyset \qquad B_k \subseteq c(Top_k) \qquad \bar{B}_k \cap T_k = \emptyset \qquad T_k \subseteq Top_k$$

Proof. It is easy to see that $B_k \cap \bar{T}_k = \emptyset$: if $i \in B_k$ and $i \in \bar{T}_k$, then $U_i \leq L^c \leq L_i$, implying $L_i = U_i$, which contradicts our assumption that the intervals are strict. $\bar{B}_k \cap T_k = \emptyset$ is similar.

The claim $B_k \cap Top_k = \emptyset$ follows from the fact that every tuple in B_k has a probability dominated by all tuples in $\bar{T}_k$, and the latter set has at least k tuples. $T_k \subseteq Top_k$ is by duality. $\square$

When the critical region becomes empty, $L^c \geq U^c$, then we have identified Top_k.

Lemma 6.2 *(1) If the critical region is empty, i.e., $L^c \geq U^c$, then $T_k = \bar{T}_k = Top_k$ and $B_k = \bar{B}_k = c(Top_k)$. (2) If $|T_k| = k$ or $|B_k| = n - k$, then the critical region is empty.*

Proof. (1) When $L^c \geq U^c$, then $\bar{T}_k \subseteq T_k$. By the previous lemma, $T_k \subseteq Top_k$. But we also have $|\bar{T}_k| \geq k$ and $|Top_k| = k$; hence, all three sets are equal.

(2) Assume $|T_k| = k$ (the case $|B_k| = n - k$ is dual, and omitted). By the definition of T_k, for every $i \in T_k$, we have $U^c \leq L_i$; thus, there are k values L_i that are $\geq U^c$. It follows that $L^c = \max_k(L_1, \ldots, L_n) \geq U^c$, proving that the critical region is empty. $\square$

Thus, our goal is to simulate the objects G_i until the critical region becomes empty or, equivalently, until T_k contains k elements, then return T_k. Our algorithm will therefore simulate the objects $G_1, G_2, \ldots, G_n$ only until the critical region becomes empty, then will return $Top_k = T_k$. The question is, which object to choose to simulate at each step.

Call a tuple t_i a *crosser* if $L_i \leq L^c$ and $U^c \leq U_i$. If the critical region is non-empty, then a crosser is any interval that contains the critical region. There are always at least two crossers because every non-crosser $[L_i, U_i]$ satisfies either $L^c < L_i$ or $U_i < U^c$; there are, at most, $k - 1$ non-crossers of the first kind (since $L^c = \max_k(L_1, \ldots, L_n)$), and, at most, $n - (k + 1)$ non-crossers of the second kind (since $U^c = \min_{n-k}(U_1, \ldots, U_n)$), and these two sets are disjoint when $L^c \leq U^c$; hence, there exists at least 2 crossers.

This observation allows us to prove that it is necessary to simulate until the critical region becomes empty: otherwise, the set Top_k is not uniquely defined.

Lemma 6.3 *If the critical region is non-empty, then Top_k is not uniquely defined by the intervals $[L_1, U_1], \ldots, [L_n, U_n]$.*

Proof. We will choose probabilities $p_i \in [L_i, U_i]$ for every $i = 1, n$ in two possible ways, such that Top_k differs; this proves that it is not possible to compute Top_k by examining only the current lower/upper bounds. If the critical region is non-empty, then $|T_k| < k$ and $|B_k| < n - k$. Furthermore, these two sets are disjoint since $B_k \subseteq \bar{B}_k$, which is disjoint from T_k. For each $i \in T_k$, we know that $i \in Top_k$, so we set p_i as high as possible, $p_i = U_i$; similarly, for each $j \in B_k$, we set $p_j = L_j$ since we know that this tuple does not belong to Top_k. Denote by $R = [n] - B_k - T_k$: these are the "rest" of the tuples: each interval $[L_i, U_i]$ for $i \in R$ has a non-empty intersection with the critical region (L^c, U^c); in other words $[L_i, U_i] \cap (L^c, R^c) \neq \emptyset$. Fix any two distinct crossers, t_i, t_j. For all tuples t_l such that $l \in R$ other than t_i, t_j, we set their probabilities $p_l \in [L_l, U_l]$ to any value in the critical region $p_l \in (L^c, R^c)$, with the only restriction that all the p_l's are disjoint: this is possible since the critical region is an open interval. For our distinguished crossers, t_i, t_j, we make two choices of their probabilities. In the first setting, $p_i = L^c$, $p_j = U^c$. The p_i larger than all other probabilities, except those in T_k: since $|T_k| < k$, we must have $t_i \in Top_k$; similarly, p_j is smaller than all probabilities except B_k, and therefore $t_j \notin Top_k$. In the second setting, we let $p_i = U^c$, $p_j = L^c$. Now $t_i \notin Top_k$ and $t_j \in Top_k$, proving that Top_k is not uniquely defined. $\square$

We have proven that one must simulate the tuples until the critical region becomes empty: this is both necessary and sufficient. Next, we show in what order we need to simulate these tuples.

Call a crosser an *upper crosser* if $U^c < U_i$; call it a *lower crosser* if $L_i < L^c$; call it a *double crosser* if it is both an upper and a lower crosser. The algorithm proceeds according to three cases, which are illustrated in Figure 6.1:

Case 1 There exists a *double crosser*, i.e., an interval $[L_i, U_i]$ such that $L_i < L^c < U^c < U_i$. Then, we apply one simulation step to G_i.

Case 2 There exists a *lower crosser* $L_i < L^c < U^c = U_i$ and a *upper crosser* $L_j = L^c < U^c < U_j$. Then, we apply one simulation step to G_i and one simulation step to G_j.

Case 3 There are only upper crossers, or only lower crossers. Then we choose a maximal upper- or lower-crossers, respectively, and apply to it one simulation step.

These cases are summarized in Algorithm 4. We prove that the algorithm is optimal within a factor of 2.

Theorem 6.4 Consider n tuples, and consider any sequence of N simulation steps, which computes the set Top_k by bringing the intervals $[L_1, U_1], ..., [L_n, U_n]$ to a state where the critical region is empty. Then Algorithm 4 computes Top_k using at most $2N$ steps.

Proof. We show that every simulation step done by Algorithm 4 is mandatory, except for case 2, when either the lower or the upper crosser is mandatory, but not necessarily both. Consider first Case 1, and let $L_i < L^c < U^c < U_i$ be the double crosser simulated by Algorithm 4. Then $t_i \notin \bar{T}_k$. Any sequence of simulations that do not touch the tuple t_i can only increase L^c; hence,

Algorithm 4 Input: n objects $G_1, \ldots, G_n$, where each G_i describes the following data:

(1) a tuple t_i

(2) an unknown probability p_i

(3) a lower bound L_i and an upper bound U_i such that $p_i \in [L_i, U_i]$.

Output: The set Top_k.

1: **while** true **do**

2: $\quad L^c = \max_k(L_1, \ldots, L_n) \; U^c = \max_k(U_1, \ldots, U_n)$

3: $\quad B_k = \{t_i \mid U_i \le L^c\} \; T_k = \{t_i \mid U^c \le L_i\}$

4: $\quad$ **if** $U^c \le L^c$ **then**

5: $\quad\quad$ **return** $Top_k = T_k$

6: $\quad$ **end if**

7: $\quad$ **if** exists $[L_i, U_i]$ such that $L_i < L^c, U^c < U_i$ **then**

8: $\quad\quad G_i$ is a *double crosser*: simulate G_i one step.

9: $\quad$ **end if**

10: $\quad$ **if** exists $[L_i, U_i], [L_j, U_j]$ such that $L_i < L^c < U^c = U_i, L_j = L^c < U^c < U_j$ **then**

11: $\quad\quad G_i, G_j$ are *lower/upper crossers*: simulate both G_i, G_j one step.

12: $\quad$ **end if**

13: $\quad$ Choose a *maximal crosser* $[L_i, U_i]$ such that $L_i \le L^c, U^c \le U_i$.

14: $\quad$ Simulate G_i one step.

15: **end while**

the condition $L_i < L^c$ continues to hold after any number of simulation steps; hence, we always have $t_i \notin \bar{T}_k$. By the same argument $t_i \notin \bar{B}_k$. By 6.2, when the critical region becomes empty, then $\bar{B}_k \cup \bar{T}_k = [n]$, but this contradicts the fact that neither $\bar{B}_k$ nor $\bar{T}_k$ contains t_i. Consider now case 2, and let $L_i < L^c < U^c = U_i$ and $L_j = L^c < U^c < U_j$ be a lower and upper crosser, respectively. Then $t_i \notin \bar{T}_k$ and $t_j \notin \bar{B}_k$. Consider any sequence of simulations that does not touch the tuples t_i or t_j but causes the critical region to become empty. That sequence must either decrease U^c, causing $t_i \notin \bar{B}_k$, or it must increase L^c, causing $t_j \notin \bar{T}_k$, both contradicting the fact that, when the critical region becomes empty, $\bar{B}_k \cup \bar{T}_k = [n]$. Finally, for case 3, assume there are only upper crossers, and that $L_i = L^c < U^c \le U_i$ is a maximal upper crosser; then $t_i \notin \bar{B}_k$. Assume a sequence of simulations that do not touch the tuple t_i: it will continue to hold that $t_i \notin \bar{B}_k$; hence, when the algorithm terminates, it must be the case that, upon termination, $t_i \in \bar{T}_k$: this means that L^c will remain unchanged during these simulations, implying that $\bar{T}_k$ also remains unchanged during these additional simulation steps. That means that at the time the algorithm inspected the crosser t_i we had $|\bar{T}_k| = k$, contradicting the fact that the critical region is non-empty. $\quad\square$

Finally, we consider the case when some probabilities are equal, $p_i = p_j$. If the set Top_k is uniquely defined, then one can show that the algorithm works unchanged. However, if the ties between probabilities cause Top_k to be ill-defined, then the algorithm will never terminate, and the critical region will never become empty. In that case, we must modify the algorithm to stop when the critical region becomes smaller than some desired precision $\varepsilon > 0$.

6.1.2   RANKING THE SET Top_k

So far we have discussed how to find the *set* Top_k. Next, we show how to rank (order) it, and, for that, we describe two algorithms: one is theoretically optimal, while the second one is better and more convenient in practice. Both rely on Algorithm 4.

The first algorithm proceeds as follows. It starts with n tuples, $t_1, \ldots, t_n$, and computes the set Top_k using Algorithm 4. Next, using this set of k tuples, it runs the same algorithm again, in order to retrieve Top_{k-1}, in the set of tuples $Top_k = \{t_1, \ldots, t_k\}$. At this point, only one tuple is left out, in other words the set difference $Top_k - Top_{k-1}$ contains a single tuple: print this tuple as the *last* tuple of the ranked list, remove it from the set, decrease k by one, and repeat. The tuple that remains in the set until the end is the top ranked tuple. Using an argument similar to Theorem 6.4, one can prove that this algorithm is optimal within a factor of 2. Notice, however, that this algorithm is impractical because it lists the tuples in reverse order, bottom-to-top.

The second algorithm is more practical. This algorithm starts by running Algorithm 4 directly on the n input tuples, setting $k = 1$. In other words, it starts by computing Top_1, which identifies the top tuple in the entire set. Then, it removes it from the set of tuples, decreases n by 1, and computes again Top_1 on the remaining $n - 1$ tuples. It stops when it has printed k tuples. One can prove that, in theory, this algorithm can perform arbitrarily worse than an optimal algorithm, if the intervals $[L_i, U_i]$ shrink unpredictably in an adversarial manner. However, in practice, it has almost the same performance as the previous algorithm, and it has the major advantage that the tuples are returned in decreasing order of the probabilities.

6.2   SEQUENTIAL PROBABILISTIC DATABASES

Sequential probabilistic databases are motivated by the observation that a large fraction of the world's raw data is sequential and low-level [IDC, 2007], such as text data, hand-written forms, audio feeds, video feeds, and data from physical sensors. And while this low-level data is rich in information, the data is difficult for many applications to use directly since applications often need higher-level information, e.g., the ASCII text corresponding to the low-level image of hand writing in a form. To make higher-level information available to applications, a popular approach is to use a statistical model, which infers the higher-level information from the lower-level, raw data. To achieve high quality, many of these models model sequential dependencies: in equipment tracking applications, where a piece of equipment is at 9:00am gives us a great deal of information of where that equipment is located at 9:01am. Sequential probabilistic models are intended to capture these types of sequential dependencies. While sequential probabilistic databases use many of the same fundamental techniques as probabilistic relational databases, we ask different types of queries on sequential probabilistic databases. Also, the probability distributions that are common in sequential probabilistic databases cannot be represent succinctly as pc-tables and require a different representation. As a result, sequential probabilistic databases require changes to our theoretical and practical infrastructure.

One popular statistical model to extract sequential structure data from raw, unstructured data are *Hidden Markov Models* (HMM) [Rabiner, 1990]. Abstractly, an HMM takes as input a sequence of *observations* and produces as output a probability distribution over a sequence of *hidden states*. HMMs can be used to extract structure that is useful in a diverse set of applications: In RFID applications, the observations are the low-level antenna sightings, and the hidden states are sequences of higher-level locations, such as rooms or hallways [Letchner et al., 2009, Ré et al., 2008]. In speech applications, the observations are acoustic signals, and the hidden states are sequences of words or phonemes [CMUSphinx, 2010, HTK, 2009, Letchner et al., 2009, Rabiner, 1990, Sha and Saul, 2007]. There are other data-rich applications that use HMMs as well: sequence matching in biological data [Durbin et al., 2006, HMMER, 2010], optical character recognition [Chen et al., 1994], and image classification [Fosgate et al., 1997]. To capture the output of statistical models like HMMs, Kanagal and Deshpande [2009] and Ré et al. [2008] defined *Markov Sequence Databases*. In this approach, a database contains several *Markov Sequences*, which are sequences of random variables that have the Markov property, i.e., a random variable is independent of its history given its predecessor. Markov sequences exactly capture the output of an HMM after the HMM "sees" the observations.

Formally, a Markov sequence μ of length n operates over a finite set Σ of *state nodes* (or just *nodes*),[2] and it comprises an *initial-state distribution* $\mu_{0\rightarrow}$ and *transition functions* $\mu_{i\rightarrow}$ for all $1 \leq i < n$, where $\mu_{0\rightarrow}$ and $\mu_{i\rightarrow}$ are defined as follows.

- $\mu_{0\rightarrow} : \Sigma \rightarrow [0, 1]$ is a function such that for all $s \in \Sigma$,

$$\sum_{s \in \Sigma} \mu_{0\rightarrow}(s) = 1.$$

- $\mu_{i\rightarrow} : \Sigma \times \Sigma \rightarrow [0, 1]$ is a function such that for all $s \in \Sigma$,

$$\sum_{t \in \Sigma} \mu_{i\rightarrow}(s, t) = 1.$$

The set Σ of the state nodes of the Markov sequence μ is denoted by Σ_μ. We may write $\mu[n]$ instead of μ to denote that μ is a Markov sequence of length n.

Example 6.5   Our example of RFID for Markovian sequences is adapted from [Kimelfeld and Ré, 2010]. In particular, we consider a hospital where transmitters are attached to medical equipment. Each transmitter transmits discrete signals with fixed time intervals in between. Sensors are spread over the hospital in known locations (e.g., rooms, hallways, laboratories, etc.). A transmission contains the *transmitter identifier* and a *sensor identifier*.

---

[2]Note that Σ denotes the nodes of a Markov sequence, whereas for an NFA it denotes the alphabet. This is not accidental since we later use the state nodes as the alphabet of an NFA.

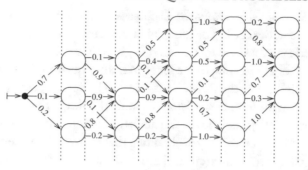

Figure 6.2: A Small Markov Sequence from RFID. Figure from Kimelfeld and Ré [2010].

In our example, we consider the transmissions of a specific crash cart. Based on the relevant transmissions, a prediction of the location of the cart at each point in time is made. Note that an actual location of the cart is typically uncertain, for several possible reasons. For instance, physical limitations may lead to erroneous reads or, more commonly, missed readings. As another example, the locations of sensors can easily introduce ambiguity (e.g., sensors located near passages or close sensors that simultaneously read the same signal). More subtly, the antenna readings themselves are at a very low-level, and there may be no 1-1 mapping to higher-level events, e.g., the same sequence could correspond to entering either of Room 1 or Room 2. Such a prediction is done by viewing the transmissions as a sequence of observations in a *hidden Markov model* (HMM) and translating this HMM into a Markov sequence.

Figure 6.2 shows a tiny example μ of the resulting Markov sequence. In this figure, we consider two rooms, numbered 1 and 2, and a lab. Each of the three contains two locations (each has a sensor). For example, Room 1 has sensors in locations r1a and r1b, and the lab has sensors in locations la and lb. The set Σ_μ of state nodes comprises the six locations (i.e., r1a, r1b, etc.). The states are represented by rectangles (with rounded corners). The functions $\mu_{0\rightarrow}$ and $\mu_{i\rightarrow}$ are represented by directed edges that are labeled with probabilities. Note that some edges are missing, and we implicitly assume that they have a zero probability. As an example, $\mu_{0\rightarrow}(\text{r1a}) = 0.7$ is indicated by the upper edge emanating from the filled circle on the left. As another example, $\mu_{3\rightarrow}(\text{la}, \text{lb}) = 0.1$ is indicated by the edge from the la rectangle to the lb rectangle between variables S_3 and S_4 (which we discuss later). Note that the sum of edges emanating from each object is 1 (as we require in a Markov sequence).

Continuing the previous example, a hospital administration can now ask queries to monitor the operation of the hospital without having to make reference to low level antenna readings. For example, we want to detect the sequence of rooms that a crash cart has visited (e.g., to detect a source of infection). This query is cumbersome to express in SQL because it requires that we combine events from several points in time. Instead, sequential probabilistic data management systems use languages that make it easy to specify sequential relationships.

Query Processing in Sequential Probabilistic Databases   Processing sequential queries is a challenging systems and theoretical task. For the sake of concreteness, we focus on a probabilistic sequential database called LAHAR [Letchner et al., 2009, Ré et al., 2008]. LAHAR is a *Markov-sequence database* that supports query processing over a set of Markov sequences. In LAHAR, as in many probabilistic databases [Dalvi and Suciu, 2004, Kanagal and Deshpande, 2009, Kimelfeld et al., 2008, Sarma et al., 2008b] and in the formalisms described in this book, queries are formulated as if the data were precise (i.e., deterministic); similar to a probabilistic relational database, each answer to a query is assigned a score, which is the probability of obtaining that answer when querying a random possible world. The query language is different from a relational database: it is based on *finite-state transducers* (or just *transducers* for short), which have been used for querying both strings [Bonner and Mecca, 1998, 2000] and trees [Ludäscher et al., 2002, Martens and Neven, 2002]. A transducer is essentially an automaton that emits output strings throughout its run on the input string (in our case, a random possible world of the Markov sequence). To make the system easier to use for developers, LAHAR does not ask users to write transducers directly and instead has syntactic sugar that makes the most common queries easy to express. To avoid introducing unnecessary syntax, we will formulate our queries using transducers themselves.

Formally, a *transducer*, comprises an NFA A and an *output function* $\omega : Q_A \times \Sigma_A \times Q_A \rightarrow \Delta^*$, where Δ is an *output alphabet*. The transducer that comprises A and ω is denoted by A^ω. We assume that Δ comprises exactly all the symbols that occur in the image of ω, and we denote it by Δ_ω. a transducer A^ω *transduces* a string $\mathbf{s} \in \Sigma_A^n$ into a string $\mathbf{o} \in \Delta_\omega^*$, denoted $\mathbf{s} \rightarrow [A^\omega] \mapsto \mathbf{o}$, if there exists an accepting run $\rho : \{1, \ldots, n\} \rightarrow Q_A$ on $\mathbf{s}$ such that

$$\mathbf{o} = \omega(q_A^0, s_1, q_1)\, \omega(q_1, s_2, q_2) \cdots \omega(q_{n-1}, s_n, q_n),$$

where $q_i = \rho(i)$ for all $1 \le i \le n$. Observe that each $\omega(q_i, s_{i+1}, q_{i+1})$ is a string over Δ_ω (which can be the empty string ϵ).

Example 6.6   Continuing our previous example: our goal is to detect the sequence of rooms that a crash cart has visited after it visits the lab (e.g., to detect a source of infection). To do so, we formulate a transducer that reads the locations, and whenever the crash cart changes rooms the transducer emits the number of the new room. Figure 6.3 shows a transducer A^ω over the alphabet $\Sigma_A = \{r_{1a}, r_{1b}, r_{2a}, r_{2b}, l_a, l_b\}$ (which, not coincidentally, is the language Σ_μ of the Markov sequence μ of Figure 6.2). Each state is represented by a circle, an accepting state has an inner circle, and the initial state has an incoming arrow. Thus, the set Q_A is $\{q_0, q_\lambda, q_1, q_2\}$, the set F_A is $\{q_\lambda, q_1, q_2\}$, and the initial state q_A^0 is q_0. The functions δ_A and ω are represented by the labels over the directed edges of the figure. Generally, the notation $\sigma : \mathbf{o}$ on the edge from q and q' means that $q' \in \delta_A(q, \sigma)$ and $\omega(q, \sigma, q') = \mathbf{o}$. We use the notation $\sigma_1, \ldots, \sigma_k : \mathbf{o}$ as a shorthand for $q' \in \delta_A(q, \sigma_i)$ and $\omega(q, \sigma_i, q') = \mathbf{o}$ for all $i = 1, \ldots, k$.

Let us examine the output of this query on the example Markovian Sequence database from Figure 6.2. Figure 6.4 lists some strings produced by the transducer on this Markovian Sequence. For example, the sequence of room and labs $r_{1a}\, l_a\, l_a\, r_{1a}\, r_{2a}$ is produced by the Markovian

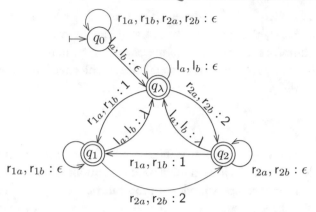

Figure 6.3: An example transducer that detects the sequence of rooms that a crash cart has visited (see Example 6.6).

string	value	probability	output
s	$r_{1a}\ l_a\ l_a\ r_{1a}\ r_{2a}$	0.567	1 2
t	$r_{1a}\ r_{1a}\ l_a\ r_{1a}\ r_{2a}$	0.007	1 2
u	$l_a\ r_{1b}\ r_{1b}\ r_{1a}\ r_{2a}$	0.002	1 2
v	$r_{1a}\ l_a\ r_{2a}\ r_{1b}\ l_b$	0.0315	2,1, λ
w	$r_{1b}\ r_{1b}\ l_a\ l_b\ l_b$	0.0032	ϵ
x	$r_{1a}\ r_{1a}\ r_{2b}\ r_{1b}\ r_{1b}$	0.007	N/A

Figure 6.4: Random strings of the Markov sequence μ of Figure 6.2, their probabilities, and the output strings into which they are transduced.

Sequence with probability 0.567. On this run, the first reading is in a room, and so the crash cart has not yet visited a lab. Thus, the transducer remains in q_0 and emits an empty string. Then, the crash cart does visit a lab followed by a sequence of rooms 1 and 2. Hence, the transducer emit 1, 2 on this run.

This simple transducer already exhibits some of the challenges in query evaluation. First, there may be a huge number of possible answers (sequences of rooms) with different probabilities, and it may well be the case that most of the answers have a confidence that is too low to be of interest. Second, many possible worlds of the Markov sequence can result (i.e., be transduced into) the same answer, as such worlds may differ in the duration of staying at each room as well as the different sub-locations inside each room (e.g., the main area versus the restroom). Initially, the LAHAR system processed a restricted subset of alert queries. Only recently have the algorithms for more sophisticated queries been discovered [Kimelfeld and Ré, 2010].

Directions in Sequential Probabilistic Databases   There are other statistical models, notably Chain CRFS [Lafferty et al., 2001], that produce output that can be modeled by Markov Sequences (in spite of requiring different techniques for inference). This opens up even more applications for Markov Sequence databases, notably more sophisticated information extraction [Lafferty et al., 2001, Sha and Pereira, 2003].

6.3   MONTE CARLO DATABASES

Some applications require a very general probabilistic model, which is not possible to decompose into disjoint-independent blocks. An important class of such applications are *financial risk assessment systems*. This has led to a more complex model of probabilistic databases, where certain attributes, tuples, or regions of the database are associated with random variables that may have complex continuous or discrete distributions. Given the rich probabilistic space, the tractable techniques for query evaluation that we discussed in Chapter 4 and Chapter 5 no longer apply. The only approach known to date to evaluate queries over probabilistic databases with rich probabilistic models is to use Monte Carlo simulations throughout query processing. Hence, their name: Monte Carlo Databases, or MCDB. These databases were introduced by Jampani et al. [2008] and further discussed by Xu et al. [2009], Arumugam et al. [2010], and Kennedy and Koch [2010].

6.3.1   THE MCDB DATA MODEL

MCDB's represent a rich data model by combining two simple primitives: a large, predefined set of random variables, and SQL queries (views). MCDB's do not encode uncertainty in the data itself but allow the user to define arbitrary *variable generation functions*, VG, which are pseudo-random generators for any random variable. The semantics of MCDB is the standard possible worlds semantics for probabilistic databases. A relation is called *deterministic* if its realization is the same in all possible worlds; otherwise, it is called *probabilistic* or *random*.

All the following examples are adapted from Jampani et al. [2008]; we allowed some syntactic variations, for presentation purpose.

Consider a deterministic table Customer(cid, name, region, gender, age). We would like to store each customer's income, which is unknown. In our first example, we will describe the income as a normal distribution, with mean 10000 and standard deviation 2000:

```
CREATE TABLE CustIncome(cid, name, region, gender, age, income)
  FOR EACH d IN Customer
  SELECT d.cid, d.name, d.region, d.gender, d.age, x.value
  FROM Normal(10000,2000) x
```

This SQL statement is in essence a view definition. Starting from the deterministic table Customer, it constructs a probabilistic table CustIncome having one additional attribute, the customer's income. Normal(mean,stdv) is a variable generating function (VG) that generates a normal distribution with a given mean and standard deviation. All VG's in MCDB are implemented using sampling; thus, `Normal` samples a value and returns its result. In general, a VG function in MCDB may return relations, rather than values. The function `Normal(mean,stdv)` returns a relation with a single row, and a single attribute `value`.

Instead of writing the parameters of the normal distribution in the view definition, we can store them in a separate table, call it `NormParam(mean,stdev)`, which consists of a single row. This allows users to change the statistical model easily by updating the `NormParam` table:

```
CREATE TABLE CustIncome(cid, name, region, gender, age, income)
  FOR EACH d IN Customer
    WITH Income as Normal
        (SELECT p.mean, p.stdev
         FROM NormParam p)
  SELECT d.cid, d.name, d.region, d.gender, d.age, x.value
  FROM Income x
```

Next, we will refine this example in two ways. First, we replace the normal function with the gamma function, which always returns a positive value and has three parameters, shift, scale, and shape[3]. Second, we store the three parameters using different approaches: customers have the same shift parameter, which is stored in a single-row table `CustShift(shift)`; the scale parameter depends on the customer's region, and it is stored in a table `CustRegionScale(region, scale)`; and the shape parameter is known for each customer individually, and stored in a table `CustShape(shape)`. The new query becomes:

```
CREATE TABLE CustIncome(cid, name, region, gender, age, income)
  FOR EACH d IN Customer
    WITH Income as Gamma
        ((SELECT s.shift FROM CustShift s),
         (SELECT s.scale FROM CustRegionScale s WHERE d.region=s.region),
         (SELECT s.shape FROM CustShape s WHERE d.cid=s.cid))
  SELECT d.cid, d.name, d.region, d.gender, d.age, x.value
  FROM Income x
```

6.3.2 QUERY EVALUATION IN MCDB

Given the complexity of the probabilistic space, query evaluation in an MCDB is approached differently from Chapter 4 and Chapter 5. Instead of searching for tractable cases, MCDBs run Monte Carlo simulations. This has the major advantage that it is a uniform approach applicable to

---

[3]The gamma distribution with shift (or threshold) θ, scale $\sigma > 0$, and shape $\alpha > 0$ has the density given by:

$$p(x) = \frac{1}{\alpha \Gamma(\alpha)} \left(\frac{x - \theta}{\sigma} \right)^{\alpha - 1} \exp\left(-\frac{x - \theta}{\sigma} \right) \qquad \text{when } x > 0$$

all, even very general, probabilistic models. The disadvantage is that Monte Carlo simulations, at least when evaluated naïvely, are costly.

The semantics of a query Q in an MCDB is given by a repeated execution of Q on sample databases: the query is evaluated N times, over N randomly chosen worlds. The overall result depends on the way the possible worlds semantics is closed in the query. For example, if probabilities of tuples are computed, this probability is estimated by returning, for a possible result tuple (i.e., a tuple present in the query result on at least one sample database), the ratio M/N, where M is the number of sample result relations in which the tuple occurs. MCDBs also allow to compute a wide variety of statistical tests and aggregates on the samples, beyond tuple probabilities. For example, consider the query:

```
SELECT age, sum(income), count(*)
FROM CustIncome
WHERE income > 12000
GROUP BY age
```

The query computes for each age bracket the sum of all incomes of all customers earning more than 12000, and their number. When the query finishes one run, its answer consists of a set of tuples $t_1, t_2, \ldots$ over all N runs. The MCDB collects all tuples, and computes a set of pairs (t_i, f_i), where t_i is a possible tuple and f_i is the frequency of that tuple over the N runs. It then returns a set of tuples $(\mathrm{age}_i, \mathrm{sum}_i, \mathrm{count}_i, f_i)$. This result can be used in many versatile ways. For example, the expected value of the sum for each age can be obtained as $E[\mathrm{sum}] = \sum_i \mathrm{sum}_i \cdot f_i$. For large enough N, the accuracy of this estimator is $+/- 1.96 \hat{\sigma}_N / \sqrt{N}$ where $\hat{\sigma}_N^2 = N/(N-1) \sum_i (\mathrm{sum}_i - E[\mathrm{sum}])^2 f_i$, by the central limit theorem. Thus, by returning multiple sample answers as opposed to a single aggregate value, the system provides much more utility.

To compute a set of sample databases and evaluate a query on each of them, it is, of course, not necessary to materialize all possible worlds – since in general, infinite and even continuous probability spaces are considered in MCDBs, this would not even be theoretically possible. Nevertheless, a naïve evaluation following the sampling-based semantics of MCDBs is not practical because the parameter N needed to obtain results of good quality may be very large. Thus, an MCDB has to use a number of optimization techniques to alleviate this high cost. In the MCDB system of Jampani et al. [2008], the following ideas are used to achieve this:

- Every query Q runs only once, but it returns *tuple bundles* instead of single tuples. A tuple bundle is an array of tuples with the same schema $t[1], t[2], \ldots$ Tuple $t[i]$ corresponds to the i-th possible world in the Monte Carlo simulation, where $i = 1, N$. This allows the system to check easily if two tuples belong to the same world: $t[i]$ and $t'[j]$ belong to the same world iff $i = j$.

- The materialization of a random attribute is delayed as long as possible. For example, if income is not directly inspected by the query, then the attribute is not expanded.

- The values of the random variables are reproducible. For that, the seed used to generate that random variable is stored and reused when it is needed again.

Even with these techniques, query evaluation remains a major challenge. It can be observed that a key challenge to efficiency is avoiding the *selectivity trap*: database queries are often highly selective, through selections and joins, and many of the tuples of the input database(s) do not survive the path through the query to the result. This has been already observed in early work on *online aggregation* [Hellerstein et al., 1997]. The same issue applies to MCDBs, and a promising solution is to postpone sampling as long as possible during query evaluation, working with summary representations of all possible worlds until operators such as tuple probability computations force the system to produce samples to proceed. The PIP system [Kennedy and Koch, 2010] does just this using pc-table representations of probabilistic databases. As shown there, pc-tables generalize tuple bundles in their power to compactly represent many samples (in fact, all possible worlds). Since, as discussed earlier, pc-tables are a strong representation system for relational algebra, the relational algebra part of a query can be evaluated by transforming the c-table representation, without touching the representation of the probability distribution modeled by the random variables in the tuple conditions. Samples are only generated after the evaluation of the relational algebra operations of the query is finished, and the costly and unnecessary sampling of data that would fall victim to filtering in the relational algebra can be suitably counteracted while preserving the correctness of the overall query result.

6.4   INDEXES AND MATERIALIZED VIEWS

In relational databases, indexes and materialized views are two powerful and popular techniques to improve query performance. Achieving high query performance is a major technical challenge for probabilistic databases, and researchers have naturally adapted indexing and materialized view techniques to probabilistic databases. Probabilistic data, however, presents new challenges that are not found in relational database management systems. A first conceptual reason that probabilistic indexing differs from relational indexing is that probabilistic databases allow new types of queries. For example, consider an environmental monitoring application where we are measuring the temperature of a physical space. The sensors can report the temperature in the room only to within some confidence. In this setting, one may ask *"return the ids of all sensors whose temperature is in some critical range with probability greater than* 0.6*"*. To answer this query, one alternative is to probe each of the sensors and ask them to report their temperature reading. Alternatively, one could use an index and quickly identify those sensors that meet the above criteria.

Indexing and materialized view techniques also need to be rethought for technical reasons. For example, in an RDBMS, each tuple can be processed independently. In turn, the RDBMS leverages this freedom to layout the data to make query retrieval efficient. In contrast, tuples in a probabilistic databases may be correlated in non-obvious ways.

6.4.1   INDEXES FOR PROBABILISTIC DATA

The first set of indexing for probabilistic databases were concerned with continuous probabilistic databases to support queries called *probabilistic threshold queries* (PTQ) [Cheng et al., 2004, Qi et al.,

2010]. The following is a canonical example of a PTQ: *"return the ids of all sensors whose temperature is in some critical range with probability greater than* 0.6*".*

To explain the main ideas, it suffices consider the problem in one dimension (of course, the problem can be generalized). The input is a set of n uncertain points $p_1, \ldots, p_n$ in $\mathbb{R}$. The query consists of a range $I \subseteq \mathbb{R}$, and a threshold confidence value τ. In our example above, $\tau = 0.6$, and I describes the critical range. The goal is to find all points p_j such that $\mathbf{P}[p \in I] \geq \tau$. The true value of each p_i in $\mathbb{R}$ is a continuous random variable described by a probability density function $f_i : \mathbb{R} \to \mathbb{R}^+ \cup \{0\}$.

A common assumption is that the probability density functions f_i are specified by (small) histograms. That is, each f_i is a piecewise uniform step function that contains a bounded number of steps. Consider the case when τ is known before any query begins: for example, we only report events if they have confidence greater than 0.5, but we do not know what is the critical range I. For this problem, Cheng et al. [2004]'s idea is to refine these regions with minimum bounding rectangles similar to an R-tree. The result is an index which is of size $O(n\tau^{-1})$ and that can answer queries in time $O(\tau^{-1} \log n)$. Later, Agarwal et al. [2009] showed that this problem can be reduced to the *segments below the line problem* from computational geometry: index a set of segments in $\mathbb{R}^2$ so that all segments lying below a query point can be reported quickly. If the threshold is known in advance, an optimal index can be constructed for the problem: it has size $O(n)$ and supports querying in $O(\log n)$ – for any choice of τ. The basic idea is to break the region using hyperplanes instead of rectangles. However, how one chooses these hyperplanes requires some sophistication. Agarwal et al. [2009] also consider the case where τ is not known in advance, and they are able to obtain indexes of size $O(n \log^2 n)$ with $O(\log^3 n)$ query time using recent advances from computational geometry.

Indexing for probabilistic categorical data has been considered as well [Kimura et al., 2010, Sarma et al., 2008a, Singh et al., 2007]. An interesting observation by Kimura et al. [2010] is that researchers have focused on secondary indexes for probabilistic data. In contrast, Kimura et al. [2010] advocate the Uncertain Primary Index approach. By making the index a primary index, they save on expensive IO that other indexes must use to fetch non-probabilistic attributes. Using this idea, they demonstrate an order of magnitude gains on several real data sets. Additionally, they develop algorithms and a cost model to maintain the index in the face of updates.

Indexes have also been applied to probabilistic databases with more intricate correlation structure than BID. For example, pDBs specified by Markov sequences [Letchner et al., 2009] or graphical models [Kanagal and Deshpande, 2010]. The central problem is that on these more intricate models, determining the correlation between two tuples may be computationally expensive. For example, in a hospital-based RFID application, we may want to know the probability that a crash cart was in patient A's room at 9am and then in patient B's room at 10am. These two events are correlated – not only with each other but with all events in that hour. Naïvely, we could effectively replay all of these events to perform inference. Instead, these approaches summarize the contributions of the events using a skip-list like data structure.

The main idea of these approaches is the following. Recall that a Markov Sequence of length $N + 1$ is a sequence of random variables $X^{(0)}, \ldots, X^{(N)}$ taking values in Σ that obey the Markov Property. A consequence of this property is:

$$\mathbf{P}[X^{(k+1)}|X^{(1)} \ldots X^{(k)}] = \mathbf{P}[X^{(k+1)}|X^{(k)}]$$

The technical goal of these indexing approaches is to compute $\mathbf{P}[X^{(i)} = \sigma | X^{(j)} = \sigma']$ where i, j, σ, σ' are specified as input. Retrieving this correlation information is crucial for efficient query processing.

The first idea is that we can write the probability computation as a Matrix multiplication and then use ideas similar to repeated squaring to summarize large chunks. Let $C^{(i)} \in \mathbb{R}^{N \times N}$ for $i = 1, \ldots, N$ where

$$C^{(i)}_{\sigma, \sigma'} = \mathbf{P}[X^{(i+1)} = \sigma | X^{(i)} = \sigma']$$

Then, observe that the product $C^{(i)} C^{(i+1)}$ gives the conditional probability matrix of two-steps, that is:

$$\left(C^{(i)} C^{(i+1)} \right)_{\sigma, \sigma'} = \mathbf{P}[X^{(i+2)} = \sigma' | X^{(i)} = \sigma']$$

Applying this idea repeatedly, we can get the conditional probability of events that are far away in the sequence. We can then precompute all possible transition matrices, i.e., store $\mathbf{P}[X^{(j)}|X^{(i)}]$ for every $i \leq j$. This would allow $O(1)$ querying but at the expense of storing all ($\approx N^2$) pairs of indexes. In some applications, this quadratic space is too high, and we are willing to sacrifice query performance for lower space. An idea due to Letchner et al. [2009] is based on the standard data structure, the skip list. We instead store the transition matrices: $\mathbf{P}[X^{2^i}|X^1]$ for $i = 1, \ldots, \log N$. The storage of this approach is linear in the original data, while achieving $O(\log r)$ query time where r is the distance in the sequence.

Kanagal and Deshpande [2010] extended this idea to more sophisticated graphical models. Here, the correlations may be more general (e.g., not only temporal). And the correlation structure is often more sophisticated than a simple linear chain as in Markov Sequences. Nevertheless, using a similar skip-list style data structure, both approaches are able to summarize large portions of the model without looking at them. In both cases, this results in a large improvement in performance.

It is natural to wonder if correlations that are "far apart" are worth the cost of computing exactly. That is, in an RFID setting, to what extent does a person's location at 9am help predicate their location at 5pm? The cost of storing this correlation information is that at query time we have to fetch a large amount of historical data. Understanding such quality-performance questions is an interesting (and open) question. A first empirical study of this question was recently done by Letchner et al. [2010] in the context of Markovian Streams.

6.4.2   MATERIALIZED VIEWS FOR RELATIONAL PROBABILISTIC DATABASES

Materialized views are widely used today to speed up query evaluation in relational databases. Early query optimizers used materialized views that were restricted to indexes (which are simple projections on the attributes being indexed) and join indexes [Valduriez, 1987]; modern query optimizers can use arbitrary materialized views [Agrawal et al., 2000].

When used in probabilistic databases, materialized views can make a dramatic impact. Suppose we need to evaluate a Boolean query Q on a BID probabilistic database, and assume Q is unsafe. In this case, one has to use some general-purpose probabilistic inference method, for example, the FPTRAS by Karp and Luby [1983] and Karp et al. [1989], and its performance in practice is much worse than that of safe plans: one experimental study by Ré et al. [2007] has observed two orders of magnitudes difference in performance. However, by rewriting Q in terms of a view it may be possible to transform it into a safe query, which can be evaluated very efficiently. There is no magic here: we simply pay the #P cost when we materialize the view, then evaluate the query in polynomial time at runtime.

Example 6.7   Consider three tuple-independent relations $R(C, A)$, $S(C, A, B)$, $T(C, B)$, and define the following view:

$$V(z) \quad :- \quad R(z, x), S(z, x, y), T(z, y)$$

Denote $V(Z)$ the schema of the materialized view. Then, all tuples in the materialized view V are independent. For the intuition behind this statement, notice that for two different constants $a \neq b$, the Boolean queries $V(a)$ and $V(b)$ depend on disjoint sets of tuples in the input tuple-independent probabilistic database. The first, $V(a)$, depends on inputs of the form $R(a, \ldots), S(a, \ldots), T(a, \ldots)$, while the second on inputs of the form $R(b, \ldots), S(b, \ldots), T(b, \ldots)$. Thus, $V(a)$ and $V(b)$ are independent probabilistic events, and we say that the tuples a and b in the view are independent. In general, any set of tuples $a, b, c, \ldots$ in the view are independent. Suppose we compute and store the view, meaning that we will determine all its tuples $a, b, c, \ldots$ and compute their probabilities. This will be expensive because, for each constant a, the Boolean query $V(a)$ is essentially equivalent to H_0 (Chapter 3); hence, it is #P-hard. Nevertheless, we will pay this cost and materialize the view. Later, we will use V to answer queries. For example, consider the Boolean query $Q:-R(z, x), S(z, x, y), T(z, y), U(z, v)$, where $U(C, D)$ is another tuple-independent relation. Then Q is #P-hard, but after rewriting it as $Q:-V(z), U(z, v)$ it becomes a safe query, and it can be computed by a safe plan. Thus, by using V to evaluate Q, we obtain a dramatic reduction in complexity.

The major challenge in using probabilistic views for query processing is how to find, represent, and use independence relationships between the tuples in the view. In general, the tuples in the view may be correlated in complex ways. One possibility is to store the lineage for each tuple t, but this makes query evaluation on the view no more efficient than expanding the view definition in the query.

To cope with this problem researchers have considered three main techniques. The first two techniques exploit the common substructure in the formula. The first idea is a sophisticated form of caching. The main idea is that the lineage formula may have common sub-components. Rather than re-evaluating these sub-components, we can simply cache the results and avoid expensive re-computation. Of course, identifying such sub-components is a difficult problem and is the main technical challenge. This idea has been applied both to BID-style databases [Sarma et al., 2008b] and to graphical model-based approaches [Sen et al., 2009].

A second approach that exploits the regularity of the lineage formula is to approximate the lineage formula. Here, the main idea is to replace the original Boolean lineage formula Φ_t for a tuple t with a new Boolean formula $\tilde{\Phi}_t$ that is smaller (i.e., uses fewer variables). More precisely, given some $\varepsilon \geq 0$, we can choose a formula $\tilde{\Phi}_t$ so that $\mathbf{P}[\tilde{\Phi}_t \neq \tilde{\Phi}_t] \leq \varepsilon$, i.e., the disagreement probability is less than ε. The size of $\tilde{\Phi}_t$ is a function only of ε, but the size can be bounded independently from the size of the original lineage formula. Simply shrinking the lineage has can improve query processing time: roughly speaking, the Luby-Karp-based algorithms of Section 5.3 that approximate $\mathbf{P}(\Phi)$ take time roughly quadratic in the size of the lineage formula. A second advantage of this approach is that the formula $\tilde{\Phi}$ is syntactically identical to a conventional lineage formula and so requires no additional machinery to process. Finding the smallest such $\tilde{\Phi}_t$ is a computationally challenging problem. Nevertheless, one can show that even simple greedy solutions still find $\tilde{\Phi}_t$ that are hundreds of times smaller. Using ideas from Boolean Harmonic Analysis, one can replace the functions $\tilde{\Phi}_t$ with multi-linear polynomials which may allow even further compression. But, the resulting lineage formula require new query processing algorithms. This approach is discussed by Ré and Suciu [2008].

A third (and more aggressive technique), discussed by Dalvi et al. [2011], is to simply throw away the entire lineage formula – essentially assuming that the tuples in the view are a new relation. Of course, using such a view naively may result in incorrect answers. However, some queries may not be affected by this choice. A trivial example is that a query which asks for a marginal probability of a single tuple can be trivially answered. But so can more sophisticated queries. Intuitively, if one can identify that a query only touches tuples whose correlations are either independent or disjoint in the view – avoiding those tuples that may have complex correlations – one can use the view to process the query. Deducing this is non-trivial (the problem is Π_2^P-Complete [Dalvi et al., 2011]). Nonetheless, there are efficient sound (but not complete) heuristics that can decide, given a query Q and a view V, if V can be used to answer Q [Dalvi et al., 2011].

Conclusion

This book discusses the state of the art in representation formalisms and query processing techniques for probabilistic data. Such data are produced by an increasing amount of applications, such as information extraction, entity resolution, sensor data, financial risk assessment, or scientific data.

We started by discussing the foundations in incomplete information and *possible world semantics* and reviewed c-tables, a classic formalism for representing incomplete databases. We then discussed basic principles for representing large probabilistic databases, by decomposing such databases into tuple-independent tables, block-independent-disjoint tables, or U-databases. We gave several examples of how to achieve such a decomposition, and we proved that such a decomposition is always possible but may incur an exponential blowup.

Then we discussed the query evaluation problem on probabilistic databases and showed that even if the input is restricted to the simplest model of tuple-independent tables, several queries are hard for #P.

There are two approaches for evaluating relational queries on probabilistic databases. In *extensional query evaluation*, the entire probabilistic inference can be pushed into the database engine and, therefore, processed as effectively as the evaluation of standard SQL queries. Although extensional evaluation is only possible on *safe queries*, it can be extremely effective when it works. For an important class of relational queries, namely Unions of Conjunctive Queries, extensional evaluation is provably complete: every query that cannot be evaluated extensionally has a data complexity that is hard for #P. The dichotomy into polynomial time or #P-hard is based entirely on the query's syntax.

In *intensional query evaluation*, the probabilistic inference is performed over a propositional formula, called *lineage expression*: every relational query can be evaluated this way, but the data complexity depends dramatically on the query and the instance and can be #P-hard in general. We discussed two approximation methods for intensional query evaluation, which can trade off the precision of the output probability for increased performance. Intensional query evaluation can be further refined to *query compilation*, which means translating the query's lineage into a decision diagram on which the query's output probability can be computed in linear time. As for safe queries, there exists various syntactic characterizations that ensure that the compilation into a given target is tractable.

Finally, we discussed briefly some advanced topics: efficient ranking of the query's answers, sequential probabilistic databases, Monte Carlo databases, indexes, and materialized views.

Bibliography

Serge Abiteboul, Paris Kanellakis, and Gösta Grahne. On the representation and querying of sets of possible worlds. *Theor. Comput. Sci.*, 78:159–187, 1991. DOI: 10.1016/0304-3975(51)90007-2 Cited on page(s) 14

Serge Abiteboul, Richard Hull, and Victor Vianu. *Foundations of Databases*. Addison-Wesley, 1995. DOI: 10.1145/1559795.1559816 Cited on page(s) xii, 17, 18, 70

Pankaj K. Agarwal, Siu-Wing Cheng, Yufei Tao, and Ke Yi. Indexing uncertain data. In *Proc. 28th ACM SIGMOD-SIGACT-SIGART Symp. on Principles of Database Syst.*, pages 137–146, 2009. Cited on page(s) 138

Charu Aggarwal, editor. *Managing and Mining Uncertain Data*. Springer-Verlag, 2008. Cited on page(s) xiv, 41

Sanjay Agrawal, Surajit Chaudhuri, and Vivek R. Narasayya. Automated selection of materialized views and indexes in sql databases. In *Proc. 26th Int. Conf. on Very Large Data Bases*, pages 496–505, 2000. Cited on page(s) 140

Srinivas M. Aji and Robert J. McEliece. The generalized distributive law. *IEEE Trans. Inf. Theory*, 46(2):325–343, 2000. DOI: 10.1109/18.825794 Cited on page(s) 14

Periklis Andritsos, Ariel Fuxman, and Renee J. Miller. Clean answers over dirty databases: A probabilistic approach. In *Proc. 22nd Int. Conf. on Data Eng.*, page 30, 2006. DOI: 10.1109/ICDE.2006.35 Cited on page(s) 11, 41, 88

Lyublena Antova, Christoph Koch, and Dan Olteanu. Query language support for incomplete information in the MayBMS system. In *Proc. 33rd Int. Conf. on Very large Data Bases*, pages 1422–1425, 2007a. Cited on page(s) 42

Lyublena Antova, Christoph Koch, and Dan Olteanu. From complete to incomplete information and back. In *Proc. ACM SIGMOD Int. Conf. on Management of Data*, pages 713–724, 2007b. DOI: 10.1145/1247480.1247559 Cited on page(s) 42

Lyublena Antova, Christoph Koch, and Dan Olteanu. MayBMS: Managing incomplete information with probabilistic world-set decompositions. In *Proc. 23rd IEEE Int. Conf. on Data Eng.*, pages 1479–1480, 2007c. DOI: 10.1109/ICDE.2007.369042 Cited on page(s) 11, 14, 15, 41

Lyublena Antova, Thomas Jansen, Christoph Koch, and Dan Olteanu. Fast and simple relational processing of uncertain data. In *Proc. 24th IEEE Int. Conf. on Data Eng.*, pages 983–992, 2008. DOI: 10.1109/ICDE.2008.4497507 Cited on page(s) 41

Lyublena Antova, Christoph Koch, and Dan Olteanu. 10^{10^6} worlds and beyond: efficient representation and processing of incomplete information. *Very Large Data Bases J.*, 18:1021–1040, 2009. Preliminary version appeared in Proc. 23rd IEEE Int. Conf. on Data Eng., 2007. DOI: 10.1007/s00778-009-0149-y Cited on page(s) 11, 41

Subi Arumugam, Fei Xu, Ravi Jampani, Christopher Jermaine, Luis L. Perez, and Peter J. Haas. MCDB-R: risk analysis in the database. *Proc. Very Large Data Bases*, 3:782–793, 2010. Cited on page(s) 11, 15, 134

Mikhail J. Atallah and Yinian Qi. Computing all skyline probabilities for uncertain data. In *Proc. 28th ACM SIGMOD-SIGACT-SIGART Symp. on Principles of Database Syst.*, pages 279–287, 2009. DOI: 10.1145/1559795.1559837 Cited on page(s) 12

D. Barbará, H. Garcia-Molina, and D. Porter. The management of probabilistic data. *IEEE Trans. on Knowl. and Data Eng.*, 4:487–502, 1992. DOI: 10.1109/69.166990 Cited on page(s) 13, 41

Michael Benedikt, Evgeny Kharlamov, Dan Olteanu, and Pierre Senellart. Probabilistic XML via markov chains. *Proc. Very Large Data Bases*, 3:770–781, 2010. Cited on page(s) 88

Omar Benjelloun, Anish Das Sarma, Alon Halevy, and Jennifer Widom. Uldbs: databases with uncertainty and lineage. In *Proc. 32nd Int. Conf. on Very large Data Bases*, pages 953–964, 2006a. DOI: 10.1007/s00778-007-0080-z Cited on page(s) 41

Omar Benjelloun, Anish Das Sarma, Chris Hayworth, and Jennifer Widom. An introduction to uldbs and the trio system. *IEEE Data Eng. Bulletin*, 2006b. Cited on page(s) 41

George Beskales, Mohamed A. Soliman, Ihab F. Ilyas, Shai Ben-David, and Yubin Kim. Probclean: A probabilistic duplicate detection system. In *Proc. 26th IEEE Int. Conf. on Data Eng.*, pages 1193–1196, 2010. Cited on page(s) 11

Anthony Bonner and Giansalvatore Mecca. Sequences, datalog, transducers. *J. Comput. Syst. Sci.*, 57:234–259, 1998. DOI: 10.1006/jcss.1998.1562 Cited on page(s) 132

Anthony J. Bonner and Giansalvatore Mecca. Querying sequence databases with transducers. *Acta Inf.*, 36:511–544, 2000. DOI: 10.1007/s002360050001 Cited on page(s) 132

Randal E. Bryant. Graph-based algorithms for boolean function manipulation. *IEEE Trans. Comput.*, 35:677–691, 1986. DOI: 10.1109/TC.1986.1676819 Cited on page(s) xiii, 121

Roger Cavallo and Michael Pittarelli. The theory of probabilistic databases. In *Proc. 13th Int. Conf. on Very Large Data Bases*, pages 71–81, 1987. Cited on page(s) 13

Chandra Chekuri and Anand Rajaraman. Conjunctive query containment revisited. In *Proc. 6th Int. Conf. on Database Theory*, pages 56–70, 1997. DOI: 10.1007/3-540-62222-5_36 Cited on page(s) xii

M. Y. Chen, A. Kundu, and J. Zhou. Off-line handwritten word recognition using a hidden markov model type stochastic network. *IEEE Trans. Pattern Anal. Mach. Intell.*, 16:481–496, 1994. DOI: 10.1109/34.291449 Cited on page(s) 130

Reynold Cheng, Dmitri V. Kalashnikov, and Sunil Prabhakar. Evaluating probabilistic queries over imprecise data. In *Proc. ACM SIGMOD Int. Conf. on Management of Data*, pages 551–562, 2003. DOI: 10.1145/872757.872823 Cited on page(s) 15

Reynold Cheng, Yuni Xia, Sunil Prabhakar, Rahul Shah, and Jeffrey Scott Vitter. Efficient indexing methods for probabilistic threshold queries over uncertain data. In *Proc. 30th Int. Conf. on Very Large Data Bases*, pages 876–887, 2004. Cited on page(s) 137, 138

Reynold Cheng, Jinchuan Chen, and Xike Xie. Cleaning uncertain data with quality guarantees. *Proc. Very Large Data Bases*, 1:722–735, 2008. DOI: 10.1145/1453856.1453935 Cited on page(s) 11

Reynold Cheng, Jian Gong, and David W. Cheung. Managing uncertainty of XML schema matching. In *Proc. 26th IEEE Int. Conf. on Data Eng.*, pages 297–308, 2010a. DOI: 10.1109/ICDE.2010.5447868 Cited on page(s) 12

Reynold Cheng, Xike Xie, Man Lung Yiu, Jinchuan Chen, and Liwen Sun. UV-diagram: A Voronoi diagram for uncertain data. In *Proc. 26th IEEE Int. Conf. on Data Eng.*, pages 796–807, 2010b. DOI: 10.1109/ICDE.2010.5447917 Cited on page(s) 12

CMUSphinx. The Carnegie Mellon Sphinx project, October 2010. cmusphing.org. Cited on page(s) 130

Sara Cohen, Benny Kimelfeld, and Yehoshua Sagiv. Running tree automata on probabilistic XML. In *Proc. 28th ACM SIGMOD-SIGACT-SIGART Symp. on Principles of Database Syst.*, pages 227–236, 2009. DOI: 10.1145/1559795.1559831 Cited on page(s) 88

Graham Cormode and Minos N. Garofalakis. Histograms and wavelets on probabilistic data. In *Proc. 25th IEEE Int. Conf. on Data Eng.*, pages 293–304, 2009. DOI: 10.1109/ICDE.2009.74 Cited on page(s) 12

Graham Cormode, Antonios Deligiannakis, Minos Garofalakis, and Andrew McGregor. Probabilistic histograms for probabilistic data. *Proc. Very Large Data Bases*, 2:526–537, 2009a. Cited on page(s) 12

Graham Cormode, Feifei Li, and Ke Yi. Semantics of ranking queries for probabilistic data and expected ranks. In *Proc. 25th IEEE Int. Conf. on Data Eng.*, pages 305–316, 2009b. DOI: 10.1109/ICDE.2009.75 Cited on page(s) 13

Paul Dagum, Richard Karp, Michael Luby, and Sheldon Ross. An optimal algorithm for Monte Carlo estimation. *SIAM J. Comput.*, 29:1484–1496, 2000. DOI: 10.1137/S0097539797315306 Cited on page(s) 108

N. Dalvi and D. Suciu. The dichotomy of probabilistic inference for unions of conjunctive queries, 2010. under review (preliminary version appeared in PODS 2010). Cited on page(s) 48, 50, 52, 70, 71, 87

Nilesh Dalvi and Dan Suciu. Efficient query evaluation on probabilistic databases. In *Proc. 30th Int. Conf. on Very large Data Bases*, pages 864–875, 2004. DOI: 10.1007/s00778-006-0004-3 Cited on page(s) 10, 15, 41, 51, 52, 74, 87, 132

Nilesh Dalvi and Dan Suciu. Management of probabilistic data: foundations and challenges. In *Proc. 26th ACM SIGMOD-SIGACT-SIGART Symp. on Principles of Database Syst.*, pages 1–12, 2007a. DOI: 10.1145/1265530.1265531 Cited on page(s) 52, 88

Nilesh Dalvi and Dan Suciu. Efficient query evaluation on probabilistic databases. *Very Large Data Bases J.*, 16:523–544, 2007b. DOI: 10.1007/s00778-006-0004-3 Cited on page(s) 88

Nilesh Dalvi, Christopher Ré, and Dan Suciu. Queries and materialized views on probabilistic databases. *J. Comput. Syst. Sci.*, 77:473–490, 2011. DOI: 10.1016/j.jcss.2010.04.006 Cited on page(s) 141

Nilesh N. Dalvi and Dan Suciu. Management of probabilistic data: foundations and challenges. In *Proc. 26th ACM SIGMOD-SIGACT-SIGART Symp. on Principles of Database Syst.*, pages 1–12, 2007c. DOI: 10.1145/1265530.1265531 Cited on page(s) 41, 47, 52, 85, 86

Nilesh N. Dalvi, Philip Bohannon, and Fei Sha. Robust web extraction: an approach based on a probabilistic tree-edit model. In *Proc. ACM SIGMOD Int. Conf. on Management of Data*, pages 335–348, 2009. DOI: 10.1145/1559845.1559882 Cited on page(s) 11

Nilesh N. Dalvi, Karl Schnaitter, and Dan Suciu. Computing query probability with incidence algebras. In *Proc. 29th ACM SIGMOD-SIGACT-SIGART Symp. on Principles of Database Syst.*, pages 203–214, 2010. DOI: 10.1145/1807085.1807113 Cited on page(s) 52, 87

Adnan Darwiche. Decomposable negation normal form. *J. ACM*, 48(4):608–647, 2001. DOI: 10.1145/502090.502091 Cited on page(s) 121

Adnan Darwiche. Searching while keeping a trace: The evolution from satisfiability to knowledge compilation. In *Proc. 3rd Int. Joint Conf. on Automated Reasoning*, page 3, 2006. DOI: 10.1007/11814771_2 Cited on page(s) 91, 121

Adnan Darwiche. *Modeling and Reasoning with Bayesian Networks*. Cambridge University Press, 2009. Cited on page(s) xii, xiii, 14, 31, 42

Adnan Darwiche. Relax, compensate and then recover: A theory of anytime, approximate inference. In *Proc. 12th European Conf. on Logics in Artificial Intelligence*, pages 7–9, 2010. DOI: 10.1007/978-3-642-15675-5_2 Cited on page(s) 83

Adnan Darwiche and Pierre Marquis. A knowledge compilation map. *J. Artif. Int. Res.*, 17:229–264, 2002. Cited on page(s) 91, 100, 101, 121, 122

Arjun Dasgupta, Nan Zhang 0004, and Gautam Das. Leveraging count information in sampling hidden databases. In *Proc. 25th IEEE Int. Conf. on Data Eng.*, pages 329–340, 2009. DOI: 10.1109/ICDE.2009.112 Cited on page(s) 13

Amol Deshpande, Minos Garofalakis, and Rajeev Rastogi. Independence is good: dependency-based histogram synopses for high-dimensional data. In *Proc. ACM SIGMOD Int. Conf. on Management of Data*, pages 199–210, 2001. DOI: 10.1145/376284.375685 Cited on page(s) 42

Landon Detwiler, Wolfgang Gatterbauer, Brent Louie, Dan Suciu, and Peter Tarczy-Hornoch. Integrating and ranking uncertain scientific data. In *Proc. 25th IEEE Int. Conf. on Data Eng.*, pages 1235–1238, 2009. DOI: 10.1109/ICDE.2009.209 Cited on page(s) 5, 12

Daniel Deutch. Querying probabilistic business processes for sub-flows. In *Proc. 14th Int. Conf. on Database Theory*, pages 54–65, 2011. DOI: 10.1145/1938551.1938562 Cited on page(s) 11

Daniel Deutch and Tova Milo. On models and query languages for probabilistic processes. *ACM SIGMOD Rec.*, 39:27–38, 2010. DOI: 10.1145/1893173.1893178 Cited on page(s) 11

Daniel Deutch, Christoph Koch, and Tova Milo. On probabilistic fixpoint and markov chain query languages. In *Proc. 29th ACM SIGMOD-SIGACT-SIGART Symp. on Principles of Database Syst.*, pages 215–226, 2010a. DOI: 10.1145/1807085.1807114 Cited on page(s) 89

Daniel Deutch, Tova Milo, Neoklis Polyzotis, and Tom Yam. Optimal top-k query evaluation for weighted business processes. *Proc. Very Large Data Bases*, 3:940–951, 2010b. Cited on page(s) 11

Debabrata Dey and Sumit Sarkar. A probabilistic relational model and algebra. *ACM Trans. Database Syst.*, 21(3):339–369, 1996. DOI: 10.1145/232753.232796 Cited on page(s) 14, 42

Yanlei Diao, Boduo Li, Anna Liu, Liping Peng, Charles Sutton, Thanh Tran 0002, and Michael Zink. Capturing data uncertainty in high-volume stream processing. In *Proc. 4th Biennial Conf. on Innovative Data Syst. Research*, 2009. Cited on page(s) 11

Xin Luna Dong, Alon Halevy, and Cong Yu. Data integration with uncertainty. *Very Large Data Bases J.*, 18:469–500, 2009. DOI: 10.1007/s00778-008-0119-9 Cited on page(s) 12

Arnaud Durand, Miki Hermann, and Phokion G. Kolaitis. Subtractive reductions and complete problems for counting complexity classes. *Theor. Comput. Sci.*, 340(3):496–513, 2005. DOI: 10.1016/j.tcs.2005.03.012 Cited on page(s) 51

R. Durbin, S. Eddy, A. Krogh, and G. Mitchison. *Biological sequence analysis*, chapter 4.4, pages 92–96. Cambridge University Press, 11th edition, 2006. Cited on page(s) 130

Kousha Etessami and Mihalis Yannakakis. Recursive markov chains, stochastic grammars, and monotone systems of nonlinear equations. *J. ACM*, 56(1), 2009. DOI: 10.1145/1462153.1462154 Cited on page(s) 88

Ronald Fagin, Joseph Y. Halpern, Yoram Moses, and Moshe Y. Vardi. *Reasoning About Knowledge*. MIT Press, 1995. Cited on page(s) 14

Ronald Fagin, Benny Kimelfeld, and Phokion G. Kolaitis. Probabilistic data exchange. In *Proc. 13th Int. Conf. on Database Theory*, pages 76–88, 2010. DOI: 10.1145/1804669.1804681 Cited on page(s) 12

Robert Fink and Dan Olteanu. On the optimal approximation of queries using tractable propositional languages. In *Proc. 14th Int. Conf. on Database Theory*, pages 162–173, 2011. DOI: 10.1145/1938551.1938575 Cited on page(s) 121

Robert Fink, Andrew Hogue, Dan Olteanu, and Swaroop Rath. Sprout^2: A squared query engine for uncertain web data. In *Proc. SIGMOD Int. Conf. on Management of Data*, 2011a. to appear. Cited on page(s) 11, 15

Robert Fink, Dan Olteanu, and Swaroop Rath. Providing support for full relational algebra in probabilistic databases. In *Proc. 27th IEEE Int. Conf. on Data Eng.*, 2011b. to appear. DOI: 10.1109/ICDE.2011.5767912 Cited on page(s) 52, 120

Jörg Flum, Markus Frick, and Martin Grohe. Query evaluation via tree-decompositions. *J. ACM*, 49:716–752, 2002. DOI: 10.1145/602220.602222 Cited on page(s) xii

C.H. Fosgate, H. Krim, W.W. Irving, W.C. Karl, and A.S. Willsky. Multiscale segmentation and anomaly enhancement of sar imagery. *IEEE Trans. on Image Processing*, 6(1):7–20, 1997. DOI: 10.1109/83.552077 Cited on page(s) 130

Nir Friedman, Lise Getoor, Daphne Koller, and Avi Pfeffer. Learning probabilistic relational models. In *Proc. 16th Int. Joint Conf. on Artificial intelligence*, pages 1300–1309, 1999. Cited on page(s) 42

Norbert Fuhr. A probabilistic framework for vague queries and imprecise information in databases. In *Proc. 16th Int. Conf. on Very Large Data Bases*, pages 696–707, 1990. Cited on page(s) 13

Norbert Fuhr and Thomas Rölleke. A probabilistic relational algebra for the integration of information retrieval and database syst. *ACM Trans. Inf. Syst.*, 15:32–66, 1997. DOI: 10.1145/239041.239045 Cited on page(s) 13, 42, 120

Avigdor Gal, Maria Vanina Martinez, Gerardo I. Simari, and V. S. Subrahmanian. Aggregate query answering under uncertain schema mappings. In *Proc. 25th IEEE Int. Conf. on Data Eng.*, pages 940–951, 2009. DOI: 10.1109/ICDE.2009.55 Cited on page(s) 12

W. Gatterbauer, A. Jha, and D. Suciu. Dissociation and propagation for efficient query evaluation over probabilistic databases. In *Workshop on Management of Uncertain Data*, 2010. Cited on page(s) 42, 83, 88

Wolfgang Gatterbauer and Dan Suciu. Optimal upper and lower bounds for boolean expressions by dissociation. arXiv:1105.2813 [cs.AI], 2011. Cited on page(s) 83

Tingjian Ge, Stan Zdonik, and Samuel Madden. Top-k queries on uncertain data: on score distribution and typical answers. In *Proc. SIGMOD Int. Conf. on Management of Data*, pages 375–388, 2009. DOI: 10.1145/1559845.1559886 Cited on page(s) 13

Erol Gelenbe and Georges Hébrail. A probability model of uncertainty in data bases. In *Proc. 2nd IEEE Int. Conf. on Data Eng.*, pages 328–333, 1986. Cited on page(s) 13

Lise Getoor, Benjamin Taskar, and Daphne Koller. Selectivity estimation using probabilistic models. In *Proc. ACM SIGMOD Int. Conf. on Management of Data*, pages 461–472, 2001. DOI: 10.1145/376284.375727 Cited on page(s) 42

Sakti P. Ghosh. Statistical relational tables for statistical database management. *IEEE Trans. Software Eng.*, 12(12):1106–1116, 1986. Cited on page(s) 13

W.R. Gilks, S. Richardson, and David Spiegelhalter. *Markov Chain Monte Carlo in Practice: Interdisciplinary Statistics*. Chapman and Hall/CRC, 1995. Cited on page(s) 14

Martin Charles Golumbic, Aviad Mintz, and Udi Rotics. Read-once functions revisited and the readability number of a boolean function. *Electronic Notes in Discrete Mathematics*, 22:357–361, 2005. DOI: 10.1016/j.endm.2005.06.076 Cited on page(s) 98

Georg Gottlob, Nicola Leone, and Francesco Scarcello. Hypertree decompositions and tractable queries. In *Proc. 18th ACM SIGMOD-SIGACT-SIGART Symp. on Principles of Database Syst.*, pages 21–32, 1999. DOI: 10.1145/303976.303979 Cited on page(s) xii

Michaela Götz and Christoph Koch. A compositional framework for complex queries over uncertain data. In *Proc. 12th Int. Conf. on Database Theory*, pages 149–161, 2009. DOI: 10.1145/1514894.1514913 Cited on page(s) 43

Erich Grädel, Yuri Gurevich, and Colin Hirsch. The complexity of query reliability. In *Proc. 17th ACM SIGACT-SIGMOD-SIGART Symp. on Principles of Database Syst.*, pages 227–234, 1998. DOI: 10.1145/275487.295124 Cited on page(s) 51, 52

Gösta Grahne. Dependency satisfaction in databases with incomplete information. In *Proc. 10th Int. Conf. on Very Large Data Bases*, pages 37–45, 1984. Cited on page(s) 14

Gösta Grahne. *The Problem of Incomplete Information in Relational Databases*. Number 554 in LNCS. Springer-Verlag, 1991. Cited on page(s) 14

Todd J. Green and Val Tannen. Models for incomplete and probabilistic information. *IEEE Data Eng. Bull.*, 29(1):17–24, 2006. DOI: 10.1007/11896548_24 Cited on page(s) 41

Todd J. Green, Grigoris Karvounarakis, and Val Tannen. Provenance semirings. In *Proc. 26th ACM SIGMOD-SIGACT-SIGART Symp. on Principles of Database Syst.*, pages 31–40, 2007. DOI: 10.1145/1265530.1265535 Cited on page(s) 7

Rahul Gupta and Sunita Sarawagi. Creating probabilistic databases from information extraction models. In *Proc. 32nd Int. Conf. on Very Large Data Bases*, pages 965–976, 2006. Cited on page(s) 5, 10

V. Gurvich. Criteria for repetition-freeness of functions in the algebra of logic. In *Soviet math. dolk.,43(3)*, 1991. Cited on page(s) 98

Oktie Hassanzadeh and Renée J. Miller. Creating probabilistic databases from duplicated data. *Very Large Data Bases J.*, 18:1141–1166, 2009. DOI: 10.1007/s00778-009-0161-2 Cited on page(s) 11

Joseph M. Hellerstein, Peter J. Haas, and Helen J. Wang. Online aggregation. In *Proc. ACM SIGMOD Int. Conf. on Management of Data*, pages 171–182, 1997. DOI: 10.1145/253262.253291 Cited on page(s) 137

Jaako Hintikka. *Semantics for Propositional Attitudes*. Cornell University Press, 1962. Cited on page(s) 14

HMMER. Biosequence analysis using hidden markov models, version 3.0, March 2010. http://hmmer.janelia.org/. Accessed in Oct 2010. Cited on page(s) 130

HTK. The hidden markov toolkit, version 3.4.1, March 2009. http://htk.eng.cam.ac.uk/. Accessed in October 2010. Cited on page(s) 130

Jiewen Huang, Lyublena Antova, Christoph Koch, and Dan Olteanu. MayBMS: a probabilistic database management system. In *Proc. ACM SIGMOD Int. Conf. on Management of Data*, pages 1071–1074, 2009. Cited on page(s) 15

IDC. The expanding digital universe: A forecast of worldwide information growth through 2010. *An IDC White Paper sponsored by EMC.*, March 2007. Cited on page(s) 129

Tomasz Imieliński and Witold Lipski, Jr. Incomplete information in relational databases. *J. ACM*, 31:761–791, 1984. DOI: 10.1145/1634.1886 Cited on page(s) xiii, 14, 41

Ravi Jampani, Fei Xu, Mingxi Wu, Luis Leopoldo Perez, Christopher Jermaine, and Peter J. Haas. MCDB: a Monte Carlo approach to managing uncertain data. In *Proc. ACM SIGMOD Int. Conf. on Management of Data*, pages 687–700, 2008. DOI: 10.1145/1376616.1376686 Cited on page(s) 5, 11, 15, 134, 136

Jeffrey Jestes, Feifei Li, Zhepeng Yan, and Ke Yi. Probabilistic string similarity joins. In *Proc. ACM SIGMOD Int. Conf. on Management of Data*, pages 327–338, 2010. DOI: 10.1145/1807167.1807204 Cited on page(s) 13

Abhay Jha and Dan Suciu. Knowledge compilation meets database theory: compiling queries to decision diagrams. In *Proc. 14th Int. Conf. on Database Theory*, pages 162–173, 2011. DOI: 10.1145/1938551.1938574 Cited on page(s) 110, 121

Abhay Jha, Dan Olteanu, and Dan Suciu. Bridging the gap between intensional and extensional query evaluation in probabilistic databases. In *Proc. 13th Int. Conf. on Extending Database Technology*, pages 323–334, 2010. DOI: 10.1145/1739041.1739082 Cited on page(s) 120

Michael I. Jordan, editor. *Learning in Graphical Models*. MIT Press, 1998. Cited on page(s) xii, 14

Bhargav Kanagal and Amol Deshpande. Indexing correlated probabilistic databases. In *Proc. ACM SIGMOD Int. Conf. on Management of Data*, pages 455–468, 2009. DOI: 10.1145/1559845.1559894 Cited on page(s) 130, 132

Bhargav Kanagal and Amol Deshpande. Lineage processing over correlated probabilistic databases. In *Proc. ACM SIGMOD Int. Conf. on Management of Data*, pages 675–686, 2010. DOI: 10.1145/1807167.1807241 Cited on page(s) 138, 139

R. M. Karp, M. Luby, and N. Madras. Monte-Carlo approximation algorithms for enumeration problems. *J. Algorithms*, 10:429–448, 1989. DOI: 10.1016/0196-6774(89)90038-2 Cited on page(s) 92, 104, 106, 121, 140

Richard M. Karp and Michael Luby. Monte-Carlo algorithms for enumeration and reliability problems. In *Proc. 24th Annual Symp. on Foundations of Computer Science*, pages 56–64, 1983. DOI: 10.1109/SFCS.1983.35 Cited on page(s) 92, 106, 121, 140

Oliver Kennedy and Christoph Koch. PIP: A database system for great and small expectations. In *Proc. 26th IEEE Int. Conf. on Data Eng.*, pages 157–168, 2010. DOI: 10.1109/ICDE.2010.5447879 Cited on page(s) 41, 134, 137

Nodira Khoussainova, Magdalena Balazinska, and Dan Suciu. Probabilistic event extraction from RFID data. In *Proc. 24th IEEE Int. Conf. on Data Eng.*, pages 1480–1482, 2008. DOI: 10.1109/ICDE.2008.4497596 Cited on page(s) 11

Benny Kimelfeld and Christopher Ré. Transducing markov sequences. In *Proc. 29th ACM SIGMOD-SIGACT-SIGART Symp. on Principles of Database Syst.*, pages 15–26, 2010. DOI: 10.1145/1807085.1807090 Cited on page(s) 130, 131, 133

Benny Kimelfeld, Yuri Kosharovsky, and Yehoshua Sagiv. Query efficiency in probabilistic XML models. In *Proc. ACM SIGMOD Int. Conf. on Management of Data*, pages 701–714, 2008. DOI: 10.1145/1376616.1376687 Cited on page(s) 88, 132

Benny Kimelfeld, Yuri Kosharovsky, and Yehoshua Sagiv. Query evaluation over probabilistic XML. *Very Large Data Bases J.*, 18(5):1117–1140, 2009. DOI: 10.1007/s00778-009-0150-5 Cited on page(s) 88

Hideaki Kimura, Samuel Madden, and Stanley B. Zdonik. UPI: a primary index for uncertain databases. *Proc. Very Large Data Bases*, 3:630–637, 2010. Cited on page(s) 138

Christoph Koch. On query algebras for probabilistic databases. *ACM SIGMOD Rec.*, 37(4):78–85, 2008a. DOI: 10.1145/1519103.1519116 Cited on page(s) 43

Christoph Koch. Approximating predicates and expressive queries on probabilistic databases. In *Proc. 27th ACM SIGMOD-SIGACT-SIGART Symp. on Principles of Database Syst.*, pages 99–108, 2008b. DOI: 10.1145/1376916.1376932 Cited on page(s) 14, 43, 108

Christoph Koch. MayBMS: A system for managing large uncertain and probabilistic databases. In Charu Aggarwal, editor, *Managing and Mining Uncertain Data*, chapter 6. Springer-Verlag, 2008c. Cited on page(s) 42, 43

Christoph Koch and Dan Olteanu. Conditioning probabilistic databases. *Proc. Very Large Data Bases*, 1:313–325, 2008. DOI: 10.1145/1453856.1453894 Cited on page(s) 41, 42, 108, 122

Daphne Koller. Probabilistic relational models. In *Proc. 9th Int. Workshop on Inductive Logic Programming*, pages 3–13, 1999. Cited on page(s) 42

Daphne Koller and Nir Friedman. *Probabilistic Graphical Models - Principles and Techniques*. MIT Press, 2009. Cited on page(s) xii, 8, 14, 42

Saul A. Kripke. Semantic analysis of modal logic. i: Normal propositional calculi. *Zeitschrift für mathematische Logik und Grundlagen der Mathematik*, 9:67–96, 1963. DOI: 10.1002/malq.19630090502 Cited on page(s) 14

Nevan J. Krogan, Gerard Cagney, Haiyuan Yu, Gouqing Zhong, Xinghua Guo, Alexandr Ignatchenko, Joyce Li, Shuye Pu, Nira Datta, Aaron P. Tikuisis, and et al. Global landscape of protein complexes in the yeast saccharomyces cerevisiae. *Nature*, 440:637–643, 2006. DOI: 10.1038/nature04670 Cited on page(s) 12

John D. Lafferty, Andrew McCallum, and Fernando C. N. Pereira. Conditional random fields: Probabilistic models for segmenting and labeling sequence data. In *Proc. 18th Int. Conf. on Machine Learning*, pages 282–289, 2001. Cited on page(s) 5, 10, 134

Laks V. S. Lakshmanan, Nicola Leone, Robert Ross, and V. S. Subrahmanian. Probview: a flexible probabilistic database system. *ACM Trans. Database Syst.*, 22:419–469, 1997. DOI: 10.1145/261124.261131 Cited on page(s) 14, 42

S. L. Lauritzen and D. J. Spiegelhalter. Local computations with probabilities on graphical structures and their application to expert systems. In *Readings in uncertain reasoning*, pages 415–448. Morgan Kaufmann Publishers Inc., 1990. ISBN 1-55860-125-2. Cited on page(s) xii

Ezio Lefons, Alberto Silvestri, and Filippo Tangorra. An analytic approach to statistical databases. In *Proc. 9th Int. Conf. on Very Large Data Bases*, pages 260–274, 1983. Cited on page(s) 13

Julie Letchner, Christopher Ré, Magdalena Balazinska, and Matthai Philipose. Access methods for markovian streams. In *Proc. 25th IEEE Int. Conf. on Data Eng.*, pages 246–257, 2009. DOI: 10.1109/ICDE.2009.21 Cited on page(s) 130, 132, 138, 139

Julie Letchner, Christopher Ré, Magdalena Balazinska, and Matthai Philipose. Approximation trade-offs in markovian stream processing: An empirical study. In *Proc. 26th IEEE Int. Conf. on Data Eng.*, pages 936–939, 2010. DOI: 10.1109/ICDE.2010.5447926 Cited on page(s) 139

Feifei Li, Ke Yi, and Jeffrey Jestes. Ranking distributed probabilistic data. In *Proc. of ACM SIGMOD Int. Conf. on Management of Data*, pages 361–374, 2009a. DOI: 10.1145/1559845.1559885 Cited on page(s) 13

Jian Li and Amol Deshpande. Consensus answers for queries over probabilistic databases. In *Proc. 28th ACM SIGMOD-SIGACT-SIGART Symp. on Principles of Database Syst.*, pages 259–268, 2009. DOI: 10.1145/1559795.1559835 Cited on page(s) 41, 42

Jian Li, Barna Saha, and Amol Deshpande. A unified approach to ranking in probabilistic databases. *Proc. Very Large Data Bases*, 2(1):502–513, 2009b. DOI: 10.1007/s00778-011-0220-3 Cited on page(s) 13

Leonid Libkin. *Elements of Finite Model Theory*. Springer, 2004. Cited on page(s) 54, 60

Leonid Libkin and Limsoon Wong. Semantic representations and query languages for or-sets. *J. Comput. Syst. Sci.*, 52:125–142, 1996. DOI: 10.1006/jcss.1996.0010 Cited on page(s) 14

Bertram Ludäscher, Pratik Mukhopadhyay, and Yannis Papakonstantinou. A transducer-based XML query processor. In *Proc. 28th Int. Conf. on Very Large Data Bases*, pages 227–238, 2002. DOI: 10.1016/B978-155860869-6/50028-7 Cited on page(s) 132

Wim Martens and Frank Neven. Typechecking top-down uniform unranked tree transducers. In *Proc. 9th Int. Conf. on Database Theory*, pages 64–78, 2002. Cited on page(s) 132

Gerome Miklau and Dan Suciu. A formal analysis of information disclosure in data exchange. In *SIGMOD Conference*, pages 575–586, 2004. DOI: 10.1145/1007568.1007633 Cited on page(s) 56

Michael Mitzenmacher and Eli Upfal. *Probability and Computing*. Cambridge University Press, 2005. Cited on page(s) 107

Andrew Nierman and H. V. Jagadish. ProTDB: probabilistic data in XML. In *Proc. 28th Int. Conf. on Very Large Data Bases*, pages 646–657, 2002. DOI: 10.1016/B978-155860869-6/50063-9 Cited on page(s) 12

Dan Olteanu and Jiewen Huang. Using OBDDs for efficient query evaluation on probabilistic databases. In *Proc. 2nd Int. Conf. on Scalable Uncertainty Management*, pages 326–340, 2008. DOI: 10.1007/978-3-540-87993-0_26 Cited on page(s) 52, 109, 121

Dan Olteanu and Jiewen Huang. Secondary-storage confidence computation for conjunctive queries with inequalities. In *Proc. ACM SIGMOD Int. Conf. on Management of Data*, pages 389–402, 2009. DOI: 10.1145/1559845.1559887 Cited on page(s) 52, 88, 121

Dan Olteanu, Christoph Koch, and Lyublena Antova. World-set decompositions: Expressiveness and efficient algorithms. *Theor. Comput. Sci.*, 403:265–284, 2008. Preliminary version appeared in Proc. 11th Int. Conf. on Database Theory, 2007. DOI: 10.1016/j.tcs.2008.05.004 Cited on page(s) 14, 41

Dan Olteanu, Jiewen Huang, and Christoph Koch. SPROUT: Lazy vs. eager query plans for tuple-independent probabilistic databases. In *Proc. 25th IEEE Int. Conf. on Data Eng.*, pages 640–651, 2009. DOI: 10.1109/ICDE.2009.123 Cited on page(s) 15, 87, 88, 108

Dan Olteanu, Jiewen Huang, and Christoph Koch. Approximate confidence computation in probabilistic databases. In *Proc. 26th IEEE Int. Conf. on Data Eng.*, pages 145 – 156, 2010. Cited on page(s) 41, 102, 108, 120, 121

Judea Pearl. *Probabilistic reasoning in intelligent systems: Networks of plausible inference*. Morgan Kaufmann, 1989. Cited on page(s) xii, 14, 42, 120

David Poole. Probabilistic horn abduction and bayesian networks. *Artif. Intell.*, 64(1):81–129, 1993. DOI: 10.1016/0004-3702(93)90061-F Cited on page(s) 41

David Poole. First-order probabilistic inference. In *Proc. 18th Int. Joint Conf. on Artificial Intelligence*, pages 985–991, 2003. Cited on page(s) 88

Michalis Potamias, Francesco Bonchi, Aristides Gionis, and George Kollios. k-nearest neighbors in uncertain graphs. *Proc. Very Large Data Bases*, 3:997–1008, 2010. Cited on page(s) 12

J. Scott Provan and Michael O. Ball. The complexity of counting cuts and of computing the probability that a graph is connected. *SIAM Journal on Computing*, 12(4):777–788, 1983. DOI: 10.1137/0212053 Cited on page(s) 46, 47, 51

Yinian Qi, Rohit Jain, Sarvjeet Singh, and Sunil Prabhakar. Threshold query optimization for uncertain data. In *Proc. ACM SIGMOD Int. Conf. on Management of Data*, pages 315–326, 2010. DOI: 10.1145/1807167.1807203 Cited on page(s) 137

Lawrence R. Rabiner. A tutorial on hidden markov models and selected applications in speech recognition. In Alex Waibel and Kai-Fu Lee, editors, *Readings in speech recognition*, pages 267–296. Morgan Kaufmann Publishers Inc., 1990. ISBN 1-55860-124-4. Cited on page(s) 130

Vibhor Rastogi, Dan Suciu, and Evan Welbourne. Access control over uncertain data. *Proc. Very Large Data Bases*, 1:821–832, 2008. DOI: 10.1145/1453856.1453945 Cited on page(s) 12

Christopher Ré and Dan Suciu. Approximate lineage for probabilistic databases. *Proc. Very Large Data Bases*, 1:797–808, 2008. DOI: 10.1145/1453856.1453943 Cited on page(s) 121, 141

Christopher Ré and Dan Suciu. The trichotomy of having queries on a probabilistic database. *Very Large Data Bases J.*, 18(5):1091–1116, 2009. DOI: 10.1007/s00778-009-0151-4 Cited on page(s) 52

Christopher Ré, Nilesh N. Dalvi, and Dan Suciu. Query evaluation on probabilistic databases. *IEEE Data Eng. Bull.*, 29(1):25–31, 2006. Cited on page(s) 88

Christopher Ré, Nilesh N. Dalvi, and Dan Suciu. Efficient top-k query evaluation on probabilistic data. In *Proc. 2007 IEEE 23rd Int. Conf. on Data Eng.*, pages 886–895, 2007. DOI: 10.1109/ICDE.2007.367934 Cited on page(s) 125, 140

Christopher Ré, Julie Letchner, Magdalena Balazinksa, and Dan Suciu. Event queries on correlated probabilistic streams. In *Proc. ACM SIGMOD Int. Conf. on Management of Data*, pages 715–728, 2008. DOI: 10.1145/1376616.1376688 Cited on page(s) 5, 11, 130, 132

Sudeepa Roy, Vittorio Perduca, and Val Tannen. Faster query answering in probabilistic databases using read-once functions. In *Proc. 14th Int. Conf. on Database Theory*, pages 232–243, 2011. DOI: 10.1145/1938551.1938582 Cited on page(s) 121

A. Das Sarma, J.D. Ullman, and J. Widom. Schema design for uncertain databases. In *Proc. 3rd Alberto Mendelzon Workshop on Foundations of Data Management*, 2009a. paper 2. Cited on page(s) 42

158 BIBLIOGRAPHY

Anish Das Sarma, Omar Benjelloun, Alon Halevy, and Jennifer Widom. Working models for uncertain data. In *Proc. 22nd IEEE Int. Conf. on Data Eng.*, page 7, 2006. DOI: 10.1109/ICDE.2006.174 Cited on page(s) 41

Anish Das Sarma, Parag Agrawal, Shubha U. Nabar, and Jennifer Widom. Towards special-purpose indexes and statistics for uncertain data. In *Workshop on Management of Uncertain Data*, pages 57–72, 2008a. Cited on page(s) 138

Anish Das Sarma, Martin Theobald, and Jennifer Widom. Exploiting lineage for confidence computation in uncertain and probabilistic databases. In *Proc. 24th IEEE 24th Int. Conf. on Data Eng.*, pages 1023–1032, 2008b. DOI: 10.1109/ICDE.2008.4497511 Cited on page(s) 120, 132, 141

Anish Das Sarma, Omar Benjelloun, Alon Y. Halevy, Shubha U. Nabar, and Jennifer Widom. Representing uncertain data: models, properties, and algorithms. *Very Large Data Bases J.*, 18(5): 989–1019, 2009b. DOI: 10.1007/s00778-009-0147-0 Cited on page(s) 41

Prithviraj Sen and Amol Deshpande. Representing and querying correlated tuples in probabilistic databases. In *Proc. 23rd IEEE Int. Conf. on Data Eng.*, pages 596–605, 2007. DOI: 10.1109/ICDE.2007.367905 Cited on page(s) xiii, 14, 88

Prithviraj Sen, Amol Deshpande, and Lise Getoor. Exploiting shared correlations in probabilistic databases. *Proc. Very Large Data Bases*, 1:809–820, 2008. DOI: 10.1145/1453856.1453944 Cited on page(s) 88

Prithviraj Sen, Amol Deshpande, and Lise Getoor. Prdb: managing and exploiting rich correlations in probabilistic databases. *Very Large Data Bases J.*, 18(5):1065–1090, 2009. DOI: 10.1007/s00778-009-0153-2 Cited on page(s) 15, 42, 141

Prithviraj Sen, Amol Deshpande, and Lise Getoor. Read-once functions and query evaluation in probabilistic databases. *Proc. Very Large Data Bases*, 3:1068–1079, 2010. Cited on page(s) 121

Pierre Senellart and Serge Abiteboul. On the complexity of managing probabilistic xml data. In *Proc. 26th ACM SIGMOD-SIGACT-SIGART Symp. on Principles of Database Syst.*, pages 283–292, 2007. DOI: 10.1145/1265530.1265570 Cited on page(s) 88

Fei Sha and Fernando Pereira. Shallow parsing with conditional random fields. In *Proc. 2003 Conf. North American Chapter of the Assoc. for Comp. Linguistics on Human Language Technology - Volume 1*, NAACL '03, pages 134–141, 2003. DOI: 10.3115/1073445.1073473 Cited on page(s) 134

Fei Sha and Lawrence K. Saul. Large margin hidden markov models for automatic speech recognition. In *Advances in Neural Information Processing Syst. 19*, pages 1249–1256, 2007. DOI: 10.1109/TASL.2006.879805 Cited on page(s) 130

Sarvjeet Singh, Chris Mayfield, Sunil Prabhakar, Rahul Shah, and Susanne E. Hambrusch. Indexing uncertain categorical data. In *Proc. 23rd IEEE Int. Conf. on Data Eng.*, pages 616–625, 2007. DOI: 10.1109/ICDE.2007.367907 Cited on page(s) 138

Sarvjeet Singh, Chris Mayfield, Sagar Mittal, Sunil Prabhakar, Susanne Hambrusch, and Rahul Shah. Orion 2.0: native support for uncertain data. In *Proc. ACM SIGMOD Int. Conf. on Management of Data*, pages 1239–1242, 2008. DOI: 10.1145/1376616.1376744 Cited on page(s) 15

Yannis Sismanis, Ling Wang, Ariel Fuxman, Peter J. Haas, and Berthold Reinwald. Resolution-aware query answering for business intelligence. In *Proc. 25th IEEE Int. Conf. on Data Eng.*, pages 976–987, 2009. DOI: 10.1109/ICDE.2009.81 Cited on page(s) 11

Mohamed A. Soliman, Ihab F. Ilyas, and Kevin Chen-Chuan Chang. Probabilistic top-k and ranking-aggregate queries. *ACM Trans. Database Syst.*, 33:13:1–13:54, 2008. DOI: 10.1145/1386118.1386119 Cited on page(s) 13

Mohamed A. Soliman, Ihab F. Ilyas, and Shalev Ben-David. Supporting ranking queries on uncertain and incomplete data. *Very Large Data Bases J.*, 19:477–501, 2010. DOI: 10.1007/s00778-009-0176-8 Cited on page(s) 13

Richard P. Stanley. *Enumerative Combinatorics*. Cambridge University Press, 1997. Cited on page(s) 66, 70

Julia Stoyanovich, Susan Davidson, Tova Milo, and Val Tannen. Deriving probabilistic databases with inference ensembles. In *Proc. 27th IEEE Int. Conf. on Data Eng.*, 2011. to appear. DOI: 10.1109/ICDE.2011.5767854 Cited on page(s) 13

Thanh Tran, Charles Sutton, Richard Cocci, Yanming Nie, Yanlei Diao, and Prashant Shenoy. Probabilistic inference over RFID streams in mobile environments. In *Proc. 25th IEEE Int. Conf. on Data Eng.*, pages 1096–1107, 2009. DOI: 10.1109/ICDE.2009.33 Cited on page(s) 11

Luca Trevisan. A note on deterministic approximate counting for k-DNF. In Klaus Jansen, Sanjeev Khanna, José Rolim, and Dana Ron, editors, *Approximation, Randomization, and Combinatorial Optimization. Algorithms and Techniques*, volume 3122, pages 417–425. Springer Verlag, 2004. Cited on page(s) 121

Jeffrey D. Ullman. *Principles of Database and Knowledge-Base Systems: Volume II: The New Technologies*. W. H. Freeman & Co., 1990. Cited on page(s) 14, 41

Patrick Valduriez. Join indices. *ACM Trans. Database Syst.*, 12:218–246, 1987. DOI: 10.1145/22952.22955 Cited on page(s) 140

L. G. Valiant. The complexity of computing the permanent. *Theor. Comput. Sci.*, 8(2):189–201, 1979. DOI: 10.1016/0304-3975(79)90044-6 Cited on page(s) 46, 51

Maurice van Keulen and Ander de Keijzer.   Qualitative effects of knowledge rules and user feedback in probabilistic data integration. *Very Large Data Bases J.*, 18(5):1191–1217, 2009. DOI: 10.1007/s00778-009-0156-z Cited on page(s) 12

Moshe Y. Vardi.   The complexity of relational query languages (extended abstract).   In *Proc. 14th annual ACM Symp. on Theory of Computing*, pages 137–146, 1982. DOI: 10.1145/800070.802186 Cited on page(s) xii, 9, 48

Vijay V. Vazirani. *Approximation Algorithms*. Springer, 2001. Cited on page(s) 104

Thomas Verma and Judea Pearl. Causal networks: semantics and expressiveness. In *Proc. 4th Annual Conf. on Uncertainty in Artificial Intelligence*, pages 69–78, 1988. Cited on page(s) xiii, 31, 42

Daisy Zhe Wang, Eirinaios Michelakis, Minos Garofalakis, and Joseph M. Hellerstein. BayesStore: managing large, uncertain data repositories with probabilistic graphical models. *Proc. Very Large Data Bases*, 1:340–351, 2008a. DOI: 10.1145/1453856.1453896 Cited on page(s) 10

Daisy Zhe Wang, Michael J. Franklin, Minos Garofalakis, and Joseph M. Hellerstein. Querying probabilistic information extraction. *Proc. Very Large Data Bases*, 3:1057–1067, 2010a. Cited on page(s) 10

Daisy Zhe Wang, Eirinaois Michaelakis, Minos Garofalakis, Michael J. Franklin, and Joseph M. Hellerstein. Declarative information extraction in a probabilstic database system. In *Proc. 26th IEEE Int. Conf. on Data Eng.*, 2010b. DOI: 10.1109/ICDE.2010.5447844 Cited on page(s) 10

Ting-You Wang, Christopher Ré, and Dan Suciu. Implementing NOT EXISTS predicates over a probabilistic database. In *Workshop on Management of Uncertain Data*, pages 73–86, 2008b. Cited on page(s) 52

Ingo Wegener. BDDs – design, analysis, complexity, and applications. *Discrete Applied Mathematics*, 138(1-2):229–251, 2004. DOI: 10.1016/S0166-218X(03)00297-X Cited on page(s) 101, 113, 121

Michael Wick, Andrew McCallum, and Gerome Miklau.   Scalable probabilistic databases with factor graphs and mcmc. *Proc. Very Large Data Bases*, 3:794–804, 2010. Cited on page(s) 10

Jennifer Widom. Trio: A system for integrated management of data, accuracy, and lineage. In *Proc. 2nd Biennial Conf. on Innovative Data Syst. Research*, pages 262–276, 2005. Cited on page(s) 15, 41

Jennifer Widom. Trio: a system for data, uncertainty, and lineage. In Charu Aggarwal, editor, *Managing and Mining Uncertain Data*, chapter 5. Springer-Verlag, 2008. Cited on page(s) 6, 15, 42

Garrett Wolf, Aravind Kalavagattu, Hemal Khatri, Raju Balakrishnan, Bhaumik Chokshi, Jianchun Fan, Yi Chen, and Subbarao Kambhampati. Query processing over incomplete autonomous databases: query rewriting using learned data dependencies. *Very Large Data Bases J.*, 18(5): 1167–1190, 2009. DOI: 10.1007/s00778-009-0155-0 Cited on page(s) 13

Fei Xu, Kevin S. Beyer, Vuk Ercegovac, Peter J. Haas, and Eugene J. Shekita. E = mc^3: managing uncertain enterprise data in a cluster-computing environment. In *Proc. ACM SIGMOD Int. Conf. on Management of Data*, pages 441–454, 2009. DOI: 10.1145/1559845.1559893 Cited on page(s) 11, 134

Jia Xu, Zhenjie Zhang, Anthony K. H. Tung, and Ge Yu. Efficient and effective similarity search over probabilistic data based on earth mover's distance. *Proc. Very Large Data Bases*, 3:758–769, 2010. Cited on page(s) 13

Qin Zhang, Feifei Li, and Ke Yi. Finding frequent items in probabilistic data. In *Proc. ACM SIG-MOD Int. Conf. on Management of Data*, pages 819–832, 2008. DOI: 10.1145/1376616.1376698 Cited on page(s) 12

Wenjie Zhang, Xuemin Lin, Ying Zhang, Wei Wang 0011, and Jeffrey Xu Yu. Probabilistic skyline operator over sliding windows. In *Proc. 25th IEEE Int. Conf. on Data Eng.*, pages 1060–1071, 2009. DOI: 10.1109/ICDE.2009.83 Cited on page(s) 13

Xi Zhang and Jan Chomicki. On the semantics and evaluation of top-k queries in probabilistic databases. In *Proc. 24th IEEE Int. Conf. on Data Eng. (Workshops)*, pages 556–563, 2008. DOI: 10.1109/ICDEW.2008.4498380 Cited on page(s) 13

Esteban Zimányi. Query evaluation in probabilistic relational databases. *Theor. Comput. Sci.*, 171 (1-2):179–219, 1997. DOI: 10.1016/S0304-3975(96)00129-6 Cited on page(s) 13

Zhaonian Zou, Jianzhong Li, Hong Gao, and Shuo Zhang. Finding top-k maximal cliques in an uncertain graph. In *Proc. 26th IEEE Int. Conf. on Data Eng.*, pages 649–652, 2010. DOI: 10.1109/ICDE.2010.5447891 Cited on page(s) 12

Authors' Biographies

DAN SUCIU

Dan Suciu is a Professor in Computer Science at the University of Washington. He received his Ph.D. from the University of Pennsylvania in 1995, then was a principal member of the technical staff at AT&T Labs until he joined the University of Washington in 2000. Professor Suciu is conducting research in data management, with an emphasis on topics that arise from sharing data on the Internet, such as management of semistructured and heterogeneous data, data security, and managing data with uncertainties. He is a co-author of the book Data on the Web: from Relations to Semistructured Data and XML. He holds twelve US patents, received the 2000 ACM SIGMOD Best Paper Award, the 2010 PODS Ten Years Best paper award, and is a recipient of the NSF Career Award and of an Alfred P. Sloan Fellowship. Suciu's PhD students Gerome Miklau and Christopher Ré received the ACM SIGMOD Best Dissertation Award in 2006 and 2010, respectively, and Nilesh Dalvi was a runner up in 2008.

DAN OLTEANU

Dan Olteanu is a University Lecturer (equivalent of Assistant Professor in North America) in the Department of Computer Science at the University of Oxford and Fellow of St Cross College since September 2007. He received his Dr. rer. nat. in Computer Science from Ludwig Maximilian University of Munich in 2005. Before joining Oxford, he was post-doctoral researcher with Professor Christoph Koch at Saarland University, visiting scientist at Cornell University, and temporary professor at Ruprecht Karl University in Heidelberg. His main research is on theoretical and system aspects of data management, with a current focus on Web data, provenance information, and probabilistic databases.

CHRISTOPHER RÉ

Christopher (Chris) Ré is currently an Assistant Professor in the department of Computer Sciences at the University of Wisconsin-Madison. The goal of his work is to enable users and developers to build applications that more deeply understand data. In many applications, machines can only understand the meaning of data statistically, e.g., user-generated text or data from sensors. To attack this challenge, Chris's recent work is to build a system, Hazy, that integrates a handful of statistical operators with a standard relational database management system. To support this work, Chris received the NSF CAREER Award in 2011.

Chris received his PhD from the University of Washington, Seattle under the supervision of Dan Suciu. For his PhD work in the area of probabilistic data management, Chris received the SIGMOD 2010 Jim Gray Dissertation Award. His PhD work produced two systems: Mystiq, a system to manage relational probabilistic data, and Lahar, a streaming probabilistic database.

CHRISTOPH KOCH

Christoph Koch is a Professor of Computer Science at École Polytechnique Fédérale de Lausanne (EPFL) in Lausanne, Switzerland. He is interested in both the theoretical and systems-oriented aspects of data management, and he currently works on managing uncertain and probabilistic data, research at the intersection of databases, programming languages, and compilers, community data management systems, and data-driven games.

He received his PhD from TU Vienna, Austria, in 2001, for research done at CERN, Switzerland and subsequently held positions at TU Vienna (2001-2002; 2003-2005), the University of Edinburgh (2002-2003), Saarland University (2005-2007), and Cornell University (2006; 2007-2010), before joining EPFL in 2010. He won best paper awards at PODS 2002, and SIGMOD 2011, a Google Research Award (2009), and has been PC co-chair of DBPL 2005, WebDB 2008, and ICDE 2011.

Printed in the United States
by Baker & Taylor Publisher Services